PENGUIN BOOKS

ROADSIDE EMPIRES

Stan Luxenberg is a graduate of the Columbia
School of Journalism and a free-lance business
writer whose articles have appeared in *The New
Republic, Harper's, Inc.,* and other publications. He
lives in New York City.

Roadside Empires

HOW THE CHAINS FRANCHISED AMERICA

by STAN LUXENBERG

PENGUIN BOOKS

PENGUIN BOOKS
Viking Penguin Inc., 40 West 23rd Street,
New York, New York 10010, U.S.A.
Penguin Books Ltd, Harmondsworth,
Middlesex, England
Penguin Books Australia Ltd, Ringwood,
Victoria, Australia
Penguin Books Canada Limited, 2801 John Street,
Markham, Ontario, Canada L3R 1B4
Penguin Books (N.Z.) Ltd, 182–190 Wairau Road,
Auckland 10, New Zealand

First published in the United States of America by
Viking Penguin Inc. 1985
Published in Penguin Books 1986

LIBRARY OF CONGRESS CATALOGING IN PUBLICATION DATA
Luxenberg, Stan.
   Roadside empires.
   Bibliography: p.
   Includes index.
   1. Franchises (Retail trade)—United States.
I. Title.
HF5429.235.U5L88   1986   381'.13'0973   86-764
ISBN 0 14 00.7734 0

Printed in the United States of America by
R. R. Donnelley & Sons Company, Harrisonburg, Virginia
Set in Aster

Preface

As I researched this book I was surprised to learn how all-pervasive franchising has become. Franchised businesses seem to be everywhere. They are in nearly every city in the country, and in many commercial districts they are on every block. They are tucked away in office buildings and hidden in schools. In those isolated places where the chains have not appeared, the influence of franchising is still apparent: independent businesses that are not part of chains copy the store designs and operating techniques of franchise companies.

The more I saw of the chains, the less appealing they became to me. As I traveled to study the franchise companies, I observed how they have helped to rob small towns of their character. They have developed a fast-food diet that ranges from bland to abominable. And during my three years of research, it became clear that the chains have introduced economic problems along with their fried chicken and mufflers.

Despite some gloomy findings, my journey through the franchised world was not wholly unpleasant. Along the way I encountered many people—particularly franchisees—whose colorful personalities have not been stifled by the standardized corporations they serve. I am indebted to these people for sharing their experiences and taking the time to explain the intricacies of the chain way of business.

Many friends and colleagues helped with this book. Gerry Howard of Viking Penguin suggested doing a book on franchising. Along with Bill Strachan he labored diligently on this project, providing valuable suggestions and helping to shape the book. Virginia Barber, my agent, offered skillful assistance. My brother, Larry Luxenberg, read the manuscript and encouraged the project in its early stages. Others who offered assistance include Len Barchousky, Lisa Bergson, Ed Frost, Daniel Guenzburger, Betty Holcomb, Robert Kahn, Deborah Luxenberg, Al Medioli, and Michael Waldholz.

Contents

1

Chains and More Chains

From the beginning the project seemed doomed. It was the wrong idea at the wrong time, friends warned David Thomas. Thomas had ambitious plans to build a franchised hamburger chain, and the last thing the country needed in 1972 was another fast-food chain. Brightly colored outposts of McDonald's, Burger King, and dozens of other hamburger companies already lined the arteries of every sizable city in the country. At hundreds of prime suburban intersections portraits of a benevolent Colonel Sanders looked down on crowds of eager customers. The fast-food market was saturated, argued the Wall Street experts. There was simply no more room.

Perhaps as well as anyone in the country, Thomas, a veteran restaurant operator, recognized the awesome success of the chains. Still, he was not impressed by the giant competitors. Millions of customers might flock faithfully to parking lots under the golden arches, but Thomas felt the famous patties were skimpy—the meat was lost in a padding of pickle and bread.

This view would become famous a decade later when commercials would ask, "Where's the beef?" Convinced that others must share his tastes, Thomas decided to offer a hamburger consisting of a quarter-pound of meat—substantially bigger than the McDonald's product, which then weighed one-tenth of a pound. The new patties would be square, with the corners sticking out over the bun, exaggerating the amount of meat in the sandwich. The larger hamburger would cost fifty-five cents, compared to McDonald's bargain-basement price of eighteen cents. Thomas dubbed his chain Wendy's, after his freckle-faced daughter, and set out to do battle with the entrenched hamburger industry.

Thomas was not new to the fast-food wars or to struggling against considerable odds. An orphan who had been adopted by a journeyman construction worker, Thomas entered the food business at the age of twelve, when he lied about his age to get a job as a soda jerk in a Walgreen's drugstore. For the next five years he scrambled from job to job in Fort Wayne, Indiana. Quitting school at fifteen, he worked as a busboy at the Hobby House restaurant, a popular establishment featuring T-bone steaks.

In 1950 the seventeen-year-old Thomas entered the Army, where he was trained as a cook and sent to Europe. His talents soon emerged as the future fast-food merchant became his unit's "outside-of-channels-procurement specialist," a position immortalized in Joseph Heller's novel *Catch-22*. The procurement wizards magically understood how to manipulate the system and avoid red tape to get their hands on the best food and scarce supplies. "The position always went to the greatest wheeler-dealer in the unit," Thomas recalled three decades later. "To keep that job I learned the meaning of resourcefulness."

As he made his scavenging rounds Thomas began to spend time at the enlisted men's club. Soon he began offering advice. The service should be speeded up. The boys didn't want a fancy restaurant; they would prefer hamburgers. When sales jumped the eighteen-year-old Thomas was rewarded with the much-coveted job of running the club. He was probably the youngest person in the Army to hold such a position.

When Thomas returned to civilian life in 1953, he came back to the Hobby House and soon advanced to assistant manager. The business prospered in the late 1950s, selling barbecue chicken and beef, and focusing on take-out. In 1962 Hobby House took over four Kentucky Fried Chicken stores in Columbus, Ohio, which were struggling to sell their then little-known product. Thomas was assigned to manage the failing operation and was given the option to buy 40 percent of the stores if he could turn them around. At the time he figured his personal net worth was three thousand dollars.

The problem the young fast-food merchant faced was considerable. The Columbus stores sold more than one hundred different products, including chicken. The wider the menu, it was reasoned, the more customers would be attracted. But with such a large selection, it was difficult to maintain quality, and the image of the stores was unclear. Thomas decided to streamline the restaurants and focus on chicken. He eliminated most items from the menu, offered a box of chicken for seventy-nine cents, and began advertising heavily.

When the young manager took over, weekly sales for the four stores totalled twenty-five hundred dollars. A week after Thomas implemented his strategy sales doubled. In 1968 Hobby House sold the now highly profitable chicken stores. As his share of the proceeds Thomas received $1.7 million. At age thirty-five he was a millionaire, but still far from satisfied. He had set his sights on entering the corporate major leagues. His vehicle was to be the hamburger.

Thomas moved slowly at first. By the end of 1972 Wendy's had nine outlets, with annual sales of $1.8 million. As the country slid into recession the judgment of the Wall Street analysts was against fast food. Gasoline prices were rising, keeping motorists away from drive-ins. Household incomes were under pressure. Ignoring the pessimists, Thomas pressed ahead. While other chains targeted their small patties at families with children, Thomas was aiming his larger burgers at young adults. He was focusing squarely on the most rapidly growing age group of the population, and they were rallying to his stands.

In June 1975 the hundredth Wendy's was opened. By December 1976 there were five hundred Wendy's. By April 1977 the figure had reached one thousand. In 1978 another five hundred units were opened. Hamburger prices skyrocketed; interest rates brought most construction to a halt. In some cases Wendy's sites were poorly selected and they folded. But still the hamburger machine pushed on. In 1980 there were two thousand Wendy's. System-wide sales had passed a billion dollars. Never had a young chain grown so quickly. By 1981 the round-faced Thomas had become a familiar figure to millions of television viewers as he explained in a commercial that there was no reason not to buy his hamburgers.

With his success the newest hamburger magnate proved once again the power of franchising. It might be true, as the fast-food experts argued, that America already had enough hamburger stands and donut shops. But the shrewd entrepreneur could always find ways to attract new customers. If the demand for a product was not growing, the national chain still might expand rapidly by taking sales away from local businesses.

In recent years franchise chains of all kinds have been created. Luring customers away from small, family-run operations, the franchise companies have exploded across the country. Swarming along the roadsides, the familiar motel chains replaced Mom-and-Pop units. The list of lodging companies has grown steadily and now includes Holiday Inns, Ramada Inns, Quality Inns, Days Inns, Rodeway Inns, and Hilton Inns, among others. People who once relied on local mechanics now turn to AAMCO Transmission, Cottman Transmission, Dr. Nick's Transmission, and Mr. Transmission. Other specialists include Midas Muffler, Meineke Discount Mufflers, and House of Mufflers. Neighborhood barbers have given way to chains called The Barbers, Edie Adams' Cut & Curl, and Mantrap Professional Hair Salons. The consumer with a toothache can gratefully turn to Dental World, Omnidentix, and United Dental Networks. And, of course, everywhere there are the food dispensers. The names run into the hundreds: Dunkin' Donuts, Mister Donut, and Tastee Donut; Burger King, Burger Chef, and Bun N Burger; Taco Bell, Taco Tico, and Taco Villa; Pizza Hut, Pizza Inn, and Pizza Rack; Dairy Queen, Dairy King, and Dairy Cheer; Church's Fried Chicken, Kentucky Fried Chicken, and Popeye's Famous Fried Chicken.

The franchise companies have entered nearly every service business, supplying home nurses, lawn care, running shoes, rental cars, and computers. Though people under twenty may find it difficult to believe, not long ago very few franchise outlets existed. More than 95 percent of today's chains started in the last three decades. The vast majority began in the last twenty years, and many giant chains have showed their greatest growth in the last ten. Century 21, the real-estate operation, was founded in 1972 and by 1980 controlled 7400 outlets. Mighty McDonald's, the king of all franchise chains, was founded in 1955. By 1970 the golden arches decorated 1500 outlets. The figure passed *6200* in 1980.

The great burst of franchise growth began in the late 1940s and accelerated in the 1950s as the postwar generation migrated to the suburbs. There the chains found their natural home, forming strips along the highways. In the 1960s franchising began invading the cities. In some cases urban neighborhoods protested the arrival of the chains. Community groups staged demonstrations and sought to block franchise expansion. In nearly every instance the activists failed, and the chains continued to advance. In the mid-1970s, having already established themselves in cities and suburbs, the chains turned their sights to towns that had once been considered too small for national outlets.

The sudden arrival of the chains produced particularly dramatic results in smaller communities. A Pennsylvania town of 12,000 I knew in the late 1960s had perhaps two or three franchised outlets. Commercial activity focused on a prosperous main street where most businesses were locally owned. Visiting the area ten years later, I was shocked to see the economic transformation. Where fields and homes had stood, franchised outlets now lined the highways leading to the town. Downtown stores that had once flourished had closed or moved to the three malls that had sprouted in outlying areas. The town supported Mister Donut, Wendy's, Long John Silver's, Pizza Hut, and two McDonald's. A Holiday Inn guarded one entrance to the community. Next to it loomed a Ramada. A local real-estate office carried a Century 21 sign.

The town's shift to the franchised economy was typical of what many larger communities experienced. By the 1980s people in Abilene, Texas, and Roanoke, Virginia, in Cheyenne, Wyoming, and Columbus, Ohio, all patronized identical-looking businesses. Frequent travelers would wake up in a chain motel uncertain where they were. Shaking sleep out of their eyes, they could peer across the parking lot at the rows of outlets and still have no clue to the city or region's identity.

Most Americans now routinely patronize franchise businesses. More than 90 percent of people over twelve eat fast food regularly, the Newspaper Advertising Bureau reported, with the average customer grabbing a quick bite nine times a month. Each night 300,000 people stay in a Holiday Inn. The Commerce Department estimated total 1983 sales of franchise companies at $436 billion. This represented one-third of all retail sales in the country and 15 percent of the Gross National Product. The figure was up from $168 billion in 1973, when franchising accounted for 10 percent of GNP. (These figures include sales for gas stations and pop bottlers, companies that are technically franchises.) Business-format franchises—the motels, fast-food outlets, and other chains that are the subject of this book—produced sales of $111 billion at 297,000 outlets. Over the last fifteen years these franchises consistently outpaced the overall economy, growing even during the recession years of 1974, 1975, and the early 1980s. Sales of business-format franchises nearly doubled from 1978 to 1983.

Despite their enormous presence, the franchise chains have largely escaped scrutiny. Academic researchers have generally ignored the subject. While sociologists and psychologists endlessly examine every aspect of human behavior, they have shown little interest in the companies that have changed the country's eating habits. Popular books on franchising have mainly been confined to accounts of how to make a fortune or to tales of unscrupulous operators bilking the unsuspecting public. Perhaps the chains have intrigued few writers because the businesses seem frivolous—gaudy outlets selling uninspired food and homogenized motel rooms. Or perhaps the chains have become so much a part of the landscape they have been taken for granted. My purpose in examining franchising was to look at the phenomenon of the chains more closely than had been done before. I sought to determine why the chains had proven so enormously successful and what they had done to the country.

In the course of researching this book I interviewed several hundred people. I talked to customers in Dairy Queen parking lots and to executives of multinational chains in their plush offices. I questioned Wall Street analysts and motel maids. During each interview I asked a variation of the same question: Why have the chains succeeded?

Why do you go to fast-food places? I asked customers. Why do people prefer patronizing real-estate chains instead of independent brokers? I asked chain executives. The interviewees offered a range of suggestions. Some cited convenience. Located on a major thoroughfare and brandishing a big, familiar sign, the chain outlet is easy to find and simple to patronize because of its standardized services. Another strength of the chains, franchise aficionados argued, is quality. Many customers are avid fans of Big Macs. Others swear that Holiday Inns offers superior rooms. Executives said the chains have lower costs. With their shiny new equipment and scientific management techniques, the chains can undersell family-run operations.

All these explanations may offer clues to why certain individuals go to particular outlets, but they fail to explain franchising's overall success. As I compared the wealthy, successful chains to the vanishing local outlets, the advantages enjoyed by the chains were not obvious. In upstate New York, for example, a small local chain called Carrols prospered until McDonald's entered the territory in the 1960s. Operating in similar outlets, the companies offered nearly identical food at identical prices. Yet McDonald's quickly decimated the local competition. It could be argued that the growing national chain was better known so that travelers would be more likely to patronize it. But in the communities where Carrols operated the vast majority of customers were local people stopping a few miles from home. For these consumers Carrols was a familiar sight.

Around the country, thousands of similar contests between national and local firms have been waged. Businesses offering similar motel rooms, sandwiches, or mufflers compete. Time after time the national chains emerge on top. Why?

As I talked to franchise executives the crucial advantage of the chains became more apparent. In the 1950s the franchise companies began their explosive growth by introducing corporate methods of finance and marketing to traditional small businesses. While once restaurants and barbershops were individual operations financed by the savings of one family, the chain builders discovered that they could raise huge sums by licensing outlets to owner-operators. Pooling funds from hundreds of small investors and borrowing from large institutions, franchise entrepreneurs could build big, eye-catching outlets. They could display standardized products in attractive surroundings. Compared to the gleaming chain stores, local businesses would seem shoddy and outdated. Unlike most local businesses, the chains could advertise heavily in the newspapers and on television. They could market hamburgers and motel rooms the way manufacturers had long packaged and sold products such as aspirin and soap.

The true genius of the chain builders was not reflected in their ability to design fast-food kitchens or pick store sites on busy highways. The franchise entrepreneurs excelled in the art of selling products in a competitive environment. Relative latecomers to television advertising, they quickly learned how to use the medium as effectively as anyone had ever done. A hamburger—like soap powder—might be an ordinary commodity, but it could be made to seem special.

As I sought to discover what made the chains prosper, I also explored how they had changed the country. The franchise expansion produced substantial economic consequences. For a relatively small group of people franchising has brought lavish prosperity. The founders of the great national chains accumulated enormous wealth, and thousands of investors and employees have enjoyed successful careers, with comfortable middle-class incomes. But for many others the rise of franchising has brought little economic cheer. Driven out by the chains, thousands of independent business owners have been forced to find other work. Lives have been disrupted, savings wiped out. Some of the bankrupt small-business people have found positions in the growing ranks of the franchise work force.

There are now more than five million jobs in franchise chains. The number of people working in fast-food restaurants, motels, and muffler shops has risen at a time when jobs on farms and in factories have declined. The expansion of franchise chains has been a major component in the shift of the country's economy from the production of goods to the providing of services. More of the nation's wealth has been used to pay for tax preparation, lawn care, and donuts. Less is being invested in the production of heavy machinery and homes. Bridges and parks have decayed as new franchise outlets rose gleaming along the highway strips.

For many of the people entering the work force of the chains, the franchise economy offers only dead-end slots. While the factory worker might earn a middle-class income and have hopes of winning promotions, the maid in the motel earns little more than the minimum wage and has a scant chance to move upward. Many of the franchise companies rely heavily on young people working part-time for the minimum wage. For the workers, the jobs are economic expedients that must be tolerated for brief periods. The employees earn no benefits and seek no future with the company. By contrast, some of the local restaurants and hotels that have been driven out by the franchise competition paid higher wages and employed older people in long-term jobs.

Along with chronicling the concrete economic results of franchising, I sought to examine its more intangible effects. How is a town different once local businesses have been replaced by units of national chains? The impact of franchising is hard to quantify. But as we will see, the loss of local businesses serves to diminish regional cuisines and regional identities. Locally run operations help create a sense of community and serve as meeting places. Franchised outlets are carefully designed to minimize personal contact. The fast-food employee does not talk to the customer. The structure of franchise strips encourages drivers to drop in quickly and then move on. Working in a depersonalized environment, the employee or manager must operate within a straitjacket of corporate regulations. Managers have little freedom to tailor their units to their own tastes or to local preferences.

This standardization of economic life, which has progressed steadily for decades, is likely to continue. Young consumers have been captivated by franchised products, ensuring a strong future for the chains. By the time they reach grade school, many children are fanatically loyal customers of the fast-food chains. As they sit absorbed in front of television sets, children are bombarded with advertisements for franchise chains. They learn to crave trips to fast-food restaurants, and to insist on celebrating their birthdays there. Many parents oblige the young consumers. "When I was growing up we didn't get fast food until we got to be driving age," explained a thirty-year-old mechanic from Fairfield, Connecticut. "Our parents never would have taken us there. Now I take my two-year-old to a fast-food place for breakfast after church on Sundays."

As children become acquainted with fast food, they also learn about the muffler chains, hair salons, and motels they will one day patronize. More important, they come to believe that nationally advertised products sold in shiny outlets are superior to local goods. Having no memories of a world without chains, children grow up thinking of a 7-Eleven as the premier neighborhood grocery store. They recognize Radio Shack and Computerland as the best places to buy the products of a new electronic era.

In recent years children overseas have been obtaining their first taste of the franchise life. With assistance from the Commerce Department, franchise missions have been journeying abroad. McDonald's is now grilling identical hamburgers in twenty-seven countries. Franchise associations have been formed in Britain and France to help the growing chains. Franchising may still be considered primarily an American way of doing business, but the Europeans should not be surprised if their landscape suddenly changes. Once franchise chains gain a foothold they can grow very quickly.

2

The Franchise Formula

If you are manufacturing sewing machines in New York, how do you sell them in Cincinnati? In the 1850s that was the question faced by I. M. Singer & Co. The problem was particularly complicated, since the young business was desperately short of cash. Sales were slow. At a time when store-bought home appliances were virtually unknown, women were skeptical about these new-fangled machines. Husbands had to be persuaded to part with considerable cash in order to buy devices that would serve no practical value except to make their wives' work a little easier. If Singer was to achieve national sales distribution, the company would need aggressive salesmen who could bring the product directly to customers and show the miracles the sewing machine could work.

In 1851 a sales representative working in Dayton, Ohio, quickly sold his allotment of two machines. Cincinnati beckoned, its women waiting to be enlightened by the labor-saving salesman. Singer's man in Ohio wired headquarters for more machines. But it cost money to make machines, and the young company was nearly broke. People would buy the devices if only they could see them in operation, the salesman believed. In desperation, the company developed a brash scheme. Instead of the company paying the salesmen, the salesmen would pay the company. Eliminating salaried salesmen, Singer established a network of what would today be called dealers. Under an agreement, independent businessmen paid Singer a fee for the right to sell sewing machines in particular territories. The dealers paid sixty dollars for machines and sold them for a hundred and twenty-five. As the company had hoped, consumers soon embraced the new machine. Sales representatives in Pennsylvania and Wisconsin were earning more than eight thousand dollars a year, a large income for the time.

For the company, though, the new scheme brought less than cheerful results. The sewing machines were successful, but Singer was earning practically nothing; thanks to steep discounts the dealers absorbed most of the profits. In some territories dealers proved lazy or inefficient, allowing rival companies to steal sales. Singer could do nothing to prevent this. Under their contract, dealers had exclusive rights to their territories. The company could not withdraw these rights or send in salaried representatives. By 1856 Singer began to back away from the distribution experiment, repurchasing rights that had been sold. In the future the company would sell its machines through salaried agents working on commission. "In no instance have we sold any territorial rights that we did not afterwards regret it," wrote Edward Clark, a Singer partner, who is quoted in *A Capitalist Romance* by Ruth Brandon.

Though the Singer scheme failed, it did break new ground. In attempting to solve its distribution problems, the company had established a primitive franchise system, probably the first used by American business and the ancestor of the elaborate networks employed by today's hamburger and motel chains. The modern chains turn to franchising for the same basic reason Singer developed its plan. The companies seek economical ways to distribute products or services. Like Singer, contemporary chains license independent operators to establish far-flung outposts.

Webster's New Collegiate Dictionary defines "franchise" as "a special privilege granted to an individual or group." The term is used in a number of contexts. In medieval times the Catholic Church granted franchises to officials who served as tax collectors, taking some money for themselves and presenting the rest to the Pope. English nobles in the eighteenth century awarded similar franchises in return for payments or responsibilities. The U.S. government guarantees its citizens the "franchise to vote." More recently, owners of professional sports teams must obtain franchises from the leagues in order to operate in particular cities. At the moment would-be cable television companies are battling ferociously to obtain franchise rights from cities.

In the business world the common franchise system consists of two parties: a parent company—called a franchisor—and a dealer—called a franchisee. The franchisor grants the franchisee the right or license to sell a product or service. The franchisee may acquire the rights to use the parent's name and methods. The most common and simplest form of franchising is product or trade-name franchising. Under this system, companies—much like Singer—license dealers to sell their products. General Motors initiated one of the first successful licensing systems. In 1898 the young manufacturing company, lacking the capital needed to open retail outlets, began selling its steamers through a system of dealers that is still universally used in the automobile industry. The first franchisees included owners of bicycle and hardware stores who sold cars as a sideline.

Detroit later tried a range of marketing techniques, such as mail order and selling cars in department stores, but franchising proved to be the most effective mode. Aggressive local dealers could buy the land, buildings, and cars and sell them more effectively than the company could on its own. Having avoided the expense of fielding a sales force, the companies were free to invest in the more lucrative manufacturing sector of the business. By 1955 dealers of all the U.S. car companies were estimated to have invested $4 billion in land, buildings, and inventory. The National Automobile Dealers Association estimated that the money invested by dealers exceeded the total capital invested by the Detroit manufacturers.

Under current contracts a car company grants a franchisee the right to sell in a particular area. The franchisee buys the cars at discount and resells them. In recent years dealers have helped protect car companies from the disastrous shifts in the market. When companies overproduce or make errors in styling, dealers must bear the initial shocks. Cars sitting unsold in showrooms have been paid for by the dealer, a fact that helps to explain why hundreds of dealers have gone bankrupt in recent years while manufacturers survive.

Gasoline service-station dealers have a similar arrangement with major oil companies. Until 1930 petroleum companies owned most of their stations, permitting only a few independents to operate. Then the independents started price wars. Central management, unable to calculate appropriate prices for locations around the country, feared losing sales to the independents. In 1930 Standard Oil of Indiana began leasing stations to managers. Other companies followed. The dealers set their own prices and took whatever profits the stations generated. The system benefitted the companies and the franchisees. The dealers gained a measure of independence and control over their businesses, while oil company profits immediately went up. The franchisees, instead of receiving salaries, now paid rents. In addition, the oil companies no longer paid the Social Security taxes or the overtime wages that New Deal legislation had recently mandated. Working for their own profits, the dealers kept the stations open longer and sold more of the gas they had purchased from the oil companies.

Soft-drink bottlers were another group who saw the advantage of franchising early on. Invented in 1886, Coca-Cola at first spread slowly along with the soda fountains where it was sold. Then in 1899 two Chattanooga businessmen, Benjamin Thomas and Joseph Whitehead, persuaded the president of Coca-Cola to grant them a license to sell the product in bottles. In a six-hundred-word agreement the entrepreneurs promised to establish a bottling plant at no expense to the company. The businessmen would produce a carbonated drink, putting a mixture of Coca-Cola syrup and water into bottles. The company agreed to sell the operators the syrup and supply labels and advertising. Thomas and Whitehead were granted rights to sell their product in most of the country, as long as the new containers did not interfere with soda-fountain sales.

As the demand for Coke skyrocketed, the partners quickly realized they lacked the money and management ability to service the entire country. To continue expanding, they began awarding contracts to operators who would bottle the drink for specific territories. Thomas and Whitehead bought the syrup from the Coca-Cola company and resold it to the franchisee bottlers. In 1901 contracts were awarded in Chicago, Cincinnati, Louisville, and other cities. In 1903 the partners awarded thirty-two more contracts. The next year they issued forty-seven. By 1909 the number of bottlers reached 379. By 1919 there were one thousand bottlers participating in the booming business. The Coca-Cola plants that had started on obscure side streets moved to prominent places and became well-known landmarks in their communities.

Other major soft-drink operators followed Coke's lead. Companies such as Pepsi, Royal Crown, and Dr Pepper came to sell the rights to their formulas to franchisees. During the first several decades of this century the number of industries using franchising began to increase. In 1902 Louis Ligget invited a group of drugstore proprietors to discuss forming a cooperative. Forty druggists each contributed four thousand dollars toward establishing manufacturing facilities. The cooperative took the name Rexall. Soon it sold the right to use the Rexall name and products to independents, who would display the familiar sign.

In 1925 Howard Johnson borrowed five hundred dollars and took over a money-losing drugstore in Quincy, Massachusetts, that had a soda fountain and newsstand. The store sold three flavors of ice cream, which it purchased from a supplier. Johnson, using a hand ice cream maker in his basement, developed a product with double the butterfat content of commercial brands. Customers soon lined up outside his store to sample the new ice cream. Gradually the soda fountain evolved into a restaurant, as Johnson added hot dogs and hamburgers to the menu. In 1929, as the country slid into depression, Johnson opened another restaurant in Quincy. He began thinking of opening more outlets and processing much of the food himself. But the Depression forced Johnson to alter his plans, and he made a decision that would help change the nation's roadsides. With sales slipping and debts from his fledgling food-processing operation piling up, the restaurant operator realized he could not open another unit himself. He would need a partner—a franchisee. Johnson persuaded the owner of a restaurant on Cape Cod to use the Howard Johnson name and to buy supplies from the Quincy store in return for a fee. Both Johnson and the new operator prospered. Johnson signed on other franchisees. By 1935 there were twenty-five Howard Johnson roadside ice cream and sandwich stands in Massachusetts. By 1940 one hundred outlets dotted the East Coast all the way to Florida, each restaurant selling the same kinds of food and sporting the orange roof Johnson had selected to attract travelers.

Following the lead of Howard Johnson and other pioneers, chain builders began operating actively after World War II. Most of the giant chains of today were started in the 1950s and early 1960s. In 1952 Holiday Inns first opened its doors, while AAMCO Transmissions started in 1958. Small service businesses of all kinds were being franchised: Roto-Rooter offered to clear drains, Manpower provided temporary workers, Culligan softened water. As the massive migration from the farms and cities to the suburbs accelerated, the franchise chains prospered along with the housing developments they were designed to serve. A flood of money poured into the suburbs. The federal government subsidized highways and single-family houses.

Families who had accumulated war bonds began to cash them in. Much of this money found its way to the franchise operations.

During the 1950s incomes rose and the new middle class expanded, snapping up consumer goods, buying on credit. Having struggled through two decades of depression and war, a generation eagerly embraced an ideal life that included ownership of a suburban split-level home with a two-car garage. Each year cars grew wider and longer, flashing more chrome and brandishing bigger tailfins. As the number of cars increased, parking spaces near downtown stores became scarce, while shopping centers, with their ample parking lots, boomed. Traditional small businesses faced new pressures. The family-run corner grocery was exterminated by the self-service supermarket. Independent hotels, restaurants, and stores in the inner cities languished, replaced by suburban chains. Big corporations expanded while small operations were swallowed up.

Returning GIs were marrying and moving into the middle-class enclaves. They were eager to begin careers. Everywhere aspiring chain magnates obliged them, offering opportunities to invest in franchise outlets. One of the most ambitious operators was William Rosenberg. In 1950 Rosenberg opened a donut shop in Quincy, Massachusetts, and began eyeing the success of Howard Johnson's chain, based in the same town. Highway donut shops were beginning to appear around the country as the nation became more tied to automobiles. It would be possible to build a chain of donut shops, Rosenberg believed. An aggressive dreamer, Rosenberg was driven to succeed. Coming from a poor family in Boston, he had quit school at fourteen in 1930 and worked as a messenger boy for Western Union. He set an office record, bicycling five miles in twelve minutes, and he would be in a hurry the rest of his life. The future entrepreneur then worked at a succession of jobs, driving an ice cream truck and selling various items door to door.

After the war he set out to make his mark in a field where a lack of education did not matter. In 1946 Rosenberg started selling sandwiches and coffee to factory workers. He operated from a freshly painted truck that bore the impressive-sounding name of Industrial Luncheon Service. Three years later Rosenberg had one hundred trucks. Donuts accounted for 40 percent of his sales. But the future of the company seemed uncertain, as vending machines were looming on the horizon. Seeking a secure business he opened a shop. Selling donuts at sixty cents a dozen, Rosenberg was soon grossing $1800 a week. Gradually he modernized the store, wrapping his product in distinctive packaging and calling the business Dunkin' Donuts. In 1955, lacking the cash to build further, Rosenberg sold the rights to open more units to friends. He was franchising, just as Howard Johnson had done.

The entrepreneur starting a chain in the 1950s had to possess a certain grandiose vision. It was not enough to own one store or two. No, the chain builder longed to see dozens of his creations spread around the country. If he couldn't afford it, others would finance the project for him. The operator had to believe his operation was so compelling that replicas of the initial store should exist in towns around the country, and that thousands of customers would forgo existing independent businesses to patronize the new entry.

The chain builder's first task was to recruit investors willing to build and operate outlets at crucial intersections and on the growing highway strips. In an age before the wide use of television advertising, chains such as Dunkin' Donuts could not attract franchisees by offering sophisticated commercials or a well-known name that would immediately produce business. That would come later. In the early days the entrepreneur would have to argue that he had developed a powerful formula for designing a shop, making donuts, and selling them. Pointing to a successful store he had already opened, the donut operator would say that the hapless independent working by himself could never hope to match the pilot unit's profits. But for a fee the chain president would be glad to tutor the franchisee in the mysteries of the donut business. He would suggest where to locate the shop and help build a replica of the parent company's unit. The franchisee and chain builder would strike a deal. The franchisee, who may have never run a business, never made a donut in his life, would suddenly find himself the owner of a predesigned store. The chain operator, meanwhile, realized the more ambitious dream of heading a corporate enterprise.

The franchise expansion of the 1950s began gradually. New to the franchising business, William Rosenberg and other pioneers slowly recruited franchisees one by one. The chain builders had to learn how to locate operators and where to build the outlets. They had to develop the track records that would attract more investors. In the early 1950s Kemmons Wilson, the founder of Holiday Inns and a man who would later turn away thousands of eager franchisees, could find few interested takers among the dozens of contractors and real-estate operators he approached. Only gradually did the entrepreneurs establish suburban presences.

Early fast-food franchisees made their debuts on the outskirts of smaller cities such as Tucson, Arizona, and Columbus, Ohio. The fledgling chains occupied sites on what had been largely empty roadsides, broken only occasionally by gas stations, drive-in movies, and carhop hamburger joints. A fast-food outlet would sprout on a straightaway, a muffler shop would open down the road, and soon the pace of development quickened. Fast-food entrepreneurs were discovering that instead of catering to teenagers, who had once been major patrons of drive-ins, the chains could attract suburban families eager to load the children in the station wagon and go out for a bite.

By 1960 the old inner-city eating places, such as White Castle, were beginning to face competition of a new kind. As the middle class fled to the suburbs, the downtown shopping areas were deteriorating. On the routes connecting inner cities with outlying districts and neighboring communities, franchise strips began to form. With their rows of pulsating signs, the strips proved fertile territory for the rapidly growing franchise chains. Attracted by increasingly familiar brand names, drivers pulled off highways for a quick bite or a new muffler.

In the 1950s franchising was a little-known idea. Most entrepreneurs stumbled on the concept, improvising arrangements with franchisees to suit particular circumstances. When Henry and Richard Bloch began their H & R Block chain of tax preparers in 1956, they had no idea that anyone else had attempted a system based on licensed operators. But gradually franchising became a widely known method of doing business. McDonald's, Holiday Inns, Kentucky Fried Chicken, and other chains led the charge. In 1969 Kentucky Fried Chicken was the largest fast-food chain, with 1800 outlets, while McDonald's operated 1000. Seeing the success of the new companies, entrepreneurs had begun thinking specifically of forming franchise chains. Whether they provided hair cuts or car washes did not seem to matter. Any kind of suburban chain was likely to prosper.

Hordes of franchise salesmen spread out around the country. An entrepreneur who lived in Louisville, Kentucky, in the early 1960s recalls that it was possible to attend a different sales presentation every week. Companies from around the country set up shop in local motel rooms, where they pitched business opportunities. A group of Harvard Business School students estimated that 40,000 people would purchase franchises in 1969.

In March 1970 *Fortune,* citing the opportunities offered franchisees, reported: "At a time when more and more people are dissatisfied with the bureaucratic forms of business and demand more individual recognition, franchising updates the success dream by promising liberation as well."

But by the 1970s many franchisees had discovered that the field was not quite as promising as the salesmen had made it seem. Many of the new chains collapsed quickly. Big chains continued to grow, but competing against the giants could be as difficult for a small chain just starting as it was for the independent businessman. The business press began carrying more reports of franchise failures and scandals.

The largest chains were now beginning to resemble giant corporations in other industries. They were advertising nationally on television and developing substantial corporate structures, consisting of market researchers, financial analysts, and lawyers. The larger chains began to account for more and more of the growing franchise sales. Throughout the 1960s and 1970s the chains grew steadily. When the Department of Commerce began tracking franchise growth in 1969, it estimated total sales at $115 billion. By 1975 the sales figure had reached $190 billion. During the six-year period thousands of gasoline stations closed, but the total number of franchised outlets still increased from 383,000 to 434,000.

Unlike car manufacturers and other product franchisors, the rapidly growing chains of the 1950s and 1960s did not earn most of their income by selling supplies. What Holiday Inns and Dunkin' Donuts sold were concepts—ideas for businesses with catchy names and distinctive ways of operating. This was a newer type of franchising, which would become the fastest-growing segment of the field—business-format franchising. Format franchises include fast food, motels, and muffler shops, the businesses that have given a uniform look to highways around the country.

In the format franchise the parent company does not necessarily sell the dealer a product. Burger King sells some supplies to franchisees, but its main function is to license operators to build replicas of the parent business and to use the company name and advertising. In effect, the parent company sells its franchisees ideas. And successful business ideas do not come cheaply.

A new franchisee pays Burger King a basic fee of $40,000 to obtain a twenty-year license. In addition, the franchisee pays 3.5 percent of gross sales to the company as a royalty. For this fee the franchisee has the right to display the Burger King sign and sell products designed by the chain, such as the Whopper sandwich. From the beginning of the relationship the company supervises the franchisee's activities. Burger King's real-estate staff selects sites, which are then offered to the franchisee. The company assists in building the store, while the franchisee must pay to construct and equip the unit. Equipment must be purchased from suppliers approved by Burger King and built according to company standards. The company maintains distribution centers, selling the franchisee supplies ranging from french fries to paper napkins. The franchisee can either buy from the company or purchase from suppliers approved by Burger King.

Before the store can be opened, the franchisee must attend the company's training center for seven weeks. There the new hamburger entrepreneur learns all phases of the business, including cooking, supervising personnel, and accounting. The franchisee is an independent operator who owns the unit and can sell it at a profit with the company's approval. But the company provides precise regulations specifying how hamburgers should be prepared and the correct way to clean seating areas. District managers and inspectors regularly visit restaurants to enforce regulations and assist the franchisee in earning maximum profits. The franchisee must implement national marketing plans, selling products promoted on national television.

The system of relying on licensed franchisees has made it inexpensive for a parent company to open identical units across the country. McDonald's, H & R Block, and Midas Muffler were among the first companies to exploit business-format franchising fully. The growth of these companies was speeded enormously by franchising. Towns where no chains had existed could suddenly be blanketed with outlets in a couple of years.

Operating without franchisees, it might take decades for a company to raise the money and hire the managers necessary to establish, say, a national chain of Mexican restaurants. But by licensing local business people to open units, the chain can spread across the country in a few years. A chain seeking to put a company-owned Mexican restaurant in a town must go through the time-consuming procedures of obtaining a mortgage and carefully assessing the risks. Will the highway be moved in two years, wiping out the business? Does the town need more tacos? Then the company must hire and train a manager.

In a franchised operation the company relies on hundreds of individual franchisees to raise the money. Local dealers mortgage their homes or borrow from friends. The franchisees serve as managers of the outlets, and they take most of the risk, not the company. If the taco haven fails, the individual operator will be bankrupt; the parent company will suffer minimal losses. Even if the business concept is bad or the economy is declining, the chain can still grow as long as new franchisees are willing to invest in opening outlets. Franchised chains can expand at explosive rates that few company operations can match.

Because of the speed factor, more and more businesses have been forced to franchise. In an age in which giant corporations crush small competitors, a fledgling company's only chance for survival may be to franchise quickly. If a new idea is worthwhile, others will copy it and try to build a national operation. When the competition succeeds it can use network television and the advantages of size to drive out the originator of the idea, who foolishly chose not to franchise.

Entrepreneurs do not necessarily like to sell off the rights to their financial children. They would prefer to own all the units outright, keeping the profits at home. But they have little choice, particularly if they wish to open more than a few units. "If you have a good idea and you move slowly, others will beat you to your market," explained Robert Barney, Dave Thomas's successor as Wendy's chief executive officer.

As Wendy's established a position near the top of the hamburger heap, it had to battle other companies that scrambled to duplicate the successful format. After Wendy's opened, Judy's, Cindy's, and Andy's began offering variations on the large-patty theme. The Wendy's concept consisted of thicker hamburgers served in restaurants featuring turn-of-the-century design motifs. Cindy's sought to bring higher-quality fast food to small towns in the Southeast that had been overlooked by the national chains. Signs over Wendy's stores read "Wendy's Old-Fashioned Hamburgers" and displayed a picture of a girl with pigtails tied with ribbons. Cindy's sign said "Cindy's Ole Time Hamburgers" and featured a picture of a girl whose hair was tied with a ribbon. Thanks to its powerful franchised network, however, Wendy's quickly became a national operation capable of fending off these challengers. Had it not been franchised, the competition might have won the edge.

Customers entering a chain outlet rarely know or care whether the unit is owned by a franchisee or a company. It is impossible to tell if a chain is franchised just by looking at outlets, though some chains do advertise that their units are locally owned. Most large restaurant chains are franchised, but Denny's, a leading coffee-shop company, does not franchise. Holiday Inns, like most large motel companies, is a franchised chain. The company owns 240 hotels and licenses 1515 units to franchisees, independent business operators who put up the cash to build the facilities and then operate them. A&P is not franchised. The company owns all its stores, hiring managers to staff them.

Most chains can be clearly categorized as either company-owned or franchised. If franchised, they are either product or business-format franchises. However, a few chains fit in more than one slot. Radio Shack is a hybrid, with elements of several different approaches. The company maintains 8700 units around the world, 5700 of them owned by the corporation. Of the rest, about one hundred of the outlets are business-format franchises, vestiges from the years before 1971 when the company sold outlets. Other units are run by franchised product dealers who operate in towns of less than 8500, where it would not pay for the company to open stores. A dealer must own a profitable business in order to qualify for joining the chain. In exchange for a five-thousand-dollar fee, the dealer obtains the right to display the Radio Shack name and to add the company's products to his store's existing lines. Though dealers are free to sell any products, they often concentrate on Radio Shack goods. "I don't want to put anyone into business," says Robert Lynch, Radio Shack's vice president for franchising. "I'd like to be the icing on the cake."

Franchising's entrepreneurial spirit has spread into company-owned stores. All Radio Shack managers receive a modest base pay determined by the volume of their stores. Since bonuses are based on the profits of the stores, the managers are not far removed from franchisees.

For the small entrepreneur who masters the franchise system, the rewards can be substantial. As one outlet grows into a dozen and then a hundred, royalties come pouring in to company headquarters. The former shop operator can become a company president. For the franchise magnate there is no more standing behind the counter wearing an apron, no more sweating eighty hours a week and pampering each customer. Dozens of franchise innovators have taken their places alongside other corporate executives. Having created empires of identical outlets, they have come to enjoy chauffeur-driven limousines and Wall Street financial manipulations.

In three decades Karl Stanley went from being the owner of one shop to president of CutCo Industries Incorporated, a chain of 473 beauty salons with sales of $89 million in 1983. As Stanley demonstrated, chains providing a service that previously defied standardization could thrive as well as companies producing uniform commodities such as donuts. His silver hair and goatee carefully trimmed, Stanley fully resembled the high-priced New York hairstylist he once was. Wearing an open-neck shirt under a double-breasted jacket, he talked in a deep, calm voice that could easily quiet a society matron's concern about her new permanent.

Stanley, who died after he was interviewed for this book, described his career with the relish of the self-made. "I was taking premed in college," he recalled. "I had to quit school during the Depression, and I got into hairdressing through a friend of the family."

Stanley demonstrated a flair for the field, winning a job at Franklin Simon, a Manhattan department store, where he worked in the 1940s. The Fifth Avenue store catered to high society, and its beauty salon served a stream of celebrities and the city's rich. Stanley became one of the leaders of his profession, seven times invited to speak at the International Beauty Show. Lecturing and granting interviews, he became well known in beauty circles. But the rewards of the job were unsatisfying for someone who once planned to be a doctor.

In 1949 he opened Stanley's Beauty Salon in the Forest Hills section of New York. Though the shop prospered, Stanley sought more. Like most beauty salon operators he made little money from his employees; he was forced to fix hair himself to make a living. Stanley sat down with his accountant to discuss the situation. He concluded that he wanted a chain. "If I had fifty stores making fifty dollars a week I'd be better off, since I could stop working as a hairdresser," he said. "I decided to get the best possible location no matter what it cost and to get a name that would stick with the public."

In 1953 Stanley opened a beauty shop he called Cut & Curl in downtown Hempstead, New York—a town in the rapidly growing Long Island suburbs. Although he had gained his reputation by providing expensive hairstyling on Fifth Avenue, Stanley determined that he would make his fortune by doing cut-rate work—lots of it—for the rising middle class.

The store opened with a sale. Haircuts cost seventy-nine cents, a fraction of the normal price. Permanent waves were five dollars, or about half what the typical beauty parlor charged. Ads running in *Newsday*, the Long Island newspaper, proclaimed, "Look smart. Be smart." The first day the new store did a hundred and twenty haircuts. "The ads were corny," Stanley observed with some pride, "but they worked. We had low prices, but we were making dough because the operators were busy from Monday right through Saturday."

The new store had opened at an opportune moment. In the 1950s women were putting a new emphasis on clothes and cosmetics. After wartime privations, conforming to a feminine ideal was suddenly important. Television commercials that had recently begun pushing pain-killers and razor blades also urged women to look their best. Clairol ads proclaimed, "If I have only one life, let me live it as a blonde."

Stanley joined this beauty crusade, applying the techniques of mass marketing to a business that had been untouched by the methods of modern corporate intelligence. At the time ads for salons were rare. And no one had ever heard of a *chain* of beauty salons. Stanley shaped his store to suit the emerging suburban life-style. The new suburbanites thrived on a casual spirit, calling each other by first names, wives venturing downtown with their hair in curlers. Stanley made it easy to patronize his beauty parlor. No appointments were necessary, a policy that was innovative. The store was cheerful and clean. After all, Cut & Curl was not just selling haircuts. It was providing an enjoyable experience, a break for the busy housewife, a chance to get away from the problems of husband and children.

Stanley devised a crude division of labor to increase the efficiency of his operation. A receptionist greeted customers at a front desk. Hairdressers did the cutting and applied permanents, the skilled work. Less skilled assistants earning minimum wages provided shampoos, neutralized permanents, and did menial tasks. Low-profit manicures were eliminated.

Over the next six years Stanley built seven stores. The former hairdresser was earning a handsome income, but his goal of owning fifty stores was still distant and seemed unattainable. Then in 1961 he realized that there *was* a way to expand quickly—franchising. Stanley had been hearing stories about how the franchising method had been used with enormous success by Howard Johnson's and the young Holiday Inns chain. He contacted these companies to learn their procedures.

Stanley drew up a primitive franchise contract and sold a license for a Cut & Curl parlor to a hairdresser who opened in prime Long Island territory. In his first year the franchisee made $30,000 on an investment of $10,000. Before joining Cut & Curl he had been making two hundred dollars a week. Stanley was off, selling units around the country.

Although the haircuts offered by Cut & Curl could not be of standard quality, it was still possible to give the chain a unified identity. Each unit would look the same and employ the techniques Stanley had perfected in his suburban market. Customers would come to the outlets because they were clean and modern. Franchisees would pay Stanley a fee because he had demonstrated outstanding skills in operating a beauty salon. The veteran hairdresser would provide the shaky novice a leg up.

To speed the process Stanley hired a consultant, a franchising expert who was also selling stores that would feature Campbell's Soup—an idea whose time seemed to have come. The consultant persuaded Stanley that he needed to add the name of a celebrity to the company. When Dean Martin declined, they turned to Edie Adams. The entertainer didn't actually do much for the company. She simply sold Stanley the right to use her name, and Stanley resold the right to others. The chain was no longer an anonymous outfit. Having suddenly acquired a famous identity, the company enjoyed a surge of growth. Women would come to the stores because they trusted a familiar name. Over the years Edie Adams provided no substantial service but continued to receive royalty checks.

Stanley opened Edie Adams' Cut & Curl shops in Georgia, California, and Arizona. The shops were aimed at women over thirty-five, and by 1980 they were in forty states. To reach younger men and women, Cut & Curl introduced Great Expectations, a unisex salon decorated with bright colors and hanging plants.

As Stanley and the other chain builders expanded their operations they came to be removed from the day-to-day problems of running an outlet. The traits that make for a successful shopkeeper were of little importance. While once they may have been sticklers for quality, concerned with making fresh donuts or pleasing individual customers, now the chain executives focused on raising money and designing storefronts. Above all, they had to be salesmen. To build a successful franchise operation, the entrepreneur would have to persuade dozens or hundreds of people to alter their lives radically, to abandon their livelihoods and stake their fortunes on the chain. The operator seeking to create a national business would have to become something of a gypsy. He would have to drive the highways scouting recruits. Wherever the entrepreneur traveled he would talk up his company. "You should become a franchisee," he would tell hundreds of people. If the salesman sold well, if he persisted, he would return home with signed contracts. New outlets would sprout; the chain would grow. For the shrewd operator there were vast opportunities. And franchising would provide a vehicle for some of the shrewdest salesmen the country had ever seen.

3

Ideas for Sale

One day in 1955 David Thomas, the future founder of Wendy's, approached a peculiar customer who had come to the Hobby House Restaurant in Fort Wayne, Indiana. Dressed in a white suit with black string tie, the heavy-set stranger had white hair and a goatee. He claimed to be an expert on fried chicken. "I'm Colonel Harlan Sanders," he told Thomas.

"Who are you with, sir?" the young manager inquired.

Two decades later the Colonel would be recognized instantly wherever he went, but at the time Sanders was an anonymous traveler on a mission. Not yet familiar with the ways of mass marketing, he was attempting to find local operators who would buy franchises. Driving along the highways of Indiana, Ohio, and Kentucky, Sanders stopped at restaurants, trying to convince owners that his secret recipe for fried chicken could transform their businesses. It was not an easy task, bringing this preposterous message. Thomas was soon persuaded, but many others slammed doors in the Colonel's face.

To win attention, the unlikely salesman would plead with the owner, offering to cook chicken for the employees of the restaurant late in the evening when the dinner trade slowed. Moist and tasty, the Colonel's product at that time was vastly superior to the standardized meal that would eventually make him famous. After winning converts among the help, Sanders would stay around for a few days, cooking for customers. If there was good response, the owner might buy a franchise, paying five cents for every bird fried with the Sanders method.

Selling franchises this way proved a slow and expensive process. For a man in his late sixties with little income, it was a foolhardy project. Sanders spent nights on the road sleeping in the backseat of his car and sometimes depending on the generosity of friends for meals.

The Colonel was a salesman of extraordinary persistence, but he claimed his real talent was as a cook. As a child living in Henryville, Indiana, he had learned to cook from his mother. After his father died and his mother went out to work, the six-year-old Harlan was left to cook for a younger brother and sister. By the age of seven he had mastered baking bread and preparing vegetables.

After his stepfather beat him, Sanders left home at twelve to take a job on a farm, earning fifteen dollars a month plus room and board. Quitting farm work at fifteen, Sanders went through a string of jobs, beginning about 1905. None of the positions lasted long, many ending with the hot-tempered young man being asked to leave. He worked as a streetcar conductor, then served in the Army in Cuba. He was fired from a railroad job because of a dispute with management. He took a correspondence course in law and served as a justice of the peace for several years, losing the position after a fight with another justice.

During the Depression Sanders operated a service station in Corbin, Kentucky. By now a skilled chef, he cooked for his wife and children in the back of the place and occasionally served a meal to a traveler to earn extra money. Word of Sanders' hearty food spread. Motorists headed from Detroit and Cincinnati to

Atlanta and Miami on U.S. Route 25 stopped at "Sanders' Servistation" for the pan-fried chicken, ham, and hot biscuits. Eventually Sanders became legendary in the region. Governor Ruby Laffon made him an honorary Kentucky Colonel in recognition of his contribution to the state's cuisine. The then cleanshaven Colonel closed his gas pumps, setting up a restaurant that could seat 142. In 1939 Duncan Hines' *Adventures in Good Eating* listed Sanders' restaurant.

As Sanders' reputation grew it became increasingly difficult to satisfy the customers clamoring for chicken. Travelers wanted meals in a hurry, and it took Sanders half an hour to pan-fry the chicken. When he tried preparing the food ahead of time, too much was wasted. Other restaurants french-fried chicken, immersing it in sizzling fat. But Sanders refused to use this shortcut, since the birds came out dry and unevenly done.

The solution to the Colonel's problem came with the invention of the pressure cooker. In the late 1930s Sanders saw a demonstration of the new device, which produced tasty green beans within a few minutes. The Colonel bought one of the machines. For weeks he experimented, learning how to cook his ideal chicken. He altered pressure, cooking time, and shortening temperature until finally he achieved a chicken the way he liked it: moist, not greasy. The procedure took only eight or nine minutes. Sanders' system would help to alter the nation's eating habits.

Using the new technology, the Colonel prospered. He built the first motel in Kentucky. Realizing the promotional value of his honorary title, be began dressing the part, wearing the string tie and white suit. In the early 1950s Sanders was offered $164,000 for his business and he turned it down. The Colonel looked forward to an easy retirement.

Then suddenly the business was destroyed in 1955 when Interstate 75 was built, taking traffic seven miles to the west. A year later Sanders was forced to auction his property. The same day he received his first monthly Social Security check of $105. At sixty-six Sanders was financially little better off than he had been at twelve, when he left home. But the Colonel from Kentucky was not prepared to accept his lot quietly. He began thinking about franchising.

In the early 1950s Sanders—who was always concerned about improving his cooking—had studied food service at the University of Chicago. At the school the Kentucky restaurateur became friends with Pete Harman, owner of a hamburger stand in Salt Lake City. In 1952 Sanders taught Harman his method for cooking chicken. Later when the Colonel visited his friend he had to push past a line of customers. Harman's business had increased substantially. He was planning to sell his Ford and buy a new yellow Cadillac. Though Harman did not realize it, he had become the Colonel's first "franchisee."

A couple of years later, Ted Cullin, who owned the Blue Bird Restaurant in Morristown, Indiana, was heading south on his vacation when he stopped at Sanders Court, an establishment whose sign then boasted of "tile baths" and "steam heat." That night he tried the house specialty—fried chicken. "It was so good that I thought it must have been an accident," he told the *Louisville Courier-Journal* later. "But then I had it again for breakfast and it was better."

Cullin reached an agreement with the Colonel, joining the half-dozen restaurant owners who by the mid-1950s were paying Sanders four cents for each chicken they cooked according to the secret recipe. In 1956, having lost his business, Sanders set out to build on this tiny beginning of a franchise system. If he could sell one hundred licenses, the franchise salesman calculated, he could earn a thousand dollars a month, enough to live on comfortably. Accompanied by his wife, who dressed in an antebellum gown, the Colonel loaded his car with pressure cookers and his secret seasoning.

Sanders was frustrated in his effort to interest well-known restaurants. "You couldn't even talk to the big operator," Sanders later explained to *The New Yorker*. "Oh, no, he was sittin' up smoking cigars. He had him a chef in the kitchen, and he knowed all about food that was to be known."

Gradually Sanders made inroads. Restaurant owners were hearing how Sanders' chicken could attract customers. They began approaching the Colonel. It was no longer necessary for him to travel. If people wanted to buy the franchises they would have to come to Kentucky. Sanders and his wife managed the growing business from their home in Shelbyville. The Colonel took care of the bookkeeping while his wife managed the shipping of the spices. By 1960 they had over two hundred franchised outlets and were earning $100,000 a year. By 1963 there were six hundred units producing profits of over $300,000. The Colonel had seventeen employees. He ran the operation from an office he had built behind his house.

While Sanders labored in Kentucky, other chain builders were discovering the value of franchising. Salesmen for McDonald's, Holiday Inns, and dozens of other companies were traveling the country, many driving battered cars and facing rejections. Though the Colonel only sold a product, most of the franchise salesmen offered complete business formats. Over the next decade Kentucky Fried Chicken also began offering complete restaurants.

In the mid-1950s a franchise salesman required the determination of a Colonel Sanders to find buyers. Wary customers wondered why they should pay hard cash in exchange for a paper license to business ideas. But by the late 1960s the success of Sanders and the other chains had become well known. Boosted by powerful advertising campaigns, Kentucky Fried Chicken created more than a hundred millionaires among its stockholders, franchisees, and employees. McDonald's produced at least as many of the newly wealthy. All this success legitimized franchising, giving it a strong appeal to investors. By 1980 there were more than six thousand Kentucky Fried Chicken stores. White Castle, a hamburger chain that opened in 1921 and did not franchise, never produced more than two hundred units. To businessmen the message was clear. Franchising could bring quick profits. The task of the franchise salesman had become much easier.

By the early 1960s chains were putting pressure on individual operators. Mom-and-Pop businesses of all kinds were quickly disappearing. Still, the idea of owning a business continued to have a powerful appeal. In corporate offices and on assembly lines, employees harbored dreams of leaving constraining jobs, of owning their own restaurant or travel agency. For tens of thousands of people, buying a stake in a franchise operation began to seem like a feasible way to achieve the goal of independence. With a franchise there would be no more scowling bosses and nine-to-five jobs. The franchisee might work a seventy-hour week, but the profits would be his. And the chances of failure with a franchise seemed much less than operating independently.

If the new franchise holder knew nothing about running a restaurant, the company would provide training. If the franchisee lacked capital, the company would help arrange a loan. The parent company would assist with bookkeeping and cost controls, crucial aspects of running a business that often destroy the new operator.

Tales of the fortunes made in franchising fueled the fantasies of would-be shopkeepers. The millworkers and school teachers who had carefully tucked away $15,000 or $20,000 in savings over twenty years eagerly turned their money over to franchise salesmen. In New York in 1961, A. L. Tunick addressed an attentive crowd that had come out for one of the first trade shows designed to sell franchises. Tunick, a millionaire thanks to his Chicken Delight chain, spoke fervently of the benefits of linking up with a franchise company. "Welcome, you unhappy people," Tunick greeted the crowd. "You're here because you are unhappy over your economic lot, your job, and your future. Maybe you are happy, but you want to be happier.

"Are you making $20,000 but want to make an easy $50,000 a year? We don't have that for you. Are you making maybe $60, $80, $100 a week, and you'd like to make about $10,000, $15,000, or $20,000 a year, and are you prepared to work hard for it, at least in the initial years?

"We have lots of opportunities for you."

Such appeals ensured a constant pool of investors ready to snap up franchise licenses. For the franchise company the benefits of winning over these entrepreneurs are clear. In the typical franchise arrangement the local operator pays an initial fee and then pays royalties on all sales. A Midas franchisee, for example, pays a $10,000 license fee and royalties of 10 percent of gross sales. Computerland charges $20,000 and royalties of 8 percent. Some companies charge considerably more. If the initial franchise license costs $20,000—a common price—and the company can sell one hundred of them, it is doing quite nicely indeed.

As the company's sales increase, it can raise the price of new franchise licenses. In 1975 Kwik Kopy, a regional chain based in Houston with 150 outlets, charged $8000 for a franchise. By 1980 the price had climbed to $29,500, since the company had become a profitable national operation with 470 units.

Franchisees must sign detailed contracts with the parent company. Philly Mignon, a sandwich chain, uses a fifteen-page document that is typical. The franchisee agrees to pay a franchise fee of $17,500 for the right to run one restaurant at a specific location. The owner-operator obtains the right to use the trademarked name and the company's system of running limited-menu self-service restaurants. The company agrees to make reasonable efforts to maintain the reputation of the chain.

Each Tuesday the franchisee must report sales from the previous week and pay the company royalty payments of 4.5 percent of gross sales. The franchisee must also spend 4 percent of gross for advertising, with one-fourth of that total going to the parent to be used for promoting the entire chain. In addition, the franchisee must pay a "Grand Opening" fee of $2500, which is to be spent on advertising and marketing in the first thirty days the business is open. The contract is for fifteen years. At the end of the period, if the franchisee has a satisfactory operating record, the company may renew the contract.

Parent companies can profit from franchisees by selling them supplies. Tunick, who started Chicken Delight in 1952, did not charge royalties to his franchisees. However, he required them to buy cooking equipment and food supplies from him. The system worked well enough when the franchisees prospered. In

1965 Tunick sold out to Consolidated Foods, enjoying a handsome profit. But in 1972 *The Wall Street Journal* reported that eight hundred franchise holders were suing the company. They had grown tired of paying inflated prices for supplies, providing the company huge profits. A federal court sympathized with the franchisees, and Consolidated Foods sold its rights to the Chicken Delight trademark, having concluded that without the old arrangement on supplies the company was no longer worth holding.

To reach franchise buyers companies advertise in publications such as *The Wall Street Journal*, *Forbes*, and *The New York Times*, as well as in the business opportunities sections of local newspapers. The companies are not shy about presenting their case. "Isn't it about time you made some *real* money?" AAMCO Transmissions asked readers of *The Wall Street Journal*. "Change your life-style," Kampgrounds of America suggested in *The New York Times*.

Hertz used a more subdued approach in its efforts to sell wealthy investors equipment-rental outlets. In fact, the company warned prospective franchisees that the new units were bound to *lose* money for the next several years because of high interest rates. Even so, hundreds applied for licenses.

The Hertz outlets rent heavy equipment to construction companies and manufacturers. In the spring of 1981 the company began advertising the franchises in *The Wall Street Journal*, pointing out that construction companies—faced with high interest rates and sporadic business—were becoming more interested in renting equipment rather than buying machinery that might be idle half the year. At first there were few inquiries. This was not completely unexpected, since the ad mentioned that investors must raise $1.5 million to open an outlet. "In the beginning we had certain doubts that people would respond," said Joseph Vittoria, former vice-chairman of Hertz.

During the following summer President Reagan began talking more about tax shelters for business and tailoring more laws for investors. Hertz decided to change its ads to emphasize the tax benefits of the franchise. The reworded ad drew hundreds of calls the first day, keeping the sales staff busy till midnight. Applicants included the chief executives of major corporations and a wildcat oil driller who had hit on one lucky well; he flew to New York in his private jet to talk to Hertz.

Despite the sizable investment requirements, most of the callers said they wanted more than one outlet. The Hertz name and the chance for tax shelters drew them. The franchise offered the same tax benefits *before* the Reagan program, but the President's campaign had encouraged investors to put tax shelters at the top of their agendas.

Besides using newspaper ads, chains locate new franchisees through referrals from banks and existing franchisees. Notices in government publications, such as the Department of Commerce's *Franchise Opportunities Handbook*, bring inquiries. For the last two decades franchise trade shows have attracted eager crowds who come to examine the rows of colorful booths where companies display their wares. Each year dozens of fairs are held in hotels and auditoriums around the country. Main Line Marketing Inc., of King of Prussia, Pennsylvania, stages about fifty "Business Opportunity Shows" a year, charging fees to companies for their booths.

A weekend show held in January 1982 at a Ramada Inn in Montvale, New Jersey, attracted about four hundred people each day. The motel ballroom took on the atmosphere of a county fair as middle-aged husbands and wives discussed the merits of exhibits that promised financial independence, while younger people with longish hair stared intently at distributorships for video games.

A dozen people crowded around someone selling distributorships of popcorn poppers. Popcorn cracked while behind the strident salesman a sign listed dozens of places where the product could be sold, such as bars, bowling alleys, and bus stations. Uniformed representatives of Uniglobe travel agencies asked passersby if they had thought of going into the travel business. They passed out literature pointing out the advantages of joining a chain, since, "Today's consumer equates quality, competence, and success with size." Uniglobe's advertising agency, the leaflet noted, worked for Century 21 and Alka-Seltzer. "People are tired of their bosses," stated Sam Damico of Main Line Marketing, explaining what draws the customers. "Or they're just curious."

The possibility of owning a business seemed very real at the show. For $3400 a customer could purchase the means to open a small part-time business-cards operation. Most people casually wandered around the ballroom, asking questions of the representatives and watching videotapes at the booths. A few fairgoers indicated interest in the franchises. Robert N. Lattomus, representative for General Business Services, said he usually sells one franchise during a weekend show for his business counseling company. When a man stopped to ask Lattomus about General Business Services, the salesman inquired if he had ever owned a business before. The man said he had had five in the last eleven years, having just sold out the last one. He came to the show looking for his next opportunity.

After locating likely franchisees at fairs or through ads, many companies invite them to formal sales presentations. There they provide more information on the company and woo the potential franchisee with evidence of profitability. VR Business Brokers runs ads for "The Businessman's Business." Those calling the advertised toll-free 800 number who seem like serious prospects are invited to a sales presentation. VRBB is perhaps the ultimate franchise—a business that sells other businesses, including franchised outlets. Small-business owners wishing to sell out can come to a VRBB dealer, who will find a buyer.

The company invited interested people to a sales presentation in October 1981 at the Roosevelt Hotel in New York City. A dozen candidates gathered in a conference room, mostly middle-aged men in business suits with several younger people and one woman. Jay Sargent, a young man with a dark blue suit and a gleaming smile, introduced himself as the company's communications director and began explaining why the economy has been kind to VRBB. People who had once sought security in large corporations were being laid off, he noted. To ensure themselves a steady income in the future unemployed blue-collar workers and executives were seeking to purchase small businesses. "They want to buy their next job," he explained. "We at VRBB feel we're at the right place at the right time."

For the next hour Sargent talked simply and clearly, spouting a stream of facts and figures without referring to notes. With the enthusiastic sincerity and expansive gestures of a television preacher he held his audience rapt. But Sargent was not selling religion; he was extolling the gospel of making money through franchising.

The communications director told the tale of George Naddaff, founder of VRBB. The rags-to-riches story was made to seem an awesome saga. A working-class youth and an underachiever in school, Naddaff sold baby carriages door to door. "How many people here have done direct selling?" Sargent asked.

The woman said she had sold cosmetics, while a man volunteered that he had sold vacuum cleaners. Sargent smiled knowingly and said they must appreciate how hard it is going door to door. Within ten years Naddaff was earning $170,000 as head of his company's sales force. After a dispute with his superiors, he left the company and faced the difficulty of finding new work. "He couldn't go become a bank president because the income would have only been a third of what he had been making and he wasn't qualified," Sargent pointed out.

To solve his problem Naddaff "bought the Colonel." In 1967 Naddaff and a partner purchased a regional Kentucky Fried Chicken franchise for the Boston area. "The Colonel taught him a system. By buying the Colonel's system and paying thirteen cents on the dollar George became a millionaire."

The message is clear: franchising is the answer—even if you pay steep royalties. And there is a suggestion that Naddaff learned the business from Sanders himself. (In fact, Naddaff did profit from his franchise, but he never dealt with the Colonel, who had sold the company some years earlier.) Next Naddaff helped develop a chain of child-care centers, which he sold in 1980 for $10 million. Then came the call of business brokerage. VRBB is attempting to build a national chain of brokers modeled after Century 21. Just as Century 21 changed the real-estate industry, VRBB claims it will alter its field. "They have been doing what we are doing," Sargent noted. "We're bringing professionalism and expertise to an industry."

Sargent explained how the VRBB system works. The company's brokers walk into businesses and ask if they are for sale. In one out of twenty cases the owner will say yes and allow VRBB to sell the property. VRBB then advertises in the business opportunity pages of the local paper. The ads run with the VRBB sign.

In each of its market areas the company tries to dominate the business opportunity pages. Sargent held up a copy of the *Philadelphia Inquirer* business opportunity page with VRBB ads highlighted in pink Magic Marker. Several dozen pink ads dominated the page. He passed around the paper. "That is impressive," one man in the audience conceded.

VRBB brokers have 1500 businesses for sale on their lists in Philadelphia and 1300 in Atlanta. Each broker can sell any of the properties listed by other brokers in the chain. A broker who lists a business and sells it receives the full commission. If the broker sells something signed on by another broker, they split the fee. There are so few business brokers in the country, Sargent said, that VRBB agents working as a team can control a market. When the market area is covered profits start pouring in. "Without a tremendous amount of money we dominate an area," Sargent said. "We leave no room for competition."

For each transaction a brokerage office charges 12 percent of the selling price of the business, or a minimum of $6000 for small deals. The $6000 minimum might seem steep in some cases, Sargent volunteered, but it isn't. VRBB recently sold a florist's shop in Memphis for $16,000. The owners wept and kissed their broker's hand as they paid him $6000, Sargent explained. They had not expected to get any money for the shop. "Where we don't exist these people lose big."

VRBB provides important support for franchisees, the salesman observed. "Could you be a business broker without us?" he asked. "I think you could. You could struggle for a few years and make critical errors."

But what VRBB offers is more security, a better chance at success and more money over the long run. In a poll of franchisees, 98.6 percent of them said if they had to do it over again they would invest in VRBB. "If you have any intelligence you will spend fifty dollars on the phone and ask our franchisees how much they make," Sargent said.

Having enraptured his listeners with tales of success, Sargent came to the point. A VRBB franchise costs $22,500 and the company gets 6 percent of gross income as royalties. In the past the company has entered cities and quickly sold its quota of outlets. Sargent sold eleven franchises in Houston after two days of presentations such as the meeting today. Houston sites were no longer available. He expected similar success in his new campaign in New York. He invited everyone to come to VRBB's Boston headquarters, where they could ask company officers "brutal questions." "I want you to come to Boston this Friday," he said at the Wednesday meeting.

Sargent suggested everyone should go right home after the meeting and call up franchisees to learn how they are doing. There was a feeling of urgency as most people in the room filled out forms to make reservations for Boston. "I have an uncle who every Thanksgiving says he could have bought Polaroid stock at thirty cents," Sargent said.

In case anyone missed the moral of this last story, he issued a final word of advice. "I suggest you move quickly to come to Boston. We will leave no room for our competition."

VRBB may indeed prove to be another Polaroid. On the other hand, chances are it won't. (In fact, the company has proved moderately successful—it now has 300 units operating.) Franchising, like any business operation, is risky. In the marketplace there is only room for a handful of contenders to succeed. If you are betting on whether a new chain will succeed, you should always assume it will fail. In nearly every case you will be right. Very few business ventures of any kind last more than a few years. This is certainly true in franchising, where entrepreneurs can start chains on not much more than a whim, using other people's money.

The business press, which should understand the odds against success, regularly carries glowing accounts of new franchise concepts. The journalists faithfully quote company officials, who explain why the country needs a chain of used-car dealers or home remodelers or visiting nurses. Often the article is accompanied by a picture of the company president, who, it is noted, was an executive at a successful established chain. One of my favorite franchise articles appeared in *The Wall Street Journal* on May 8, 1978, when the newspaper alerted readers to Command Performance, a haircutting chain that was providing executives with impressive profits:

"'I'm an ex-Marine with a short haircut and I'm very conservative,' says a highly placed financial officer at a big international corporation. 'When somebody suggested I buy a franchise for a unisex hairstyling salon, I said, "You've gotta be kidding.'"

"Nonetheless the financial executive bought. What he bought is already becoming one of the hottest franchise deals going. The lure: For ten or twelve hours a week of management, a potential yearly pre-tax operating profit of 20 to 30 percent of sales of $50,000 or better on a total investment running only $50,000 to $80,000.

"The franchise or license gives its buyer a hairstyling shop for men and women called Command Performance. The franchisor is Command Performance Systems Inc., Westport, Connecticut, the brainchild of Richard J. Wall and Walter J. (Bud) Wright. Mr. Wall, a veteran marketing man, was a founder and key figure in the success of Bonanza, the steakhouse franchisor. Mr. Wright was an insurance executive for Burger King."

The article went on to explain that the chain had sold 134 licenses in six months. Franchisees included many former executives who were giving up their jobs to take on shops. It seemed impossibly easy. And it was. In April 1981 the company filed Chapter XI bankruptcy proceedings. A new owner took over the company and tried to revive it.

Such setbacks are not unusual. For a chain to grow it must serve some need of a large group of people. It must be adequately financed and properly managed. When all these elements fall into place a chain can expand with breathtaking speed. However, the response of customers is unpredictable. The life of a national chain depends on intangible qualities that are not easily controlled. "The success of new concepts, as rare as it is, is largely a matter of good fortune rather than any special prescience on the part of their founders," writes Robert Emerson, a fast-food expert and investment manager for Fred Alger & Company.

No major chain has ever been able to establish a second successful national chain. Kentucky Fried Chicken certainly has the financial resources and management experience to start another chain. Yet the company has been unable to succeed with attempts at Mexican, seafood, and roast-beef operations. The magic that enabled the original fried chicken concept to sweep the country was absent in later attempts.

Hoping to hit on a successful concept, entrepreneurs start dozens of franchise companies every year. And every year dozens die. Many entrepreneurs toying with a business idea immediately think of franchising. It is the best way to milk big profits from an idea quickly, they reason. Whenever a need seems to arise in the economy, would-be chains rush to satisfy it.

If a chain survives for several years and manages to build a substantial network of franchisees, its chances for enduring may be quite good. But the route to success is uncertain. Chains that start strong may suddenly collapse. In August 1978 Tantrific Sun Inc. opened its first suntanning parlor in Searcy, Arkansas, a town of 14,000. Judy Moody, a local woman working in real estate, developed the idea of charging people to use sun lamps. Her husband, James, who taught vocational agriculture, designed the tanning equipment, which consisted of a booth that was seven feet high and three feet across, lined with lamps on all sides. A customer walked into the booth and simply stood to receive an even suntan on all sides. The customer began with a one-minute exposure and in later visits increased to about ten minutes. A package of twenty visits cost about thirty-five dollars.

After the original salon proved successful two more were opened in Little Rock, financed by a group of real-estate operators headed by Grady Mason, who became president of the company. A franchise was sold and began operating in Memphis in March 1979. When a newspaper ran an article about the parlor the company was flooded with requests for the right to franchise. Tantrific was unprepared for the intense interest in its product. "We didn't even have a sales force," Mason later told *The New York Times.*

To handle the rush they occupied several suites at a Holiday Inn in Memphis. Mason said that "in three days we sold a quarter of a million in franchises; people were waiting in the hallways for a chance to talk to us."

Within a year there were one hundred salons ranging from Nevada to North Carolina, most of them owned by doctors and lawyers. The company hoped to open five hundred more over the next several years. Customers poured in. Franchisees paid the company a $25,000 fee for the equipment and help in setting up. In addition, they gave Tantrific 10 percent of their sales. Franchisees reported grossing seven thousand dollars a month. Half of that was profit. The first salons sported patio furniture to go with the sun theme. But with more money pouring in, parlors switched to expensive wicker. "People want to keep their tans all year round," James Moody said, explaining the success.

Competitors rushed to join what seemed to be the beginning of a huge industry. The earliest entrants would certainly become rich. By 1980 the International Tanning Manufacturers Association reported twenty-two franchise chains in operation, with names such as Tanique and Tantilize.

Then the growing empires came under attack. Dermatologists began suggesting to the Federal Trade Commission that improper use of tanning bulbs could lead to cancer and aging of the skin. As the industry expanded some companies were throwing together equipment in garages without considering safety procedures. Articles began appearing pointing out the dangers of suntan parlors. Customer traffic, which had been slow in summer anyway, began to vanish. By 1980 Tantrific was headed toward bankruptcy. Other companies soon followed. The next year the tanning manufacturers association reported that *all* its members had stopped franchising tanning parlors.

Stories of failures do little to discourage the hordes of would-be franchisees. Part of the reason chains continue to win supporters is that franchise salesmen keep refining their pitches. On more than one occasion I have been swept up by a salesman's enthusiasm, convinced that a young chain had real potential to become a national operation. I would feel the excitement of being present at the beginning of a company whose name would become a household word. Fortunately, I was listening as a journalist, not a potential investor. I lost only time, not money. None of the promising companies proved more than modestly successful. My biggest disappointment came with Dentcare, the first dental franchise.

In December 1981 I went to White Plains, New York, to interview Myles Sokoloff, the company's vice president. Sokoloff escorted me through the plush headquarters offices to a conference room, where he proceeded to narrate a slick slide presentation. The chain had thirty-five offices drilling away, trying to tap the huge market of unfilled cavities. A 33-year-old dentist with a round face and a serious manner, Sokoloff recited the Dentcare story in a bit of a singsong, punctuating the tale with enthusiastic predictions of a bright future.

"What is Dentcare? Dentcare is the largest developer of dental centers in the United States and Canada. By 1982 we expect to be in markets around the country. We originally decided we were not going to market in the Northeast because the competition was too keen. But there has been so much interest in the Northeast we have sold two franchises in New York, two in Connecticut with an option for seventeen, and two in Boston. We have sold a franchise in Portland, Oregon, and in Jacksonville, Florida. So we are expanding at a rapid rate.

"Why does a dentist want to get involved in Dentcare? One, because of our size and experience. Two, because of our marketing muscle. Three, because of our financial resources. Dentists are becoming interested in the franchise concept because of articles such as 'The Birth of Franchised Dentistry,' in *Dental Economics*. Dentcare has been written about in many publications. *Fortune* magazine is currently doing an article on us, which should come out in the next couple of months.

"The dental industry, according to the U.S. Department of Labor, was a $13 billion industry in 1979. It was estimated that by 1985 it would rise to $36 billion and by 1990 it would rise to $60 billion. That represents dollars spent on getting your teeth fixed in the United States. The latest statistics for 1980 are about $17 billion. The rise is meteoric. Part of the reason for the rise in dental expenditures has been the result of the employers offering dental plans as a benefit. On the graph you see that in 1972, 18 million people were covered. In 1977, 35 million, and in 1980 it was estimated that 60 million people would be covered. But according to the Health Insurance Institute of America 74 million were covered."

Sokoloff then explained how the chain was luring the new customers. Located in a mall or department store, each Dentcare center was a modern facility designed to resemble a retail outlet, rather than a dentist's office. Customers entered the front of the wood-paneled store, where a receptionist greeted them in a plant-filled waiting area. Walls featured murals with lake or forest scenes. For the first visit no appointment was necessary. Patients could simply walk in. The chain would attract the millions of people who had never visited a dentist because it was frightening or inconvenient or expensive.

For a dentist-franchisee the profit potential was enormous. Franchisees hired recent dental graduates to staff the facilities. While a prosperous private practitioner typically grosses $110,000 and earns $45,000, the Dentcare operator could do substantially better, Sokoloff said. An outlet in West Mifflin, Pennsylvania, grossed $600,000, and several units had reached

$1 million. Some franchisees owned more than one outlet. People were pouring into the stores, Sokoloff said. After an advertising blitz in Richmond, Virginia, the center handled a hundred new patients in a week. The chain was impressive enough to win the assistance of well-known companies. J. Walter Thompson, the giant advertising agency, was producing a campaign for the chain. General Electric Credit Corporation was underwriting credit cards that customers could use at Dentcare centers around the country. Sokoloff handed me an elaborate packet of information about the chain that included articles printed in the *Chicago Tribune*, *U.S. News and World Report*, and the *St. Paul Dispatch*. An article about Ronald F. Saverin, who headed Dentcare, appeared in *Forbes* under the headline "Ronald McDentist." The company was going to be joined by many competitors, the then thirty-one-year-old Saverin told the magazine. "This business is just too lucrative," he said.

I left the interview thoroughly impressed. Mass-market dentistry was about to arrive. The Dentcare sign would appear in malls around the country and flash out from network television ads. Shoppers would get their teeth fixed on impulse. I was not at all surprised to see an article in the February 21, 1983, issue of *Fortune* under the title "Here Come McDentists." The article described efforts of several franchise chains and showed a picture of Sokoloff and Saverin, who was now identified as thirty-two. But something curious had happened. The caption identified the pair as founders of Dwight Systems. Where was Dentcare? I had talked to Sokoloff in December, and by June *Fortune* said, "Saverin and Sokoloff walked away from the enterprise, leaving such major creditors as Montgomery Ward and E. F. Hutton Credit Corporation to sue the empty corporate shell for hundreds of thousands of dollars." Faced with mounting losses, the scrappy pair of dental entrepreneurs had not given up. They simply started a new company.

The problem, it seemed, was that the chain founders had been too ambitious. In its rush to grow, Dentcare signed up mall leases for which it did not have franchisees. Franchisees complained of buying equipment through the company that never arrived. Apparently confident of their impending success, the partners had been "taking some rather extravagant salaries," *Fortune* noted. Despite this history, the revived dental franchise operation was to all appearances finding new operators willing to sign on.

What brings so many investors to chains like Dentcare is the opportunity to make a fortune. But the odds against striking it very big in franchising are considerable. For a franchisee to become a millionaire requires an unusual set of circumstances. An aggressive individual must join forces with a growing company at an opportune moment.

The Ideal Operator

Flying in the front seat of a small airplane, Harold Fulmer surveys Pennsylvania's Lehigh Valley like a baron inspecting his realm. Noted for its steel mills and rich farm land, the valley is home to 700,000 people. Fulmer feeds and houses a large percentage of them. "Over there," he says, pointing to a factory, his voice rising above the whirr of the engines, "they're adding six hundred employees, and they're putting up more housing. That will bring us more business."

Across the road from the growing industrial complex is a shopping mall whose entrance is marked by the famous arches that appear tiny from the air but are still instantly recognizable. It is one of Fulmer's fourteen McDonald's. The store now does $1 million in annual sales, and the figure undoubtedly will shoot up when the factory expands.

In the backseat of the plane Mike Krajsa, Fulmer's executive director, points out the franchisee's other properties that stand out dark against the blanket of week-old December snow sparkling in the sunshine. There are apartment buildings, commercial areas, more McDonald's outlets. The plane sweeps out to nearby Kutztown and circles the community's airport, which Fulmer owns. From the plane Fulmer observes traffic patterns and the developments spreading out from Allentown and Bethlehem, the two largest cities in his territory. The airborne perspective helps him decide where to place new McDonald's units and how to lure customers to old ones, he claims. But one suspects that the working-class boy who became very rich flies only partly in search of profits. For Fulmer flying, like making money, is a recreational activity.

A six-foot-three-inch, 275-pound giant who wears a cowboy hat and string necktie, Fulmer greets friends with hearty handshakes and tells people he is—and always will be—a small-town boy. But he discusses McDonald's finances with the polished intelligence one would hope to find in, say, the Secretary of State. At forty-one, Fulmer is worth over $60 million. The McDonald's stores register about $14 million sales a year and probably produce about $2 million a year in profits. Fulmer has become a prominent member of the valley's ruling elite, a group once dominated by Bethlehem Steel executives and department-store owners. People who in the past would have paid little notice to a hamburger operator treat the McDonald's franchisee with deference. College presidents and clergymen beseech him for donations. Charities ask him to serve on their boards. Every week dozens of hopeful callers try to sell him something or request an appointment to learn the secret of his sudden rise.

Fulmer's success came because of his keen eye for underpriced property and deft sense of timing. And he was lucky. During the 1960s and 1970s, Fulmer's two businesses—real estate and McDonald's—thrived. By 1980 he owned, among other things, one thousand apartment units and four shopping malls. His chief indulgence was a collection of one hundred antique cars that featured a string of Bentleys and the Rolls-Royce used in the movie *Goldfinger*. In recent years, to protect his enormous income from the tax collector, Fulmer constantly invested in what seemed to be losing propositions. The strategy did not always work. One oil-drilling partnership that was supposed to provide a write-off immediately produced a gusher. The investment brought an unexpected $1 million.

Some of Fulmer's acquisitions are bought to complement existing holdings. Other properties seem to be purchased by a man who plays while he works. In 1980 Fulmer bought a radio station and began using it to advertise McDonald's. He later bought a helicopter for radio traffic reports, a big old hotel in Allentown to use as headquarters, and a thousand-acre camp that his three thousand employees can visit for summer vacations. Any business Fulmer purchases, he operates flamboyantly. Above all, the franchisee is a promoter, an old-fashioned salesman. "You've got to excite the customers," he lectures. "You've got to create interest. You've got to have something going on all the time."

Acting on this philosophy, radio station WSAN, which is 1470 AM, periodically has announced that everyone who comes to a McDonald's in the next fourteen minutes and seventy seconds will get free food. Drivers screech in. In the fall of 1981 Fulmer's restaurants raffled away a BMW. The radio station occasionally announced that for the next hour the $10,000 car would be parked in the lot of a McDonald's, where anyone could fill out entry slips. The previous summer Fulmer put twenty tons of ice in a parking lot and held a contest to guess how long it would take the ice to melt. The winner won a trip for two to Hawaii. Fulmer once bought a building and discovered that the structure contained thirty abandoned wooden rocking horses. Not one to pass up an opportunity, he set up a rocking horse marathon in a mall near a McDonald's. The thirty participants rocked as long as they could with the last person moving receiving a car. The winner went for over four days and the feat was entered in *The Guinness Book of World Records*.

Some local critics said Fulmer went too far when he ran a billboard-sitting contest to publicize the radio station. In the event three entrants were to sit on the ledge of a billboard. The last one to climb down would be awarded an $18,000 mobile home. The radio station received half a million applications to enter the event. Three "lucky" contestants were selected and they began their marathon wait, living in tents on a platform on the ledge of the billboard that is six feet wide and forty-eight feet long, standing thirty feet above an interstate highway. A sign promoting the station towered over the men. The billboard sitters caused traffic tie-ups as people driving by paused to stare. Brownie Scouts brought the valiant three cookies, and college students asked for their autographs. Some people charged that Fulmer was exploiting the men in the manner of the Depression-era dance marathons. The contestants said they welcomed the event, since it might be the only way they would ever get a house of their own.

Life was cramped on the billboard, but the men told the many reporters who journeyed to the site that they were determined. Almost two hundred days into the contest one of the entrants was arrested for selling marijuana to a plainclothes policeman. Shortly afterward Fulmer declared the contest a draw and awarded the two remaining men mobile homes, proclaiming he would make donations to the Boy Scouts and other causes as well since the contest had gained so much publicity.

All Fulmer's activities bring attention to the McDonald's stores and help to explain the chain's strength in the Lehigh Valley. The Allentown operator is hardly a typical franchisee. One of the richest fast-food operators in the country, Fulmer is an extreme case of zealous dedication producing mountains of profits. Still, the contribution he makes to McDonald's is similar to the role thousands of lesser franchisees play in chains of all kinds.

Companies often lavish praise on their franchisees, saying that they make chain success possible. Besides putting up money to develop new stores, franchisees provide parent companies with a unique brand of management talent. Owner-operators are said to bring more energy to a store than salaried managers do. "A franchisee is motivated far better than an employee," said Leo Lauzen, president of Comprehensive Accounting. "He is building his own future and takes pride in his work."

Though it may be true that franchisees are motivated, they do not necessarily produce better results than company-operated stores. In most chains the parent companies typically own some outlets, while the majority of units are operated by franchisees. In nearly every category of franchise chain the outlets owned by parent companies and administered by salaried managers have greater average sales than units owned by franchisees. In automotive products and services the average company-owned unit in 1983 had sales of $665,000, while the franchisees averaged $174,000, according to the Department of Commerce. Company-owned real-estate offices had sales of $553,000, compared to $215,000 for franchisees. In hotels, motels, and campgrounds, company units averaged $3,043,000 compared to $1,501,000 for franchisees. In restaurants, auto rentals, tax preparation, and printing, the company units had substantially greater sales than the franchisee units.

Somehow the parents manage to produce more sales than the hardworking franchisees. Franchise companies often set the rules of the chain, so that company-owned units operate with advantages. Franchisors are not necessarily concerned about the franchisee's profits. In some chains the parent takes most of the best locations for itself. Franchisees are then used to fill out less profitable areas and to give the chain the full coverage needed to finance national advertising and bulk purchases of supplies. Hertz only franchises rent-a-car units in smaller cities where sales are lower. H & R Block, which has covered all major cities in the country, sells only what it calls satellite franchises. These go to people in towns of less than 15,000 population. The franchisees must already have existing businesses, such as real-estate brokerages. During the tax season their offices double as Block centers. By relying on part-time franchisees Block can penetrate areas that would not be large enough to support a full-scale company unit.

Franchisees may be used to pioneer untested areas where sales are uncertain. If a franchisee does achieve strong sales, the parent may buy out the unit or place another franchised outlet near the successful operator. This will cut into the sales of the first franchisee but overall chain sales will increase and royalties to the parent will rise. Companies often outsell franchisees because the parent units have more cash available and can spend more heavily on local advertising. In all cases the parent company holds the edge and will use the franchisees to the parent's benefit.

Franchisees have provided cheap labor for many chains. Some companies make special efforts to recruit couples. Dunkin' Donuts encourages husband-and-wife teams to open outlets, since the couples and their children are willing to work long hours. Typically companies suggest that the wife keep the books, while the husband oversees operations and purchases supplies. To find competent franchisees companies develop selection procedures. Minuteman Press talks to prospective investors half a dozen times before granting a license. Chains vary in the qualities they seek in franchisees. Holiday Inns accepts only experienced real-estate developers who can manage large operations and raise the more than $6 million needed to put up a new motel. To run one of its sandwich shops, Blimpie merely wants a stable person with some experience in business or at a job such as teaching. General Business Services, which provides business and accounting advice to small businesses, looks for people with substantial experience; a master of business administration degree is considered a plus. Dunhill Personnel looks for middle-level corporate executives who are typically making around $30,000 to $40,000 and are personable.

Many companies welcome teachers or corporate executives who see little future in their careers. Of the three hundred franchisees of Dunhill Personnel in 1980, fourteen were former Xerox employees; most had been middle managers or engineers. During periods of recession, when layoffs increase and winning promotions in corporations becomes more difficult, applications for franchises increase. Kwik Kopy, a Houston-based company, received a surge of inquiries in 1975 when the space program slowed down and NASA employees were looking for work. Some franchisees struggled first with their own small businesses. Larry Fasciano, who worked in his family's shoe store for twenty years, took over a Dunkin' Donuts franchise in New York after he concluded there was little hope for the old business. "We were being eaten up by the chains," he said.

For the franchisee, opening a chain unit for the first time can be an exciting and terrifying procedure. Many new investors sell possessions and take out huge loans. They look to the company for support and general handholding. "It is a frightening situation when all of a sudden, after years of working for someone else, suddenly they find themselves running their own business," a franchise salesman said. "It is a real gamble."

Though the ideal franchisee must be willing to take a chance, many companies shy away from innovative risk-takers with broad backgrounds. Fast-food companies in particular like plodding operators who will not challenge corporate policies. The franchisee must be willing to toe the line. He must be motivated, but not too freewheeling. Franchisees enjoy the support of large corporations with sophisticated marketing procedures. In exchange for the supposed security of belonging to a chain, the local operator gives up the right to engage in the kind of experiments that make running a small business exciting. "Everything is spelled out for the franchisee in detail," explained Joseph Koach, former executive vice president of the International Franchise Association. "It's enough to drive a lot of entrepreneurs up the wall."

People who buy franchise licenses seeking creative freedom may become caught in the same procedural straitjackets that ensnare company employees. In some chains hundreds of regulations are enforced by inspectors who insist that everything be done by the book. In order to open more units the franchisee must receive permission from the parent, a sometimes lengthy and frustrating process.

McDonald's regulations often inhibit Harold Fulmer, who likes to run his business with a free-ranging zest. Though the Allentown franchisee enjoys some liberty to develop marketing campaigns, his hamburger production procedures are rigidly controlled. And Fulmer must sometimes abandon his own zany concepts to participate in the standard games and contests emanating from corporate headquarters. Using his own ideas may require negotiations with company executives. In 1974 Fulmer decided to stay open twenty-four hours a day. The company, learning about the schedule change, objected. Staying open all night would hurt McDonald's wholesome image, officials argued. However, the franchise contract only specified stores should remain open from six a.m. to eleven p.m. The regulations did not forbid staying open all night. No one ever considered it. Recognizing that Fulmer had discovered a loophole, the company officials shrugged and let him try the scheme. Fulmer's all-night operations proved profitable. Utility bills were not increased substantially, since refrigerators and signs had been operating all night anyway. Truck deliveries and cleaning could be done more efficiently when traffic was light. The stores also did a surprising amount of business from people up at night. Acknowledging Fulmer's success, the company encouraged twenty-four-hour operations in units around the country.

Over the years McDonald's regulations have become increasingly cumbersome. While the fast-food outlets generally have been profitable for Fulmer, his task has become less joyful. McDonald's began by selling franchises to businessmen who had the money and were willing to take a chance on a struggling young company with a bold idea. In recent years the chain has selected colorless types who are eager to follow corporate dictates. "I feel like a dinosaur in the system," Fulmer complains. "In the beginning McDonald's wanted individualists and people that were aggressive. As the system gets more and more sophisticated it gets more and more controlled. I feel more and more boxed in. I don't have the liberties I had before. When I first opened the store I got an eight-page mimeographed sheet. That was the manual. Today they have it so sophisticated almost every question is answered."

Purchasing his first McDonald's franchise license was a brash step for the young entrepreneur. While he was in high school in 1959 Fulmer took a job working behind the griddle at the new McDonald's in Allentown, the sixty-first outlet in the system.

From the beginning the store was successful as people who were accustomed to paying fifty cents for a hamburger lined up for the cheap McDonald's patties. Local restaurant operators couldn't believe the prices McDonald's charged and thought the store must be using dog meat. Fulmer loved the excitement of the new restaurant, the assembly-line production, the cars lined up for a block. The young workaholic had found something to absorb his compulsive energies. "There was always something going on," he told the *Allentown Evening Chronicle* two decades later. "It was a constant hustle. I enjoyed working fast with my hands, and the faster you were the better it was."

Two years later Fulmer was promoted to manager. Then when the owner decided to open another drive-in, he agreed to make Fulmer a partner with a 40 percent share. To obtain the franchise license Fulmer had to be approved by McDonald's. Although the nineteen-year-old was too young to have a legally binding signature under Pennsylvania law, McDonald's did not notice the problem. Fulmer already talked with the certainty of a much older businessman. To secure the $20,000 loan he needed for his share, the young franchisee badgered a local bank, making five visits before a loan officer caved in. Fulmer poured himself into the business, working two straight years without a day off. On days when the store was closed, he labored in the back office monitoring inventory, checking his books. When young employees stumbled, when errors erased profits, Fulmer raged with table-thumping fury.

The business prospered, and by 1964 Fulmer was realizing $60,000 in profits a year. He paid himself a salary of $125 a week. The extra money went to investments. He bought every property he could. In a period of steadily inflating real-estate prices the value of his acquisitions climbed, helping him to make other purchases. Salesmen began coming to the McDonald's where Fulmer spent most of his time and offered him properties. He bought anything under $5000 almost automatically.

The original operator sold his interest to Fulmer, and by 1969 the young franchisee owned the two McDonald's stores outright. He set out on a development spree. Over the next ten years Fulmer's annual sales increased an average of 47 percent a year, as he opened more and more McDonald's and sales of individual stores climbed. Fulmer promoted his product vigorously, constantly inventing new sales ideas and using gimmicks from corporate headquarters. One year he ran fifty-six promotions.

Fulmer now looks on his rapid growth as a thing of the past. He expects to open only another two or three McDonald's outlets, since he considers his territory almost fully developed. He cautions would-be McDonald's franchisees that expansion in recent years has proved difficult. "If you get a McDonald's today you can't expect to be a millionaire," he observes. "If you have a good location and you run it well you'll have a comfortable living."

In the early 1960s Fulmer faced little direct competition. Now fast-food outlets dot the Lehigh Valley. Customers no longer line up for a block to sample McDonald's fare. Burger King was the first major chain to follow McDonald's into the area, in some cases taking sites Fulmer wanted to acquire. Now every McDonald's faces competition from a nearby Burger King. Other franchise companies have rushed to win a share of the local market. In the two years ending in 1981, Fulmer estimated that fifty franchised chain restaurants opened in the Allentown area, including Wendy's, Roy Rogers, and Perkins Cake and Steak.

Besides facing increased competition, franchisees now pay higher license and royalties fees to the company than Fulmer did when he acquired his business in the 1960s. In addition, it is now much harder to obtain rights for good locations. Fulmer was free to buy licenses quickly as the chain expanded. Now it is difficult for a new investor to buy rights for even one McDonald's, since most licenses go to proven operators. "Getting a second license is tough," Fulmer explains. "Getting a third is almost impossible today."

Of course, a McDonald's franchise is still a valuable property. Opening a store costs about $330,000, including the price of the franchise license, equipment, and supplies. The stores average about $1 million annual sales, while the franchisees are said to earn about $100,000 for each store they own. To win a coveted license, candidates must endure a thorough screening of their finances and background. Prospective franchisees who pass the initial test are then required to work for three hundred hours without pay in a McDonald's. They must do all jobs in the store, from flipping hamburgers to mopping floors. This provides a basic education in McDonald's techniques. At the same time the practice forces the franchisee to demonstrate a commitment to the business and allows the company to see if the future operator can handle a job that may involve doing grubby labor. The fact that thousands eagerly line up to submit to this demanding initiation is a tribute to the appeal of the McDonald's franchise.

What motivates many prospective franchisees are the tales of operators building mini-chains, like Harold Fulmer's. By gradually acquiring a string of outlets the franchisee may leave the middle class to enter the ranks of the truly wealthy. Dozens of franchisees have taken this route. Virgil Conard of Corpus Christi, Texas, owns fifty-six Pizza Huts. A former employee of Southwest Bell Telephone, he quit his job in 1966, convinced of the strong future of pizza chains. Since then Conard has bought and sold a series of franchises. During one period in the late 1970s he owned—beside Pizza Huts—five Orange Julius outlets, one TraveLodge, and twenty-five Church's Fried Chicken restaurants. "I consider all opportunities that come my way," he said.

The typical franchisee does not achieve wealth. Saddled with royalty payments and advertising costs, most operators cannot expect to earn much more than $25,000 a year from one outlet. Owners of parent companies have a better chance of succeeding, since they can strike it rich in one or two good years selling franchises. Bruce Kinmoth has been struggling to build up his Philly Mignon outlet. Kinmoth owned two gas stations when he began shopping for a fast-food franchise in 1980. At the time gasoline profits were minimal, and his rent was about to go up

20 percent. With the help of a loan backed by the Small Business Administration, he purchased a Philly Mignon outlet for $118,000 in the Rockaway Townsquare mall in Rockaway, New Jersey. He opened in June 1981. After three months at the griddle cooking the steak sandwiches that are the mainstay of the chain, Kinmoth was not yet turning a profit. He expected that the big money was still somewhere in the future. The franchisee had made mistakes in his first weeks, hiring too many people. In addition, the mall location had not proved as strong as expected, though he hoped that new developments being built might bring more traffic. "The mall is too far out," he explained. "But give it a couple of years and we think things will pick up."

Kinmoth was selling about four hundred dollars a day, with much of his business coming during the lunch hour. One noon in September a half-dozen adults sat at the tables of his store, which was decorated with hanging plants. Meanwhile, across the mall corridor the large McDonald's was mobbed with young mothers bringing toddlers, who sat in the special high chairs the store provided. Kinmoth said he was not discouraged. He had high hopes for the young Philly Mignon chain, which at the time had 35 stores open and 190 franchises sold. "I think this is going to be a big company," he predicted.

When a franchisee succeeds, the parent company tends to believe it should take most of the credit. The parents often see franchisees as inexperienced amateurs who owe whatever profits they achieve to the chain's formulas. Using the chain approach the local operator can make more money than he ever thought possible. From the franchisee's view it is the local investor who puts up the money, takes the risk, and works to make an outlet prosper. Franchisees sometimes say the companies treat them like second-class citizens, charging exorbitant royalties for services that diminish in value as the years go on. The reality is that to create a successful chain both parties must contribute. Without strong franchisees the parent cannot operate over the long run. If the parent is weak the franchisees have little chance of success.

As the chains have proven their ability to support successful businesses, they have courted more sophisticated franchisees. In some cases wealthy corporations have snapped up franchise licenses. While the company executives may lack the dedication of husband-and-wife teams, giant companies can bring valuable assets to a franchised chain. Several years ago Greyhound began opening Burger King units in bus stations. For the Burger King Corporation bus stations were prime locations that would not be available to the chain unless Greyhound—which owns the properties—ran the outlets. For the bus company the fast-food stores solved the problem of finding an alternative to the lackluster Greyhound Post House cafeterias in the stations that many considered overpriced outlets relying on captive customers. "Passengers always felt that Post Houses were ripping them off," explained John Teets, vice-chairman of Greyhound. "With Burger King bus travelers are getting a known quantity.

A Greyhound Burger King opened in the Philadelphia bus station in 1975. In its first year the store produced $1 million in sales, four times the Post House record. By 1978 the figure had climbed to $1.7 million. Greyhound now has twenty-five Burger Kings in stations in cities such as Buffalo, Pittsburgh, Tampa, and Houston. The bus company has proved to be a profitable franchisee for the parent company. Greyhound now runs some of the highest volume fast-food outlets in the country because of the company's busy locations and its policy of hiring experienced store managers. The stores average over $1 million a year in sales, with some doing $2 million. Encouraged by this success, Greyhound is now opening Burger Kings on sites outside bus stations.

Even when the franchisee is a sophisticated corporation, franchise companies can never be certain that a new license holder will prove to be an able operator. In their efforts to determine what kind of franchisee is most suitable, companies experiment, trying older or younger people. Some companies seek those with experience in the field, while others actively avoid the knowledgeable. When Karl Stanley of CutCo Industries began franchising his beauty salons in the early 1960s, he naturally turned first to experienced haircutters. But soon he soured on veterans of beauty salons. Too often they had developed their own methods and were not willing to adopt the franchise company's system. More important, the former salon workers might be adept at cutting hair, but they knew little about running a business. Licensed beauty operators could be hired easily, Stanley decided. The franchisees should be capable of handling the real problems of running a chain outlet— negotiating leases, buying supplies, managing workers. In addition, the operators had to have enough money to make a substantial investment. They should have the potential to open more than one shop so the chain could grow. Following these criteria Stanley began selling licenses to doctors, lawyers, and airline pilots.

William Gaderick, a franchisee of CutCo Industries' Great Expectations unisex salons, has never given a haircut. Still, two years after he began operating the shop it was becoming profitable. Gaderick is a computer executive who spends only a few hours a week at the store, while his wife, Myrna, drops in twice a week and keeps a vigilant eye on the place. In his forties, with graying hair and wearing a neat business suit, Gaderick speaks with the articulate precision of a sophisticated executive. He talks enthusiastically about the shop, apparently fascinated by the details of a business that is still new to him.

In the fluid computer business several of Gaderick's employers had closed. And although he had always done well at the jobs and found new ones, he sought a stable income source that could tide him through any shaky periods. "For many years I had thought about going into my own business without knowing what it would be," he says. "I didn't care what the business was. I felt I could run any business."

Once he sold computers to the Carvel ice cream company and talked about franchising with the chain's president. At times he vaguely considered buying a Burger King or other fast-food outlet. During one job search he answered a want ad that turned out to be for Command Performance, a franchised haircutting chain. Though he had not come to discuss a franchise, Gaderick began to think about going into the salon business. After checking various chains he settled on Karl Stanley's Great Expectations because the company had long experience. "Since I didn't know anything about haircutting, I decided to go with a company who did know," he explains.

In buying the $15,000 franchise license, Gaderick did not purchase the right to benefit from the national TV advertising and instant name recognition that fast-food chains provide. Out-of-towners passing by his store were not likely to give him much business. What he was getting from Great Expectations was skilled help in setting up the business. The company provided assistance throughout the start-up period.

Gaderick already knew the mall location he wanted in New York's World Trade Center. Great Expectations approved the location and offered advice on negotiating the lease. After reaching agreement with the landlord, Gaderick bought his furniture and beauty supplies from Great Expectations. Company staff helped Gaderick's architect design and lay out the store. Gaderick spent a week at a company store learning the ropes, then two weeks before the opening date Great Expectations took out ads for haircutters and hired a staff for the franchisee's new store. The parent company recruited a manager who had run another store. Gaderick's expenses to begin the store totaled $150,000.

The outlet's location proved to be ideal. Each day 20,000 people hurrying past the big front windows can look in on the brightly colored salon. The first day the store opened, seventy-five customers stopped in. Since then there has been a steady flow of secretaries and junior executives, many coming before or after work. Gaderick, while generally pleased with the parent company, had some criticisms. Members of the initial crew hired by Great Expectations proved unsatisfactory. In the first two years of operation the entire crew turned over several times. "They didn't take as much care in hiring as we do now," Gaderick said. "The store started out on the wrong foot. Some customers came out dissatisfied with their haircuts."

Still, the store in late 1981 was recording seven thousand dollars in weekly sales, serving four hundred customers a week compared to the three hundred that came in the first year. When Gaderick finishes paying off his start-up costs, he said he expected to be earning 30 percent profits on sales. As the franchisee has learned to run the store, he has turned less to the parent company. The company has continued to provide annual styling classes for the haircutters, and if Gaderick's profits slipped the company would provide advice. But generally the franchisee is operating on his own.

When a franchisee like Gaderick begins functioning smoothly the parent company can watch the profits mount. While in the process of establishing units the parent company must spend heavily to field a staff that can sell licenses and support the new franchisee. Once these expenditures stop, the franchised outlet becomes particularly valuable to the parent. In fact, a strong franchised unit may produce a higher rate of return than an outlet owned outright by the parent where expenses are greater. In 1980 McDonald's Corporation owned about 25 percent of its 6200 units, with the rest franchised. Revenues from the company-owned stores were $1.69 billion, and profits were 16 percent. From the franchised stores the parent received only $486 million in royalties and fees, but 84 percent of that figure went to profits.

To attain maximum profits chains try to come up with the right balance between franchised and company-owned units. Minuteman Press has only one company-owned store in its chain of more than four hundred outlets. The parent operator simply found it easier and more profitable to focus on franchising. This arrangement is often used by companies who are skillful at creating and overseeing a franchise system but not at operating the units themselves. Other companies find it profitable to own and operate more units. Holiday Inns, which relies on franchisees to provide investment capital, tries to keep 80 percent of its rooms in franchised units. In 1983 CutCo Industries owned 52 salons and franchised 439.

Beside producing revenues the company-owned units help

the parent lead and control its chain. Company units serve as models and places where experiments can be conducted. If the franchisee says it is simply not possible to get 425 servings of french fries from a 100-pound bag, as McDonald's specifies, the parent can point to company-owned units where the standards are being met. The franchisee can then visit the successful unit to learn how things should be done. Franchisees who grow lackadaisical may be motivated by the success of the model units.

Not everyone enters franchising for the chance to make big money. Some merely seek to run their own shop. Near Allentown, Pennsylvania, on a wooded plot that is about twenty miles from Harold Fulmer's office and a world removed from his hamburger kingdom, Bill and Kathleen Weber operate a Kampgrounds of America site. Owning a campground is hardly a stepping-stone to wealth. But the Webers like the outdoor life that comes with running the site. "When we went into it we didn't look at it from a business standpoint," noted Kathleen Weber, an outgoing woman who talked eagerly about the franchise.

Sitting in her hundred-and-fifty-year-old house located on the campground, she was explaining about the operation when someone interrupted to warn that a dog had slipped out of its pen. Excusing herself, she stepped out her door to check. She returned a minute later. "My husband was a chief draftsman in an architect's office in Allentown for twenty years," she said, resuming her explanation. "He wanted out. I had a beauty shop. This was something the whole family could participate in. We felt it was a good way to raise children."

The Webers, longtime campers, once stayed at a KOA during a cross-country trip. In 1970 they opened their campsite. The camp is on a grassy clearing that has trees scattered among the one hundred fifty sites. A covered bridge crosses a stream running through the lot. There is a basketball court and picnic shelter. Most sites are taken by trailers and motor homes. The business grosses only $130,000 a year, bringing thin profits. But the family lives on the campground, and the business pays many of their expenses, such as insurance and utilities. It has been more than a full-time occupation. With the four children pitching in, the Webers put in sixty-hour weeks during the summer, checking in campers, maintaining sites, running the camp store, and attending to the swimming pool. If an electrical hookup isn't working, they fix it. "I think I can run the UN after this," Mrs. Weber said.

KOA normally looks for families to run its outlets. In a few instances franchisees have bought two campsites near each other; the husband oversees one and the wife the other. But the company believes that running a camp requires the full-time attention of a live-in family. KOA franchisees must meet company specifications for maintaining adequate facilities. Even in the open air of campgrounds the parent company is careful to maintain its control of the franchise. The rules governing the KOA units are not as rigid as the standards maintained by McDonald's. But like many franchise companies, the campground business looks to the hamburger chain for ideas on how to operate a chain. Whether it provides campsites or chicken wings, a franchise company can learn a great deal by studying the hamburger operation's profitable system.

5

The Franchise Factory

At first Ray Kroc was not impressed with the simple hamburger stand he had traveled halfway across the country to see. A small eight-sided building with high windows, it reminded some employees of a fishbowl. MCDONALD'S FAMOUS HAMBURGERS, a sign on the roof proclaimed. The drive-in located in San Bernardino, California, seemed little different from hundreds of establishments Kroc had seen in his thirty years as a salesman. As he sat in the parking lot one desert morning in 1954, Kroc wondered if the store could live up to its awesome reputation.

Shortly before the eleven a.m. opening time employees began pulling up, dressed in crisp white shirts, trousers, and hats. With carts they hauled potatoes and meat from a nearby shed into the store, bustling "like ants at a picnic," Kroc later wrote. Then the customers began to appear, lines of them filling the parking lot. They swarmed up to the drive-in, ordering hamburgers at the front windows and french fries at a side window.

In a few minutes customers made purchases, then returned to their cars carrying bags of hamburgers. Kroc watched in disbelief. Curious to learn more about this ritual, Kroc stopped some customers and asked how often they visited the place. Every day, one workingman volunteered. A fashionably dressed young woman explained she stopped by as often as possible.

The customers came from miles away. What drew them was the best food at the lowest price in the area. The menu was fixed. Hamburgers cost fifteen cents, while a bag of fries was a dime. The sixteen-ounce milk shakes cost twenty cents. The plain fare never varied and neither did the quality. It was the most efficient money-making machine Kroc had ever seen. His excitement grew as he pondered the possibility of making this elegantly simple restaurant available to people around the country.

Most of his life Kroc had been on the prowl for ways to make a fortune. At fifty-two, he was comfortably middle class, but the big success he had long sought eluded him. Short and cocky, the ebullient Kroc had pushed a variety of products, speaking in his flat Midwestern accent. For a time in the 1920s he worked as a paper-cup salesman for the Lily Tulip company in the Chicago area, selling to pushcart vendors and to concessions at the zoo and ballpark. One winter when business slowed Kroc decided to try his luck in Florida.

A skilled pianist, he landed a job playing with the Willard Robinson band at a swank speakeasy on Palm Island, called The Silent Night. Owned by a rum runner who brought illegal liquor from the Bahamas, the nightclub featured marble floors, Grecian pillars, and an unusual pricing policy. All drinks, whether champagne or whiskey, cost a dollar. There were only three choices on the menu—lobster, steak, and roast duckling. Years later Kroc recalled the stylish simplicity of the club and the efficiency achieved by serving only a few items.

After a brief career at the keyboard, Kroc returned to Chicago and selling cups. One of his customers was the young Walgreen Drug Company, which used pleated cups to serve sauces at its soda fountain counters. For drinks the drugstore used traditional glassware. Watching the lunch-hour crowds waiting for seats, Kroc developed a novel idea. With a new kind of Lily cup, Walgreen could sell milk shakes "to go." Instead of waiting, the overflow customers could take their drinks with them. Walgreen—and Kroc—would increase sales. The Walgreen executive Kroc approached thought the idea was ridiculous. The company was charging fifteen cents for each shake served in a glass. If the drugstore bought cups at one and a half cents apiece, profits would melt away.

Kroc suggested opening a special take-out counter. Walgreen resisted. Finally the salesman offered to *give* the store a supply of cups to try his idea for a week. From the first day the innovation succeeded. Kroc had won a big account, and each time Walgreen opened a new unit, cup sales increased. The big profits, Kroc had learned, came from the chains and large corporations. From then on he would spend less time chasing pushcart vendors and concentrate on a few big companies such as Swift and Armour, who ordered thousands of cups.

In 1938 Kroc began selling the Multimixer, a device that could produce five milk shakes at once. After the war, as the economy picked up, the salesman began doing business with a new breed of companies, franchised chains such as Dairy Queen and Tastee-Freeze. These growing operations provided steady demand for more milk shake makers. Even so, the profits of most soft-ice-cream stores were dwarfed by the earnings of a hamburger stand in San Bernardino that Kroc had heard about.

Kroc's curiosity was aroused when he learned that the drive-in had ordered eight Multimixers. How could one hamburger stand need to produce forty shakes at a time? The salesman flew to Southern California to find out.

The McDonald's outlet was one of dozens of drive-ins that had sprouted in Southern California, a growing region where cars had already assumed a special importance. In the early 1930s drive-in restaurants began appearing in city parking lots, then spread along the highways, most of them featuring chicken, barbecue beef, and pork. While the food in most places was similar, the restaurants competed by trying to come up with novel service ideas. Some hired aspiring Hollywood starlets as carhops, who dressed in outlandish costumes or worked on rollerskates.

Maurice and Richard McDonald took a different approach. The brothers came from New Hampshire to California in the late 1920s, hoping to find jobs in the movie industry. After handling props on Hollywood sets for a few years they bought a movie theater, then in 1940 turned to running a hamburger stand. The McDonalds knew little about the food business, but they learned quickly. By 1948, when they opened the San Bernardino restaurant, they had developed their powerfully streamlined operation.

From long experience on the road, Kroc appreciated how rare the McDonald's drive-in was. At most roadside stands the quality of the food might vary considerably from day to day. McDonald's provided a reliable meal. For the traveling salesman clean restrooms were an unexpected bonus. The McDonald brothers kept theirs immaculate.

Kroc eagerly introduced himself to the creators of this wondrous fast-food factory. The brothers were delighted to meet the salesman they called "Mr. Multimixer." The next day Kroc returned and again witnessed the long lines of customers. He envisioned hundreds of McDonald's restaurants around the country, each one using six of his Multimixers. "I've been in the kitchens of a lot of restaurants," he told the brothers, "and I have never seen anything to equal the potential of this place of yours."

But the brothers were not interested in expanding. They were already making $75,000 a year and owned three Cadillacs. Living in a big white house on a hill overlooking the restaurant, they enjoyed sitting on their porch watching the desert sunsets. They were not interested in a venture that would only create problems. The scrappy salesman was not easily discouraged. By franchising, he argued, the McDonalds could continue living their quiet lives while the royalty checks poured in. The brothers need only find someone to sell the franchise licenses. He, for example, would be willing to assume this headache.

Kroc returned to Chicago, having reached an agreement. He would sell franchises and split the proceeds with the McDonalds. In late middle-age the salesman threw himself into the project. Kroc's wife was furious at him for abandoning a secure business for this risky one. But Kroc had always hoped to become rich, and this seemed like his last chance.

The first step was to build a pilot unit in Des Plaines, Illinois. Franchise chains typically start with an experimental outlet where the business can be refined and new ideas can be tried. The pilot store can build a track record that will entice franchisees seeking a profitable business.

For a year Kroc and his staff worked on the Des Plaines store, making it into a smooth-running operation. Though the McDonald brothers' drive-in was an efficient model, Kroc saw areas where wastage could be reduced, pennies saved. He would no longer hand-dip ice cream for shakes as the McDonalds had done. The new store began using a soft product taken from a tank.

Kroc also began developing the uniform specifications that would serve as guides for franchisees around the country trying to reproduce the McDonald's formula. The chain would offer a limited menu. This simplified purchasing, while quality could be controlled. By using assembly-line techniques and not offering any variety in hamburgers or condiments, the chain's labor costs could be kept to a minimum. McDonald's under Kroc could continue to sell hamburgers for fifteen cents, a price that seemed suspiciously low even in the 1950s.

Above all, the Kroc system aimed to achieve speed of service. The goal was to serve a hamburger, fries, and a shake in fifty seconds. After much discussion and experimentation Kroc settled on what he considered the ideal hamburger that would be simple to make yet appeal to the majority of palates. The patty weighed 1.6 ounces and measured 3.875 inches across before cooking. It was 19 percent fat and did not contain any lungs, hearts, or cereal. The bun was three and a half inches wide.

In the first years of operation Kroc and his staff refined their procedures. They determined how high to stack the patties so that the bottom ones would not be crushed out of shape. After considerable experimentation they settled on how much wax had to be in the wax paper, separating the patties so that the burgers could easily slip off the paper onto the grill.

In the 1950s french fries were an unimportant side dish that brought in little profit at most restaurants. The McDonald brothers, however, lavished considerable attention on their fries. Many customers were fiercely devoted to the product. Kroc believed the McDonald's fries were the best he had ever tasted. Convinced that they would be crucial for his chain he set out to master french fry production. "The french fry would become almost sacrosanct for me, its preparation a ritual to be followed religiously," he wrote in his autobiography, *Grinding It Out*.

Kroc cooked his first batch, carefully duplicating the brothers' method. He peeled the potatoes, leaving a bit of skin for flavor, then cut Idaho shoestring strips and soaked them in cold water. After the water was white with starch he rinsed off the potatoes and then fried them in fresh oil. Out of the grease the batch looked just right, golden brown. But something was amiss. The McDonald's fries were always crispy, but this batch was mushy. Kroc struggled to reproduce the perfect fries. After several phone calls to California he learned that the McDonald brothers stored their potatoes in bins where they naturally cured in the dry desert air. Kroc put an electric fan in the basement of his Illinois store, blowing on the potatoes to reproduce the desert drying effect. After three months of trying he achieved the correct formula.

Kroc insisted that his stores be clean and wholesome to appeal to the middle-class suburban families. All windows would be washed every day. Employees would be well-groomed. Kroc furnished the kitchens with gleaming stainless steel equipment that would flaunt the cleanliness of the operation. All the cooking was done in full view of customers. The open work area enabled patrons to see that the cheap patties were prepared in a spotless environment. In addition, the employees laboring over the grills provided diversion for customers standing in line.

Like the McDonald brothers Kroc wanted to keep away unsavory teenagers, whose loud cars and reckless ways might scare away the family trade. There would be no jukeboxes, cigarette machines, or pay phones that would encourage loitering at the stand. While the carhop system invited teenagers to linger in the parking lot, the McDonald's self-service window insured that customers would eat their meals and quickly return to the highway. For extra protection no young females would be hired, since they might attract ill-mannered young men.

With the hamburger production system designed, Kroc set out to sell franchises. By the end of 1957 there were thirty-seven McDonald's outlets operating. By 1959 the total had reached one hundred. Each unit was designed along the lines that Kroc had laid out. Operators who signed on with the young chain were carefully indoctrinated in the McDonald's system. They listened as Kroc hammered away at his theme of "QSC/TLC" or "Quality Service Cleanliness/Tender Loving Care."

In the 1950s the new McDonald's outlets caused a sensation. People traveled miles to witness the phenomenal stand dispensing cheap hamburgers. In later years Kroc would be compared to his hero, Henry Ford. The praise was exaggerated but Kroc, like Ford, had extended the techniques of mass production into a new area. Before Ford's great Michigan assembly lines screeched into production, cars had been individually crafted conveniences for the rich. Relying on standardized parts and economies of scale, the young company produced the Model T—a simple vehicle that came in one color, black. Selling at a price the masses could afford, the Ford became wildly popular. By extending the mass-production concept to hamburgers Kroc brought the ways of the factory into a service industry. At McDonald's unskilled workers repeatedly performed specialized tasks. The hamburgers were identical units, like the Model Ts. Thanks to Kroc's innovativeness, activities that had once been conducted in the household or by small businesses could now be accomplished on a large scale. Giant corporations could be built to run restaurants, barbershops, and motels. With standardization, these businesses, which had once been low-profit operations, could create fortunes for distant central mangements. Already accustomed to the use of factory-produced goods, Americans accepted motels that looked alike and muffler shops that promised uniform service.

Kroc's innovation came at a time when services were beginning to dominate the economy. As Daniel Bell pointed out in *The Coming of Post-Industrial Society*, at the turn of the century seven out of ten American workers were engaged in production of goods, laboring in fields, mines, and factories. The other 30 percent of workers were in the service sector, attending to goods produced by others. They labored as domestic servants or worked in businesses such as banking or insurance. After 1920 the number of jobs in industry increased, but the percentage of jobs claimed by the goods sector declined. Jobs in finance, real estate, and retailing were growing at a relatively faster rate. By 1950 employment was evenly divided between goods and services. As farms became mechanized, a lower proportion of national income was being spent on food. At first this additional money went to pay for durable goods, such as housing, automobiles, and clothing. Gradually people began spending on services that had once been luxuries—dry cleaning, restaurants, and travel. These were fields in which the Kroc methods could be applied.

Kroc inspired thousands of chain builders. Some attempted to duplicate every detail of the master's operation. One of the more succesful imitators was Burger Queen, a company that began operating in Louisville, Kentucky, in 1961. (The chain later changed its name to Druther's.) George Clark, one of the founders, recognized that Kroc had developed a winning formula. "Most everybody copied McDonald's," he recalls, "either through observing or maybe they copied subconsciously. Our food was exactly the same as McDonald's. If I had looked at McDonald's and saw someone turning hamburgers while he was hanging by his feet I would have copied it. We were aware that they didn't have music or pinball machines, which every other drive-in had at that time. They didn't have a phone. So we followed them."

Kroc standardized all aspects of his business, not just the kitchen. Bookkeeping, personnel practices, and building construction were the same throughout the chain. Howard Johnson and other chains had been heading in the direction of standardization, but Kroc introduced an extreme regimentation that had never been attempted in a service business. McDonald's purchasing and quality-control procedures became a model for chains of all kinds. For the last three decades entrepreneurs have looked at McDonald's and said, "Well, if Kroc can make so much money selling hamburgers, why not apply his system to motels or real-estate offices?" What the imitators have particularly admired is the chain's unified image. This has come to be a hallmark of McDonald's and all the major franchise companies. Each outlet in a chain attempts to be like every other outlet. The service provided must be similar in all parts of the country. Kentucky Fried Chicken tastes the same in Vermont and New Mexico. Holiday Inns operates on a policy of "no surprises."

Following Ray Kroc's example, companies who decide to franchise begin by standardizing operations. The chef of the would-be franchise company can no longer cook by the seat of his pants. Recipes must be sharply defined and simplified so that others can reproduce them. Procedures for all phases of management must be carefully charted so that they may be taught to others. Product selection must be extremely limited. By establishing uniform standards companies can maintain control of costs. More important, standardization allows chains to project a brand image, advertising identical outlets over wide areas.

(Inevitably, local franchisees devise systems they believe are superior to the parent company's approaches. Anyone naturally welcomes profitable ideas, but in a franchise chain free-lance experiments are seriously discouraged. Deviations can destroy the company's standardized image. In addition, the parent companies provide what they believe are proven methods. An inexperienced franchisee who tampers with a recipe or architectural design may lower profits. Still, if a local operator does develop a profitable idea, it may be adopted by the parent and then introduced in all units of the chain.)

To ensure uniformity companies supply franchisees with a complete standardized package. The larger, more sophisticated companies supply precise specifications for equipment, food supplies, and signs. Minuteman Press, for example, details the type of printing press the franchisee should use and helps make the purchase. It provides a sign for the store and copy and design for Yellow Page ads. The company explains how to hire a printer and solicit business by calling on potential customers.

The level of detail companies try to regulate varies. KOA franchisees are free to sell any groceries they want as long as the camp stores provide customers with basic staples. Great Expectations insists that all its haircutting shops have bright orange-and-white fixtures. Some companies issue franchisee manuals containing hundreds of regulations. Dunhill Personnel System employment recruiters must make seventy phone calls a day in their efforts to match job vacancies with eligible executives. To use time effectively they are told not to open their mail until the end of the day. H & R Block tax returns must be checked twice for accuracy. A medium Pizza Hut pizza should measure thirteen inches across. Minuteman franchisees are supposed to join at least two service clubs in their communities, such as the Rotary and Kiwanis, so that they can meet influential businessmen who will provide customers.

Dunkin' Donuts offers detailed cooking instructions for each kind of its donuts. Honey-dip donuts, for example, should be fried at 375 degrees Fahrenheit. The donut company supplies a chart that shows symptoms of common problems. If the grid pattern in the cake donuts forms erratically, the dough may be too wet.

Some companies regularly send bulletins announcing new regulations. McDonald's franchisees complain that they receive so many volumes of materials they could spend all their time just trying to read and digest the information. The *H & R Block Tax News* bulletin of October 1981 informed franchisees about tax regulations covering the rental of a vacation home to relatives and surgical hair transplants for cosmetic purposes. An issue of *The Block Connection*, a newsletter, carried a word of caution under the headline WINDOW BANNERS FOR FARM RETURNS. "There are two different window banners for farm tax returns, one saying, 'We specialize in farm returns,' and 'Farm returns prepared here,'" the newsletter explained. "In using the window banners, be sure that if you use the 'specialize' banner someone in your office is very familiar with farm tax returns."

One issue of Dunkin' Donuts' *Journal of Quality* warned that the frozen wild blueberries used in the company's muffins should arrive at the store at a temperature no higher than zero degrees Fahrenheit. If the berries thaw and then refreeze they will bleed in the muffins. "You should not accept the delivery of blueberries that do not meet the criteria," the *Journal of Quality* cautioned.

Unfortunately, in a winter issue the donut journal editors could offer only a makeshift solution to the problem of "melting soup lids." "Now that you are, no doubt, in the midst of the peak soup season, you have probably had occasion when a customer may order more than one take-out soup. The end result many times may be the top container falling through into the bottom one. The most effective method found, to date, to inhibit the melting lid on multiple take-out soup orders is to have your hostesses place one or two napkins between the containers. The napkins seem to serve as a buffer and steam absorber between the lid and the container bottom.

"An industry check with all the prominent take-out container manufacturers tells us that the problem is a national one with no real answer to date. The usage of take-out containers for hot items probably does not warrant the mold and material investment necessary on the part of the manufacturers. Please contact us if you have any questions on this matter or other container problems you may have."

Fighting to survive in an increasingly franchised market,

companies have come to regulate their operations even more tightly. All aspects of the business are examined to keep costs down. In the crowded restaurant industry, the quality of food may be sacrificed in the interest of maintaining profits.

Fast-food chains rely on portion control, calculating precisely the food supplies that will go on each sandwich. Prices are adjusted to ensure profits on each item. Arby's, a roast-beef-sandwich chain, carefully avoids waste. The Arby's meat is shipped to stores in "roasts" that weigh ten pounds each. A beef product minus the bones, the roasts are brown and gummy-looking masses covered with fat.

The meat is cooked slowly for about three and a half hours in an oven at 200 degrees Fahrenheit, until the internal temperature of the roast is 135 degrees as measured by a thermometer inserted into the beef. The beef is then removed from the oven and allowed to continue cooking in its own heat for about twenty minutes until the internal thermometer reads 140 degrees. The slow process is designed to keep shrinkage to a minimum. If cooked correctly the finished roast will weigh between nine pounds, four ounces, and nine pounds, seven ounces. The final figures are carefully recorded and sent to headquarters. Managers are held responsible for any inordinate weight loss. The ounces are closely watched because they quickly add up. Each Arby's beef sandwich contains three ounces of sliced meat. Managers are expected to produce around forty-seven sandwiches from each ten-pound roast. If the process is done improperly, each roast will yield fewer sandwiches and profit margins will be trimmed. In a business where thousands of roasts are sold each week, losses soon mount. McDonald's once attempted to sell roast beef sandwiches but soon abandoned the product. Profits were slim partly because the company could not control meat shrinkage.

In their efforts to achieve standardization and portion control most franchised restaurants have come to rely heavily on frozen and precooked food. As chains become larger, using fresh products becomes increasingly uneconomical. Ray Kroc managed to hold the price of McDonald's hamburgers to fifteen cents until 1967, when it rose to eighteen cents. To hold down prices the company soon resorted to frozen patties. Eventually McDonald's even abandoned the fresh potatoes Kroc cherished for his revered french fries. Franchisees had long complained about the labor involved in peeling and slicing potatoes. The peels caused sewer backups. Since the stores constantly needed shipments of potatoes, many kept railroad cars full of them at all times. Bad weather could disrupt deliveries. As the demand from chains for fresh Idaho spuds increased, it became impossible to buy the highest grade at certain times of the year. Franchisees were forced to use inferior products.

Aficionados mourned the passing of McDonald's homemade fries, but franchisees watched their profits increase with the arrival of frozen precut potatoes. Today french fries are one of McDonald's most profitable items, accounting for $1 billion in sales annually.

To serve the fast-food industry, suppliers have developed a range of different french fries, many of them precooked. It is possible to buy shoestring fries, fries with a tip of skin still on, and fries so thin they are called noodle potatoes. All of them are promoted as products designed to cut labor costs and encourage efficiency. Manufacturers claim their products look good. There is little concern for how they might taste. The fries are expected to offer good "plate coverage," taking up as much space with as little potato as possible. Ore-Ida makes a brand of large fries called "Potato Planks" and promises that "fifty percent are over three inches and a maximum of seven percent are under two inches."

Chains constantly find new products that can be frozen and presented in standardized packages. Charlie Chan, a chain of Chinese restaurants located in malls, offers quick meals. All the food is prepared by a large processor company and shipped frozen to the restaurants every week. Each unit stores enough in its freezers to feed twelve hundred people a day. Using microwave ovens and mechanized techniques, most dishes can be prepared in thirty seconds or less. Richard D'Onofrio, president of the chain, told *Fast Service* magazine that supermarkets carry a wider selection of the frozen egg rolls, fried rice, and other Chinese products than Chan sells. People patronize the chain only because it is convenient. D'Onofrio says that about 20 percent of his sales come from people who work in the malls. Many "use the take-out service and bring the fast meals home for dinner."

Relying on frozen, controlled portions, the Burger King outlet at 45th Street and Avenue of the Americas in New York City is a gleaming representative of the current descendants of the McDonald brothers' drive-in. The restaurant is one of the largest fast-food units in the world, selling over $3 million a year and staying open twenty-four hours a day. Each day the store feeds about five thousand customers, who are served by as many as sixteen clerks working the cash registers during the noon rush hour. Built on what was once the site of a Horn & Hardart Automat, the giant Burger King features a cavernous dining area that could contain several typical roadside restaurants.

It is staffed by one hundred five employees, most of them around nineteen or twenty years old, who generally stay with the store four months or less. Mike Barnes, a short, solidly built Burger Kng veteran of ten years, oversees this unskilled workforce. Every day the manager must serve an enormous amount of food to customers who are not prepared to wait. "We have to provide fast service," Barnes noted. "People come in and they only have a half hour for lunch."

Since about 40 percent of the restaurant's business comes between noon and two p.m. each day, food must be prepared in advance. Preparations for the rush hour begin each day at seven a.m. when a worker starts slicing tomatoes and pulling the pre-shredded lettuce out of a refrigerator. All the condiments must be warmed to room temperature so that they do not cool down the hamburgers when placed on the bun. Meanwhile, a skeleton crew serves the steady trickle of customers who come for the Burger King breakfast.

Mike Barnes believes that the Burger King hamburger is superior to the McDonald's product. To an outside observer the difference in quality between the two is not clear. As the Burger King television ads have indicated, the chain prepares its meat in a broiler system while McDonald's fries its burgers on a grill. The frozen Burger King patties are placed on wires on a conveyor system that slowly moves the burgers through an oven. Gas flames above and below the hamburgers cook them on both sides. About eighty seconds after the patties enter the system they emerge done. The broiler can produce more than seven hundred Whoppers an hour.

McDonald's workers place patties on a grill, then set an automatic timer that signals them when to flip the hamburger. Burger King has eliminated this responsibility. Its workers need only put the patties on the beginning of the conveyor and then remove them from the end. Some of the finished hamburgers are put in buns and stored in a steam cabinet. Another worker puts on condiments according to precise specifications. The Whopper takes four pickle slices. For a cheeseburger one slice of cheese is placed on the patty and then the sandwich is put into a microwave oven to melt the cheese. After a sandwich is prepared it is wrapped in paper, then placed in a rack that is always kept loaded. When a customer orders a Whopper, a sandwich is already waiting.

Like the hamburgers, Burger King french fries receive careful mechanical care. First the frozen fries are thawed in a refrigerator. Then they are put in a basket that is lowered into the sizzling shortening. A young worker operating the device sets a switch to cook for about two and a quarter minutes. After the allotted time the basket automatically rises out of the shortening. The worker shakes the basket to drain off grease, then dumps the fries in a tray. The machine must be calibrated so that the fries do not cook too long and become brittle and break. If they snap in two, more french fries would be needed to fill a bag and food dollars would be lost. Burger King, like most fast-food chains, must rely on automatic timers since it is difficult to tell by sight when the potatoes are done. Because the fries are coated with sugar the outsides turn brown before the centers cook through.

With all the mechanization, the employee has little opportunity to ruin his product. A bored, half-asleep teenager can perform most tasks. Even so, fast-food companies experience difficulties achieving results they seek. Burger King once struggled with a steak sandwich that required thawing the meat slowly over twenty-four hours. Workers often failed to follow the carefully outlined instructions, and the sandwiches came out tough.

Although each chain has its own special french-fry equipment, McDonald's deserves much of the credit for developing basic concepts. In 1962 the company invented the computer-controlled cooking basket that automatically adjusts frying time according to the temperature of the shortening. McDonald's also developed the french-fry scoops used by Burger King and most other chains. The triangular scoops are designed so that an unskilled teenager can fill bags with exactly the right amount of french fries. The scoops shovel in enough fries so that each bag appears to be overstuffed, leaving customers feeling they have received generous portions.

By eleven-thirty each weekday morning the giant Burger King in New York begins stepping up its production of hamburgers and french fries. The full crew of thirty is on duty. All night and throughout the morning only one broiler has slowly produced the hamburgers. For the rush hour a second one is added. Production of sandwiches is speeded up so that a backlog of Whoppers is stacked up ready for hungry customers. All eight cash registers are staffed. Mike Barnes, the manager, begins shifting his crew to where they are most needed. "The manager has to allocate people to different jobs so that the work gets done," he explained. "If the Whopper bin is filled, maybe I'll pull someone off that and tell him to mop floors."

Barnes must be careful not to cook too much. According to company regulations, hamburgers must be served within ten minutes after they are cooked. Fries may sit under heat lamps for seven minutes. After a sandwich is prepared a worker marks a number on the wrapping indicating the deadline for selling. If the food sits too long it must be thrown out. Barnes is allowed to dispose of .3 percent of his food supplies, which amounts to about one hundred eighty dollars' worth a week. "You have to stay alert to keep losses low," he said.

Customers at the counter give their orders to uniformed Burger King workers, who push buttons labeled with the item. The traditional job of the cashier, which requires knowing the price of items and being able to press the right keys, has been eliminated. The machine automatically totals the bill and figures the change. It also keeps a running tally of how much the store has sold.

Just as each movement of the workers is carefully regimented, the behavior of customers is engineered. Television ads prepare customers for new products, such as the pita salad, and show how they are eaten. In the store people line up, studying the brightly colored menu boards that highlight the limited choices. Having been served, customers sit in seats that are deliberately hard. After eleven or twelve minutes their backsides begin to feel a little uncomfortable and patrons find themselves hurrying out. At various stations there are containers labeled THANK YOU. There are no signs instructing customers to dump their garbage, but most people do. The whole store is designed so that customers will quickly spend their money and leave. There are no opportunities to talk to the help. The bustling atmosphere is totally unconducive to a leisurely lunch.

Shortly after three p.m. Barnes pushes a button on a cash register to see how he is doing. The tape says that in the hour between two and three o'clock the store recorded $300.15 in sales. The machine can also calculate how many Whoppers or other items have been sold. The day is a typical one for the store. Bad weather or an unexpected busload of tourists can cause sudden shifts in sales patterns. But Barnes can normally predict his sales figures. Many customers are regulars. "Some people come in every day about the same time and they always want a Whopper," he explained.

In most cases customers were not disappointed. Their sandwiches tasted just as expected. If fast food meets uniform specifications, part of the credit must go to the army of inspectors

Burger King and other chains employ. One such dedicated enforcer of rules for Kentucky Fried Chicken is Amjad Chisti. On a warm fall day Chisti stabs his thermometer into a chicken leg. Then, after waiting a minute, he withdraws the instrument to read the results. Perplexed, he stares at the Kentucky Fried Chicken piece. Something is amiss. "The chicken is supposed to be at least 135 degrees," Chisti explains. "It's a couple of degrees too low."

Chisti must determine what has gone wrong at the outlet in Highland Park, New Jersey. As an area manager, he oversees eight Kentucky Fried Chicken restaurants in northern New Jersey owned by Gino's, a company that has franchises for forty-three outlets of the chain. Chisti's bible is the Colonel's detailed operations manual. Constantly consulting the rules, he ensures that all units maintain company standards. The regulations governing food temperatures are a major concern. The chain believes that customers who receive cold chicken may be discouraged from returning. "You have to make sure that everything is done right," Chisti says. "You want to provide the kind of product that the customer expects."

After the chicken pieces are cooked, they are stored in a steam cabinet that maintains a constant heat. Since the cabinet seems to be properly adjusted, Chisti is baffled about what the problem might be. Finally the store manager solves the mystery. A few minutes earlier the outlet had received several large orders for barrels of chicken. Heat must have escaped while the cabinet doors were held open. The chicken's temperature should return to normal in a minute, Chisti is told.

The area manager is preoccupied with solving such problems. Every day he drives throughout his territory in New Jersey, visiting three or four stores. A stocky native of Pakistan, the outgoing Chisti greets his workers by their first names, flashing a broad smile as he teases young employees. He began working for Gino's in 1972 as an assistant manager and served as a manager before being promoted to his current job. On most of his trips he simply checks to make certain things are running smoothly and helps managers solve problems such as budget overruns. But a dozen times a year he spends over an hour performing what may be his most important function: conducting a formal inspection. Using the standard Kentucky Fried Chicken checklist, he rates his managers on a scale of one hundred points. The store in Highland Park earned an eighty-eight on one inspection because of several problems. The front case displaying salads was smeared. The extra-crispy chicken was not flaky enough.

The company's checklist begins with a review of the food. The inspector must examine the dates on products. Chickens must be less than six days old; the gravy mix must be used within six months. Chicken fat and tails must be pulled from the thighs. Then the inspector watches salespeople to make sure that they greet customers and are "not engaged in horseplay." Chisti's company insists its people surpass the parent chain's requirements. Kentucky Fried Chicken says that if five customers are in line they must be served within ten minutes. Gino's insists that the transactions be completed in seven and a half minutes. To conduct the inspection, Chisti moves about the store, making observations with a thermometer and stopwatch.

Inspectors from the parent company also review Chisti's stores. Using the standard checklist they monitor the franchisee's performance. In addition, Kentucky Fried Chicken relies on "mystery shoppers," employees posing as customers who make purchases. Unknown to the workers they carefully observe the operation of the store and report to central headquarters. Franchisees are informed of shortcomings.

Inspectors like Chisti, bearing clipboards and uniform regulations, represent an arm of the parent reaching to exercise control over the chain. With aggressive inspection programs chains can act to head off problems and revive themselves when quality declines. Inspections help maintain the disciplined standardization. Franchisees who fail inspections may eventually lose their licenses. Such severe penalties are necessary, franchise companies say, since the value of all units in a chain may be diminished if some outlets develop poor images.

Kampgrounds of America periodically withdraws licenses.

When a franchisee fails an inspection, the company will send a consultant who spends up to three weeks trying to improve the camp. At the end of sixty days franchisees who fail inspections again are required to attend a special school. After these efforts, if the camp still does not meet standards the franchise contract will be canceled. "We're reluctant to take away a franchise," said Arthur Peterson, president of KOA. "But dirty camps are unforgivable."

In recent years Holiday Inns has stepped up efforts to eliminate dilapidated units. The chain withdrew the licenses of fifty-one motels in 1981. In some cases the troublesome motels were owned by doctors, lawyers, or other investors who purchased franchises as tax write-offs or long-term investments. Units also fall into decay when a motel is passed on from parents to children who serve as absentee owners. To avoid these problems the company has begun selecting franchisees more carefully, choosing professional real-estate operators who are committed to maintaining their properties.

Holiday Inns is well aware that some consumers associate the chain with flimsy walls and clashing color schemes. Spending millions, the chain has sought to alter its public face. Most chain motels are located near other chain units. Wherever there is a Holiday Inn, a Ramada or Howard Johnson's is usually nearby. They all compete for the same prime customers, business travelers who visit an area regularly. When a motel declines or a new, more modern competitor rises on the scene, business at the inferior units quickly drops.

To ensure it keeps a lead over other companies, Holiday Inns keeps a staff of fifty-three inspectors traveling constantly, patrolling their territories. The inspectors, arriving unannounced, tour the facility with the manager in tow. Many managers dread the surprise guests and complain bitterly that the company representatives dwell on minor details. The anxiety over the review procedures may be justified, since managers sometimes receive bonuses for good inspection ratings and are fired for poor ones. The company has tried to ease the tension by downplaying the police role of inspectors, who are now called "quality consultants." In fact, the inspectors can provide managers with good advice. Veteran members of the "Quality Assurance" department have visited hundreds of motels and are willing to pass on tips that will simplify a manager's life.

The inspectors spend about three hours thoroughly reviewing a unit from floor to ceiling. Randomly selecting about 10 percent of the rooms, they look at the ceiling for marks. Light bulbs must be the correct wattage. On the walls they search for dirt. Checking for dust, the inspectors run their fingers around edges of baseboards. They examine mattress covers and peek under beds. Carpets cannot be frayed or discolored. Locks must be proper for the doors; smoke alarms should be in working condition. Managers concerned about passing these exacting inspections complain that they must train maids to clean more thoroughly than they have ever done in their own homes.

Motels rated fair or poor are inspected again in sixty days. If they fail the second round the franchisee may be declared in default and lose the license. Inspectors occasionally catch well-run hotels at bad moments, such as the day after a rowdy convention. But no allowances are made for what may be untypical chaos. The unit is given a two-month warning of the next review and told to do better. When Holiday Inns asks its guests to rate the hotels, the traveling public generally agrees with the inspectors. In 61 percent of the cases where the guests rated a hotel inferior, the inspectors also gave poor marks.

While revoking the license is the ultimate sanction, the company inspectors commonly take lesser steps at substandard units, requiring the franchisee to invest in replacing worn-out facilities. This can be expensive: Renovating a typical 150-unit motel costs as much as $800,000. An absentee investor, unwilling to pay the price, may decide instead to sell the unit, close it, or continue to operate without the Holiday Inns sign attracting guests. Most franchisees, while understanding the need to upgrade properties, would be slow to make heavy expenditures without prodding by the parent company. Indeed, the parent might be reluctant to make the improvements if the corporation was spending its own money instead of relying on the franchisees.

Holiday Inns will negotiate with franchisees, extending deadlines or overlooking minor defects. However, in recent years the company has become less patient with franchisees requesting exceptions. In the early 1970s, when the Arab oil embargo raised gasoline prices and drove motorists off the roads, Holiday Inns' business dipped sharply. Franchisees pleaded that they simply could not afford the repairs needed to pass inspections. Sympathizing with the operators, the company slackened its enforcement efforts. Franchisees were not pressured to make renovations. Many motels declined: Mattresses went unchanged; old wallpaper was covered with cheaper materials. They began to look cheap and shabby.

Though gas price increases in the late 1970s again hurt Holiday Inns, the company reversed its lenient policy. Profits might be down, but the franchisees would have to scrape by. Standards would be maintained so that when drivers returned to the roads they would stay at Holiday Inns. With increased enforcement the number of Holiday Inns receiving unacceptable company ratings dropped from 42 percent in the mid-1970s to 22 percent in 1981.

Holiday Inns sets *minimum* standards. Though rooms must be at least a certain size, franchisees can choose to build them larger. Franchisees may add special features to their motels and use more expensive materials than the company requires. This differs from some fast-food companies where operators must follow regulations to the letter. In some cases franchisees have made elaborate improvements on Holiday Inns that would not seem warranted in a chain aiming at the broad middle-priced market. "Some people overbuild their units in order to impress their friends at the local country club or for a tax loss," a Holiday Inns executive explained.

The goal of enforcing standards is to achieve predictable mediocrity. The nature of chains dictates that they strive to provide limited offerings of minimal quality. The very reason to franchise is to build a large chain. And in a chain of a thousand franchised outlets, it is difficult to offer a wide selection. If one outlet carries a product, all units must follow. This requires procuring enormous amounts of supplies and training franchisees in new procedures. Of necessity, a hardware chain can only offer limited selection; offering high-quality service is out of the question. In a large chain work must be specialized and customers treated in an impersonal manner. Good cooking requires the individual touch of a skilled chef. It is difficult to imagine a quality standardized meal—or tax return.

A nation where one town is indistinguishable from the next, where mediocrity rules, is likely to have a deadening effect on its citizens, particularly the young. The eighteen-year-olds I interviewed could not remember when they first ate in a McDonald's. For them Holiday Inns had always been the main hotel in town, the 7-Eleven was the best place to pick up a six-pack, and Radio Shack offered the latest electronic miracles. Immersed in a world dominated more and more by large impersonal corporations, the current high school generation may be more susceptible to feelings of powerlessness that contribute to a host of psychological problems.

People originally went to McDonald's for its novelty. But as the chains grew and became institutionalized they soon offered tedium instead. Burger King, perhaps sensing a craving for something different, introduced its famous "Have it your way" campaign. The promotion claimed customers had a choice. In fact, at Burger King you cannot really have a custom-designed sandwich. You get exactly what the corporate headquarters has determined you and millions of others will get, and you sit on seats designed by corporate headquarters. The only power you have—the choice you make—is to tell the clerk to leave off certain ingredients. Customers who say nothing get the standard hamburger. Burger King made the "Have it your way" offer secure in the belief that most people would passively accept the uniform model. If too many customers had revolted and demanded that the pickle or lettuce be held, the system would have collapsed. Mass production cannot meet the desire for variety. After twenty years of producing uniform hamburgers, Burger King and some other chains began offering salad bars. This was partly a concession to the fad for health foods and dieting, and partly a concession to those people who wanted to assert their individuality in some way.

In the early days of nineteenth-century industrialization, Marx wrote about the plight of the factory worker, whose work had been depersonalized. Large-scale production, bureaucratization, and specialized jobs had made it impossible for workers to feel they played a significant role or that work had a value in itself. Marx talked of the alienation of the worker whose job does not provide creative self-expression. In *Marx's Concept of Man*, Erich Fromm points out, "Alienation or estrangement means, for Marx, that man does not experience himself as the acting agent in his grasp of the world, but that the world (nature, others, and he himself) remains alien to him."

It is no longer necessary to work in a factory to experience alienation. Some express their powerlessness by saying, "You can't beat the system." Others complain of a sense of meaninglessness. Recent writers have suggested that more aspects of contemporary life have taken on the qualities of the assembly line, even while fewer people are employed in the repetitive jobs of classic heavy industry. "The social and cultural malaise affects not only disenchanted intellectuals, industrial labor, and the poor classes," argues René Dubos in *So Human an Animal*, "but also all those who feel depersonalized because circumstances compel them to accept mass standards which give them little chance to affirm their identity."

Dubos, like a number of biologists and psychologists, argues that a diverse environment is necessary for humans to develop their potential and maintain normal behavior. Children require a rich range of experiences in order to develop the capacity for conceptual thinking. The young growing up in today's suburbs may suffer from a lack of stimulation. In a society of limited choices people are prevented from acting creatively, from developing new ideas. Their lives become poorer and they begin to act in the stereotyped ways necessary to survive.

"Cultural homogenization and social regimentation resulting from the creeping monotony of overorganized and over-technicized life, of standardized patterns will make it progressively more difficult to exploit fully the biological richness of our species and may handicap the further development of civilization," Dubos writes. "We must shun uniformity of surroundings as much as absolute conformity in behavior and taste. We must strive instead to create as many diversified environments as possible."

While it is difficult to measure with clinical precision the effects on people of an increasingly standardized society, it does seem clear that the coming of franchising has impoverished the environments of many communities. As each eccentric roadhouse and corner grocery is replaced by a franchised outlet, diversity is lost. The replacement of regional cuisines with standardized foods means that citizens have less reason to feel ties to their areas, to be proud of their communities. If all communities look the same, the native might ask, what reason is there for me to care about my town?

The defenders of franchising argue that the coming of chains represents progress. Independent businesses have simply been replaced by a more efficient modern system. Just as the car replaced the horse, the fast-food outlet drove out the diner, and the chain motel with its computerized reservations system eliminated the tourist court. Because of their systematic purchasing programs and standardized procedures, franchise chains have often been applauded as examples of efficiency. In 1980 *Fortune* cited Burger King as a company that had improved productivity by turning hamburger cooking into a science.

While franchise chains have been praised, American car and steel makers have been much criticized for their low productivity growth. Japanese companies, it is noted again and again, are more efficient. Productivity is measured by the output of a business per unit of labor. The Japanese companies produce more steel per worker than the Americans. Low productivity is bad news for the economy: If Americans produce fewer goods and services, they must consume less, and the standard of living will necessarily fall. Much of the decline in the U.S. standard of living relative to other countries has been blamed on productivity problems. While once the United States had the highest standard of living in the world, by the late 1970s there were four non-OPEC countries with higher per-capita Gross National Products: Switzerland, Denmark, West Germany, and Sweden.

The Department of Labor's Bureau of Labor Statistics maintains records on productivity rates of many major industries. In businesses where franchise chains have been replacing independents it might be expected that productivity rates would be climbing. The Labor Department's category of "eating and drinking places" would seem a likely area for growth. According to the National Restaurant Association, limited menu restaurants accounted for 24 percent of all sales in eating and drinking places in 1970. In 1975 the figure was 32 percent and in 1979 fast food accounted for 38 percent. Over the period thousands of neighborhood taverns and restaurants vanished while fast-food chains sprang up. But the Labor Department reports that during the period of 1965 to 1981 the average annual rate of productivity increase for eating and drinking places was 0 percent. For the period of 1975 to 1980, when Wendy's was undergoing its great expansion and Burger King and McDonald's were both opening new outlets, productivity actually dropped an average of 1.4 percent a year. Laundry and cleaning services, another heavily franchised industry, also showed no productivity increase in the period of 1965 to 1981, while hotels and motels increased 1.8 percent a year. By comparison, all U.S. manufacturing in the period showed an average rise of 2.4 percent and automobile makers climbed 2.6 percent.

From 1948 to 1965 overall U.S. productivity increased at the healthy clip of 3.2 percent a year. Since then the rate has dropped markedly. Interestingly, it was in the middle 1960s that the greatest growth of franchised chains began. Lester Thurow, the MIT economist, writing in *Technology Review* in 1980, argued that part of the reason for the decline of productivity was the move into the services sector. Services, he noted, have relatively low productivity growth. As workers shift from higher-productivity industries to the services, overall productivity slows. By 1978 service productivity had fallen to 62 percent of the average for all industries. In 1977 a man-hour of work produced $4.92 worth of output in services, compared to $8.09 for the whole economy. "Services have acted as a brake to productivity growth since World War II, and the brakes have gradually tightened as service productivity has fallen relative to the national average," Thurow observed.

Some observers believe there is little that can be done to improve service productivity. Daniel Bell examines the productivity question in *The Coming of Post-Industrial Society*. "The simple and obvious fact is that productivity and output grow much faster in goods than in services," he writes. "Productivity in services, because it is a relation between persons, rather than between man and machine, will inevitably be lower than it is in industry." Bell points out that a barber is limited in how many haircuts he can give. A teacher teaches only a certain amount. The problem becomes particularly dramatic in the cities. Municipal expenditures cover hospitals, education, police, and other services where only limited productivity gains are possible. While service productivity stagnates, factories achieve gains. The unions demand to share the benefits of the increased productivity, and this is only fair. The factory worker who produces more should receive a fatter paycheck. However, workers in government and other low-productivity services demand pay as high as the factory workers'. Bell says that the labor component of efficient manufacturing is about 30 percent of the cost, while in services labor acounts for 70 percent. A 10 percent wage increase in industry means a 3 percent rise in production costs. If city workers demand a similar 10 percent wage increase, the costs of the service will rise 7 percent. This in large part explains why from 1965 to 1970 the price of cars rose 15 percent while the price of medical care, schooling, and insurance climbed 42.5 percent.

While service industries generally suffer low productivity growth, still the question remains: Why hasn't productivity increased in such franchised areas as eating places and motels? Jack Viegle, an economist at the Bureau of Labor Statistics who compiles the data on hotels and motels, suggests an explanation for his industry's slow performance: "With hotels you are to some extent limited in what can be done to improve productivity," he says.

Whether the business is a modern chain motel with a computerized reservations system or a small family operation, much of the work to be done is similar. Somebody has to make the beds and sweep the floors. The chains have failed to improve substantially on the old ways. In the eating and drinking category there is the same lack of progress. If outsiders are impressed with the gleaming fast-food outlets, industry people worry about productivity problems. *Restaurants and Institutions* magazine runs a regular feature on productivity. In its January 1, 1983, issue, the magazine sounded a note of criticism: "Compared with other industries, food service is amazingly underengineered. . . . The basic technologies of cooking have not changed much since the first time somebody placed a pot over a fire. And major changes do not seem to be on the horizon."

Jack Penrod, a former McDonald's franchisee, believes that all the shiny equipment has not improved fast-food efficiency. He argues that the chains such as McDonald's have not developed a system that truly saves labor. In September 1981 he told *Fast Service* magazine that "there's nothing really new—the basic equipment packages are still being used: the flat grill (around for one hundred years), the deep fat fryer (fifty years), the electronic tie-in with a cash register bank for a tape or visual readout in the kitchen (at least five years)."

The McDonald's worker takes as long to grill a patty as the

lunch counter's short-order cook requires. The chain employee probably does achieve higher output because of steadier flow of customers. However, the short-order cook's output can be attributed to his labor along with the efforts of perhaps three or four other workers in the business. At McDonald's there are hundreds of people working behind the scenes. There may only be a half-dozen people visible to customers. But in order to calculate productivity—output per worker—it is necessary to figure in the contributions of everyone in the company. At the lunch counter the owner probably hires the cook or cooks himself. McDonald's has a personnel staff where assistant vice presidents ponder the problems of overseeing an international workforce. There are armies of inspectors and staff architects to plan buildings. Whatever efficiencies may be achieved in the McDonald's kitchen may be partially negated by the inefficiencies involved in running a large chain.

One obvious example of how a chain may lose productivity can be seen in city outlets where the major fast-food companies post guards who pace the premises, looking menacing. Lunch counters do not hire uniformed guards. The guard, of course, adds nothing to output. The productivity of the store drops, even though the uniformed presence may be necessary for the store to operate. A major cause of the lack of productivity growth in fast food is the inefficient use of labor, as we will see in a later chapter, "Help Wanted."

The basic low productivity of franchised businesses is reflected in an annual survey conducted by *Forbes*. The magazine ranks companies according to various categories. In a chart labeled "Jobs and Productivity," the magazine rates 808 companies for sales per employee for 1982. McDonald's is 806, with $20,800 in sales per employee, while Holiday Inns is 798. In order to achieve a sales-per-employee level that matches McDonald's, your local diner with a staff of ten must produce annual sales of about $200,000, or about $700 a day. A prosperous old-fashioned operation can do this without too much trouble.

This is not to suggest that McDonald's is an unusually inefficient or overstaffed company. Like the other fast-food chains, the hamburger company is performing a service that can be done by small independent businesses. Uniting local operators into large chains does not substantially increase productivity. Building bigger car factories produces economies of scale and greater productivity. Building bigger franchised chains apparently does not offer similar benefits. "Eating places had low productivity growth before the chains," said Richard Carnes, an economist in the Bureau of Labor Statistics. "They still have low productivity growth."

The Bureau of Labor Statistics does not keep data on such franchised areas as car repairs, tax accounting, or barbershops. However, it seems that these businesses would be less likely than restaurants or motels to show productivity improvement. A Midas Muffler installer works at about the same pace as an independent operator did twenty years ago.

If a larger size does not help to increase productivity, still it would seem that the chains would enjoy economies of scale in purchasing. Franchise salespeople, listing the advantages of chain membership, typically cite low-cost bulk purchasing. Someone buying for one hundred stores can presumably negotiate a better price than the owner of one outlet can ever hope to obtain. However, most of the franchisees I talked to said that they got few if any price breaks by buying through the franchisors' purchasing programs. The company programs simplify the franchisees' efforts in buying, but since the parent companies make profits on these sales, the franchisees do not necessarily get bargains. Whatever economies of scale chains achieve are not passed on to the franchisees or the public.

When Frank Gaderick opened his Great Expectations hair salon in New York City, he bought all the furniture and beauty supplies from the company. Gaderick could have purchased furnishings—which must be white with bright orange stripes—from other suppliers, but this would have required hunting for a supplier and negotiating a price. The advantage of buying from the company was not the cost. "When you're coming into a business completely cold it makes it simpler to buy from the company," he explained.

Having become a successful operator, Gaderick now no longer buys most of his beauty supplies from CutCo Industries, the parent company, which sells a complete line of private-label products. The franchisee found that customers prefer items with brand names such as Clairol, and the prices are comparable or cheaper than what the company offers.

Holiday Inns sells its franchisees everything the well-appointed motel requires, from furniture to cleaning supplies. To display the offerings the company maintains a large show-room at its Memphis headquarters. The facility contains model guest rooms, lounges, and restaurant settings. For the forward-looking franchisee there are meeting rooms with chrome chandeliers and chrome frame chairs. The operator seeking to liven a staid property can select the latest in exotic lighting for a disco lounge.

Despite the convenience of the showroom, franchisees with more than one motel find it economical to buy from the manufacturers. "We get better prices by buying direct from the factories," said Richard Metz, vice president of purchasing for American Motor Inns, a large franchisee.

Business Week, in its December 13, 1982, issue, noted that the president of Howard Johnson's, desperately trying to improve the profitability of the chain, decided to allow restaurants "to buy foods from a variety of sources rather than exclusively from HoJo's food operations."

Hamburger franchisees do obtain limited price benefits. The fast-food franchisors do not sell hamburger to dealers. The franchisees typically form co-ops to make bulk purchases. McDonald's uses its muscle in negotiating with large suppliers for franchisees. The parent company insists that it certify the supplier meets standards before franchisees make any purchases. Having won the prize of certification, Golden State Foods Corporation now serves only one major customer, McDonald's. After World War II William Moore, the supplier's founder, began peddling meat to corner foodstands in Los Angeles. In 1953, having heard about the McDonald brothers' amazing restaurant, Moore visited the San Bernardino business. Seeing the long lines of customers, he made a sales pitch to Maurice McDonald. "Old Mac McDonald took a liking to me for some reason, but he wouldn't buy any meat from me," he explained to *Dun's Review*. "And I hounded him; I was drooling for that business."

After Ray Kroc set the hamburger chain on its upward course, Moore hurried to win business from the first three franchisees in Los Angeles. He expanded his facilities, buying out a bigger meat-processing company. Then, lacking the sales to support this larger operation, Moore approached Kroc, explaining sorrowfully he was about to go bankrupt. Don't worry, the confident hamburger salesman told his supplier, things will improve. They did indeed. In the 1960s McDonald's stands sprouted like weeds along California highways. Kroc, remembering those who remained loyal during difficult times, rewarded Moore beyond the meat peddler's wildest imaginings. By the late 1960s Moore was supplying one hundred fifty McDonald's stores throughout California. In 1972 Moore began selling stock in his company. On the opening day shares were priced at $13. By the close of the day the stock sold for $30, thanks to a report that McDonald's was enjoying record earnings. By 1975 Moore's personal worth was estimated at $7 million.

At first Moore sold the chain patties. Then he expanded to cheese, shortening, ketchup, soft-drink syrups, and milk shake mixes. With each new product Moore catered to his prize customer's whims, meeting whatever arbitrary standards Kroc imposed. In the early days Moore won approval for products easily, receiving quick nods from top McDonald's officials. As the company's bureaucracy grew, Moore found himself dueling with product-development staff members, who examined recipes with laboratory precision, forcing minute changes. The inspectors refused to certify the tartar sauce for a year and a half, and Moore labored for two years to win approval for his Big

Mac sauce. "I used to get a lot of things done with one phone call," he groused to *Dun's*. "It doesn't work that way anymore. They've got a corporate ladder there that is very difficult for me to relate to."

McDonald's purchased hamburger from as many as one hundred eighty suppliers in the 1960s. By 1981 the figure had dropped to five. In its search for uniformity, McDonald's developed a few large suppliers. Smaller meat processors vanished from the fast-food picture as quickly as neighborhood restaurants. As the surviving processors came to depend more heavily on the hamburger chain, McDonald's exercised more control over them.

Today McDonald's biggest supplier is Keystone Foods, a company that provides hamburger to more than 2600 of the chain's outlets. Thanks to its prosperous customer, Keystone's sales zoomed from $158 million in 1977 to $418 million in 1981. The company was conceived in the middle 1960s by Jack Catt, a salesman who traveled the country pushing frozen meat products. Everywhere Catt went he saw McDonald's arches rising above the highways. Recognizing that a consistent product was the key to fast-food success, Catt wondered why the growing chain relied on fresh hamburger purchased from a host of suppliers. The salesman began calling on McDonald's purchasing officials, telling them that frozen patties would permit greater uniformity. In 1969 the chain agreed to test a frozen product. Catt and some partners began developing a process where hamburger moved through sixty-foot tunnels cooled by liquid nitrogen to minus-200 degrees Fahrenheit. The frozen patties proved profitable for the standardized chain. Most customers did not notice the change.

Keystone today purchases, feeds, and slaughters beef cattle, which are then processed into patties and distributed to stores. While Keystone is listed as an independent company on the New York Stock Exchange, it is in fact tightly controlled by McDonald's. The meat processor has no contract with the parent company or the franchisee-owned purchasing cooperatives that decide what suppliers to use, but McDonald's still determines the standards Keystone products must meet. Company purchasing agents negotiate what they consider to be a fair price. Since 95 percent of Keystone's revenues come from McDonald's, it has little choice but to bow to the dictates of the chain.

Keenly aware of who pays the rent, Keystone employees walk through their company headquarters wearing McDonald's ties and blazers. Company cafeterias are decorated in McDonald's red and gold. Just to make sure its giant customer remains satisfied, Keystone maintains a force of sixteen inspectors who venture into the McDonald's restaurants to advise franchisees and make certain no one violates company specifications. Keystone's attention to detail has helped it win expanding markets. In 1981, when McDonald's began introducing chicken products, Keystone became a major source of McChicken Sandwiches and Chicken McNuggets, serving 3700 outlets.

McDonald's franchisees probably buy hamburger at lower prices than anyone else. If that is so, I naively asked several industry executives, why is it the company does not cut prices and undersell competitors? Customers around the country pay similar prices for fast-food hamburgers whether the operator owns one store or is in a chain of a thousand units. A president of a regional chain explained that part of the reason for the uniform prices is that McDonald's takes its savings out in higher profits. In any case, the cost breaks franchisees receive are not substantial. "If you are buying hamburger for two hundred restaurants you are going to get a better price than the guy who is buying for one," he explained. "If you are buying for two thousand you can't save that much more than if you are buying for two hundred. The distributor can't give it away. He has to make some profit. So someone who is buying for two thousand may have a slight price advantage that works out to a quarter of a cent for each hamburger. For a company selling millions of hamburgers that means a lot of extra profits. It doesn't mean very much for the price the individual customer pays."

Since standardization did not provide the same benefits to franchising as it introduced to manufacturing, the contributions of Ray Kroc and Henry Ford should be viewed differently. Ford developed a way to increase productivity substantially. A stubborn perfectionist, the car maker clung to his basic design, only allowing fundamental improvements such as shock absorbers and more reliable brakes. As he constantly improved the factories, the cost of his product dropped. In a fifteen-year period the price of the Model T dipped from $780 to $290 because the productivity increases allowed lower prices. Ford used standardization to make cars affordable.

Before the fast-food chains were developed people could already afford hamburgers. One outlet—like the original McDonald brothers' unit—can produce cheap, quality food. It is not necessary to standardize procedures and build a large company in order to offer products like the chains provide. What standardization did allow Kroc to do is produce a uniform product that could be packaged and advertised around the country. It could be sold—like the Ford—by franchisees. The gleaming McDonald's assembly line is not substantially more productive than the traditional diner, but it produces a product that seems special. Theodore Levitt, a professor at Harvard Business School, writing in the *Harvard Business Review* in September 1972, pointed out how car makers put standardization to a different use than the fast-food chains. "While in Detroit the significance of the technological process lies in production, at McDonald's it lies in marketing," he wrote.

Marketing, as the business professor uses the term, refers to all the processes involved in presenting the product to the public and persuading customers to buy. Marketing is where franchising realizes its great economies of scale. One store alone could not advertise on TV. But a thousand stores can afford the best persuasive power the networks can offer.

Battling Brand X

Henry and Richard Bloch had reached a decision. They would abandon their tax-preparation operation, focusing instead on providing bookkeeping and management assistance to small businesses. The tax practice was a disagreeable venture, the brothers concluded, requiring them to spend frustrating hours earning little money. One of the Blochs' clients, learning he was about to lose a valuable accountant, protested strenuously. An employee of the *Kansas City Star*, he argued that the brothers could improve their business by advertising. Henry hesitated. Just try one ad, the man urged. Reluctantly the brothers agreed. Promising to complete tax returns for five dollars, the ad ran on January 25, 1955. The day the ad appeared Richard was manning the office while Henry paid calls on clients, going over their checkbooks and records. When Henry arrived at one client's business there was a message for him to call Richard.

"Get back as soon as you can," Richard told him. "We've got an office full of people."

Though the brothers knew nothing about newspaper promotions, their ad had run at an opportune moment. "We couldn't have picked a better time," Henry recalls, talking in the somber voice that has persuaded millions of Americans to use his service. "People were just getting their W2 forms."

During that tax season the brothers collected $25,000 in fees, an astonishing figure for them. They had found a spacious niche for themselves. Changing the spelling of their name to make it easier to pronounce, they called their company H & R Block. Sober, intelligent accountants, the brothers were also aggressive risk-takers, rare in their profession.

Quickly the Blochs opened two more offices in Kansas City. In October 1955 Henry started seven outlets in New York City, each located near an Internal Revenue Service center, where people seeking help with taxes formed long lines. Backed by the simple newspaper ads, the New York Block operation recorded $56,000 in sales the first year. For years tax accountants had relied on classified ads to attract attention, but Block's use of larger display presentations was a powerful innovation. Coming at a time when taxpayers were feeling increasingly resentful of the government's outstretched hand, the newspaper campaign reached a responsive audience. "We knew we had something good," Henry says. "It was like a winning hand at poker."

Running the New York office proved a difficult proposition. Since neither brother wanted to live away from home, they took turns serving two-week shifts at the Eastern outpost. Then, tired of commuting, they decided to sell out. Several accountants answered an ad the Blochs ran in *The New York Times*, but none of them could afford the brothers' price. Faced with the obstacle, the imaginative Blochs tried an untested approach. They persuaded the New York accountants to pay $10,000 down and then a royalty for the right to the H & R Block name and methods. The brothers had not set out to franchise; in fact, they had never heard of the practice. They had simply improvised a makeshift solution to a problem.

In 1956, impatient to expand, the brothers advertised for local operators in Des Moines, Oklahoma City, and Little Rock. At first established accountants had no interest in the unknown Block operation. Working in solo practices or small partnerships, prosperous tax preparers saw little reason to solicit customers actively. They viewed themselves as professionals who provided a personal service to a few clients. The Bloch brothers were offering a kind of business that was foreign to accountants. In the chain approach the operator would hire others to prepare forms. The franchisee would be more concerned with advertising and renting of offices than with tax laws.

To run these new offices the brothers turned to the few young people who answered the ads. Meeting with prospective operators in hotels, Henry and Richard explained how advertising could expand a business. To demonstrate how Block's sales had increased, Henry showed a graph that formed what he called a stair pattern; step by step the line indicating sales moved up each year. During the first several years joining the chain in the Midwest cost nothing. There was no initial fee, Henry pointed out, and H & R Block paid for the first year's advertising. If the franchisee's sales were higher than the previous year, he paid a percentage of the gains to the company.

The first newspaper ads did not rely on the soft-sell approach. "How to tame your income tax," said one, featuring a lion tamer and his animal. "Having illusions about your income tax?" inquired one, showing a magician holding a hoop in the air through which a comely assistant floated. "I was never too proud of those ads," Henry Bloch confesses. "I thought they looked cheap."

The brothers' first franchisees included accountants who could not afford advertising themselves or were afraid to try the new media tactics themselves. In 1958 Pat Merriman, then a twenty-four-year-old tax accountant with clients in Lubbock and Amarillo, Texas, met the Bloch brothers, who then oversaw thirty-nine offices. Merriman had been doing five thousand dollars a year in business and was amazed at the results of H & R Block's offices. Impressed with the intelligence of the brothers, Merriman feared that they represented the wave of the future. "I didn't want to have to compete with them," he recalls. "I didn't have the nerve to spend money on ads the way they did."

Merriman acquired the right to open Block offices in all of Texas. In his first year with the chain he ran an office in Lubbock. The following season the franchisee opened a second unit in Amarillo and then a third one in Austin. The parent company's central office continued to provide Merriman and other franchisees the newspaper display ads that were proving so effective. In 1961 Block took a careful step into television advertising. The home office provided scripts, sending them to franchisees who read them on local TV. Merriman appeared on a Texas station explaining who he was and saying he could help blue-collar workers use itemized deductions. H & R Block was for the common man, the ad said. Another spot explained that the tax preparer could be of special value to nurses.

By 1963 television was boosting the Block name in cities around the country. Offices opened in Cleveland and Fresno, losing money the first several years, then moving into the black to stay. Then the rapidly expanding company made the big jump into national advertising. John Cameron Swayze, the well-known television announcer, became the company's first national spokesman. In one ad Swayze stood in front of a map of the country, explaining how big Block was and how the convenient offices could save people money. This direct talk proved effective. Franchisees around the country opened offices as fast as they could. In 1965 Pat Merriman's mini-chain had one hundred offices; by 1970 the figure had reached three hundred. In 1977 he reigned over four hundred twenty offices in Texas.

From the beginning competitors tried to copy the Block system. In some cities they took out full-page ads mimicking the brothers' five-dollar offer. But no rival firm moved as quickly to build the large chain needed to support network advertising. By the late 1960s H & R Block was firmly entrenched as a national system with a television identity. By the 1980s the company was filling out ten million tax returns a year. Any competitor wishing to duplicate the feat would have to spend heavily to do battle with Block. The new firm would have to be prepared to lose millions for a number of years in order to buy the brand-name identification Block had already created.

With their advertising campaigns, the Bloch brothers were introducing a powerful tool to franchising—they were creating a brand name for a service chain. The harried citizen could struggle with taxes himself, take his chances with a "Brand X" accountant, or rely on a trustworthy, familiar name. "Stop burning the midnight oil," said one Block ad featuring an unshaven, haggard taxpayer. Advertised brand-name products first began to prosper around the time of the Civil War as the public was offered a range of "miracle" patent medicines and cleaning powders. By 1900 companies were spending half a billion dollars a year on advertising in newspapers and magazines. N. W. Ayer & Son of Philadelphia, one of the early advertising agencies, handled accounts for Hires Root Beer, Montgomery Ward, and Burpee seeds. In a classic campaign for the new National Biscuit Company, Ayer introduced an approach to marketing that is still used by companies around the world.

The product to be sold was an ordinary cracker. In the nineteenth century, before the predecessor of Nabisco opened, crackers and cookies were unbranded products sold loose in roughly made cracker barrels. In 1899 Adolphus Green, president of National Biscuit, decided the time had come for a standardized, nationally advertised soda cracker. To make the product look different from local competitors' he chopped off the corners of the squares, creating an eight-sided cracker. Then, along with the advertising agency, he brooded about selecting the right name. They toyed with Taka Cracker, Hava Cracker, and Wanta Cracker, but the winning entry was Uneeda. Next the marketers needed a package. For months they tried different containers before Green's partner developed a cardboard box lined with wax paper. To add a touch of dignity the product was called a biscuit instead of a cracker. The company backed the Uneeda Biscuit with the largest advertising campaign of the time, spending a million dollars a year on newspapers, magazines, billboards, and streetcars. The first ads were teasers displaying the word Uneeda. To show off the waterproof container, Ayer produced a design featuring a boy in a raincoat carrying the box through a storm. A year after the Uneeda Biscuit entered the market, the company was selling ten million packages a month.

With Uneeda the basic elements in selling a nationally branded product had been established. The process required standardizing a product, packaging it, selecting a name, then advertising as much as possible. The Uneeda campaign helped to establish an unwritten rule governing advertising expenditures: The most heavily advertised products would be those that were not necessities or that were little different from competitors'. Until World War I, sugar, a basic staple purchased by most households, did not advertise. Cocoa, which was not a necessity, advertised heavily.

The advertising industry grew slowly until the end of World War II. War had lifted the country out of the Depression. Men found jobs in the military, while many women for the first time worked in factories. With the end of war production, the country faced the possibility of sinking back into a depression, but companies soon determined that factories could be shifted to turn out new consumer goods. To ensure prosperity businesses would have to manufacture and sell more goods than ever before. For the economy to grow it was not enough for workers to perform their jobs diligently; they would also have to buy voraciously. The consumer ideal of the 1950s was a family living in a single home in the suburbs with a big car, power lawnmower, washing machine, and other conveniences. This acquisitive life-style was championed in the new television advertisements. Television, which had been developed in the 1920s, was now providing the ideal advertising medium. It grew rapidly in power and influence, along with the companies that paid to promote their goods on the broadcast airwaves.

John Kenneth Galbraith in *The Affluent Society* (1958) argued that America had achieved an economy of plenty, where more people died from eating too much than from eating too little. Increasing production was needed to create employment and limit the social tensions caused by economic inequality. To maintain production more demand had to be created. This could be accomplished by making people perpetually discontent. The consumer's material needs for food, clothing, and shelter might be satisfied, but he would always yearn to own everything the neighbors had. Galbraith wrote that advertising's "central function is to create desires—to bring into being wants that previously did not exist." The hungry man need not be told of his need for food. Only those removed from physical want don't know what they need. "Is a new breakfast cereal or detergent so much wanted if so much must be spent to compel in the consumer the sense of want?" Galbraith asked. The modern business would have to focus on advertising and selling products. It would be just as important to spend money manufacturing *demand* for the product as it was to spend money manufacturing the actual product. Deodorant manufacturers would become particularly adept at the marketing game. Body odor was something to be feared and carefully fought against, the ads cautioned. Millions of people who had never been concerned about body odors decided "to take the worry out of being close." They were educated by television advertising to paste gluelike chemicals over their sweat gland pores.

Some companies spent millions persuading the public that ordinary commodities had unique functions. Images of all kinds could be attached to the same product. Proctor & Gamble promoted its Ivory Soap with wholesome ads speaking of mother and family. Camay, a soap produced by the same company, and a commodity that performs exactly the same function as Ivory, was advertised as a sophisticated product for the seductive woman. When franchise chains stepped into the advertising arena, they applied techniques developed by the packaged goods manufacturers. It was not good enough to do taxes yourself or to go to an ordinary accountant, H & R Block argued. As Henry Bloch's grave television manner suggested, the chain was special—reliable and solid.

Like many soap makers who advertised heavily, Block offered a product that differed little from that provided by less famous competitors. An unknown accounting firm might produce as large a tax refund as the chain outlet. And unlike branded soap, which promised uniformity, the Block tax return could never be of completely consistent quality. Inevitably some tax preparers would be better than others.

One of the most unlikely franchise successes came with the humble automobile muffler. Until the 1950s, the muffler had been a mundane product. One of many parts needed to operate a car, they were sold in grimy garages. Then a few garage owners made a profitable discovery. By posting signs promoting mufflers the dealers could double sales, as uneasy motorists bought replacements more often. The lowly muffler could become something of an impulse item. In 1956 Midas took the process a step further, introducing shops *specializing* in mufflers. The new chain painted its mufflers gold, a color easily associated with the company's name. Midas began a multi-million-dollar advertising campaign, much of it aimed at housewives. Mufflers are important products, the women were told, and Midas offers a special device. Midas was following precisely the approach developed for the Uneeda biscuit: It was taking a readily available product, packaging it in a new way, and causing consumers to associate the brand name with desirable qualities.

Franchise developers would often claim that they were creating new industries and producing thousands of jobs. In fact, the franchisors merely reformulated existing ideas, marketing old concepts in shiny new packages. In some cases the chains entered stagnant markets and grew by taking business away from existing independent outlets. During the period of Holiday Inns' early rapid expansion, the demand for hotel rooms did not grow. Holiday Inns filled new units by taking customers away from independent motels and city hotels. In 1952 Holiday Inns built its first unit. In 1964 number five hundred was completed, and number one thousand opened in 1968. In March 1966 the staff of the Board of Governors of the Federal Reserve System issued a report on the hotel and motel industry. In 1965 there were 2.5 million hotel and motel rooms, about one-third more than the figure in 1946. Despite the increased capacity, the number of rooms *occupied* had stayed about the same. The expanded capacity was created by a boom in motel construction that pushed up the number of rooms an average of 8 percent a year. "During recent years, the hotel-motel industry has shown more and more signs of excess capacity in relation to current demands," the Federal Reserve report noted.

At the same time the price of rooms doubled, a considerably greater increase than the consumer price index showed. Cheap older rooms were being torn down, while more expensive new rooms were being put up. Before Kemmons Wilson, a Memphis builder, opened the first Holiday Inn, motels had been small roadside operations of ten or twenty units that rarely featured telephones or air conditioning. Often run by husband-and-wife teams, the motels or tourist courts offered spare, functional rooms at low prices. Bigger was better, Wilson believed, and he set out to construct more substantial accommodations. He combined features of city hotels with the motels. With one hundred twenty rooms, the first Holiday Inn was an imposing building by the standards of the time, far larger and more impressive-looking than the typical motel. Wilson had placed a familiar service in a modern, shiny package. The Holiday Inn was superior in some ways to its predecessors. It did provide a swimming pool, free ice, and two double beds, things other motels had never offered. Within five years the gap in accommodations between Holiday Inns and most other units had practically vanished. Still, Holiday Inns had gained a lead it would never lose. In the motel marketing battles the company remained preeminent. The bright green and orange "Great Sign" gave the chain a strong identity. Though lacking the elegance and personal service of city hotels, most of the new Holiday Inns were soon jammed. By the mid-1960s the distinction between hotels and motels was becoming blurred. Hotels were offering free parking and Holiday Inns had built six-hundred-room units in Chicago and Manhattan.

Like the motel and muffler chains, the fast-food operations had simply repackaged a long-familiar item. All the finely tuned aspects of McDonald's business discussed in preceding chapters should be seen as the packaging needed to sell an ordinary product nationally. The McDonald's kitchen performs the same functions as the traditional lunch counter grill. But the chain's cooking facilities are deliberately displayed to the public so that customers will be entertained by young people bustling about gleaming stainless steel equipment. Watching a McDonald's crew working in their bright uniforms is fascinating. Watching a short-order cook sweat over a grill is mildly distasteful. Advertising and heavy condiments make very ordinary meat patties seem special. The hamburgers are packaged in bright containers so that the customers feel they are getting something delightful like a toy, not just a meal. The triangular scoops that overstuff french fry bags are not so much an efficiency as a marketing tool aimed at creating an impression of abundance. "A carefully planned design is built into the elaborate technology of the food-service system in such a fashion as to make it a significant marketing device," notes Theodore Levitt, a Harvard Business School professor, who argues that every aspect of the McDonald's store, from the french fryers to the garbage cans, aids in marketing products.

The main reason for the phenomenal success of fast-food chains clearly has been effective packaging and advertising. Industry executives, though, confronted with this statement, heartily disagree. They invariably cite low prices and convenience. In their early years franchised outlets were, in fact, cheaper than conventional restaurants, but by the 1980s, the cost advantage had evaporated. An adult filling up on fast-food hamburgers would spend four dollars or more, the price of a meal (including tip) at a cheap independent restaurant. Having conditioned customers, the leading chains could raise prices and still keep sales.

Of course, the cheapest alternative is eating at home, but not everyone knows this. In a 1977 survey by A. C. Nielsen, only 29 percent of respondents knew that fast food cost more. The price difference between eating out and at home increased throughout the 1970s, a time when people increasingly bought fast food. The Bureau of Labor Statistics reported that families in 1973 spent 28.1 percent of their total food expenditures on meals away from home. By 1981 the figure had climbed to 32.4 percent. In the same period the cost for food at home rose 84.6 percent, while the cost of eating out rose 95.7 percent. "An entire fast-food meal, including entree, fries, soft drink or shake, and dessert, will usually cost twice as much as the same meal prepared at home," the American Council on Science and Health reported in 1981.

Those people who say they patronize fast-food chains because they save time may be fooling themselves. Fast food genuinely does save time and effort for the truck driver or salesman who needs a quick bite and is driving past an outlet. McDonald's fries patties in ninety seconds, and customers spend about two minutes in line at well-run outlets. At a truck stop or conventional diner, the customer might wait ten minutes for a similar meal. But for fast food's traditional bulwark, families, the time advantage is less pronounced or important. To obtain a franchised meal the family must typically pile into a car, drive ten or twenty minutes to an outlet, stand in line, pay the check, and sit down on the store's not necessarily comfortable seats. The whole procedure takes as much time as pulling patties and fries out of a freezer and cooking them. A reasonably competent home chef can produce a meal at least as good as what the fast-food outlets serve.

Even if fast food does not save money or much time, some would argue it saves energy. For the exhausted working mother or the person living alone, it is easier to pick up a pizza than to cook dinner. "Fast food is a real life-saver," a working mother in Bethlehem, Pennsylvania, told me. "I don't know what I would do without it." While it may be understandable that the working mother wants someone else to do her cooking, it still does not seem that her selection of fast food is based on rational criteria. The ideal, rational consumer wanting to serve children fast food could cook at home. Shopping for meals a week or two in advance, the efficient parent could use a microwave oven and paper plates to serve the same prepackaged pizzas and hamburgers the chains sell. The home cook would eliminate driving time and the complications of shepherding children through a checkout line. Chain fast food is a luxury item that corporate marketers have transformed into a product many people consider a necessity. Customers eating fast food half a dozen times a week become hooked on a carefully advertised, packaged commodity.

The intense loyalty of children and lunching workers for fast food is surely not the result of cold calculations about price and quality. The appeal of fast food is related to intangible qualities. For many customers the outlets seemed to possess a certain Hollywood magic. Bombarded with television ads, children and adults learned that fast food represents a special experience, superior to eating at home. "You deserve a break today," McDonald's promised. Eating out may represent a break for the mother cooking every day, but the ads were aimed at children and men as much as women. Eating at home, the ads said, was not fun. Eating at McDonald's is fun.

Part of what the fast-food dispensers sell is entertainment. For kids, a trip to a fast-food outlet is an exciting event that immediately increases parents' popularity. Teenagers seek out the highway stands as destinations on unhurried nights and places to rendezvous with friends after school. The gaudy interiors and bright signs create a fantasyland, a bit of glamour that seems to provide a connection to the distant worlds portrayed on television. People in small towns would feel a certain pride when the chains first located in their areas. The old hometown must not be so obscure, after all, if an important company like McDonald's had decided to locate there. (In fact, this is the theme of one of their recent television commercials.)

Robert Emerson, a fast-food analyst for Fred Alger & Company, argues that connoisseurs who scoff at Big Macs and compare them to thick charcoal-broiled hamburgers are missing the point. The franchised chains are not attempting to provide a traditional meal. They have developed a different kind of product with its own appeal. "What McDonald's is serving is a peculiarly sweet, salty tasting item," he writes. "The addition of sugar to the buns, french fries, and perhaps to the ketchup may be the key to producing what is, in effect, salty candy."

Michael Culp, a restaurant analyst at Prudential Bache who often eats in chain outlets, finds there is little relation between whether he likes the food and the sales performance of the company. "If I consistently dislike the food the company might still do well," he says. "There are cases where I think the food is terrific and the company fails."

To quantify his research and amuse clients Culp compiles a fast-food index based on his ratings of whether meals are "edible" or "inedible." The highest-rated chains recently were two new chicken outfits, Mrs. Winners and Sisters. Other high scorers include Shoney's and Chart House steak houses.

Over the years fast food has become an increasingly sophisticated form of entertainment. In 1979 Pizza Time Theatre was developed by Nolan Bushnell, who invented the electronic game Pong that gave rise to video games. More thrilling than a Burger King, a more desirable spot for a birthday than McDonald's, Pizza Time Theatre is the ultimate fast-food treat for youngsters aged two to twelve. The chain may become a major force in the fast-food industry eventually. But in March 1984 the company suffered a serious setback, filing for reorganization under Chapter XI of the federal bankruptcy laws. Adding stores at a rate of one a week, the company had been too ambitious, *Business Week* reported. The chain opened "too many units, too soon, too close together," an analyst told the magazine. While the parent company is troubled, individual outlets thrive. Young customers, unaware of the chain's complex financial straits, clamor to visit the restaurants.

In Louisville, Kentucky, a sign in the front of the parking lot of a shopping center announces Chuck E. Cheese's Pizza Time Theatre. Chuck E. is the chain's symbol, a human-sized mouse

Bushnell hopes to make as famous as Mickey Mouse. Judging by one night's turnout the creature is beginning to accomplish his creator's goal. At eight on a Friday evening there are about a hundred cars parked near the Pizza Time Theatre and more people are swarming in. Meanwhile, the rest of the shopping-center lot is mostly empty. Across the street a Taco Tico has two customers. Down the road Kentucky Fried Chicken, Burger King, and McDonald's are doing a moderate trade. Chuck E. Cheese's receptionist greets the customers lining up between ropes and asks how many are in each party. Many of the people have come in groups of ten or more, a few adults herding excited children. On a wall there are posted a dozen names of youngsters who will be celebrating their birthdays that night. As space in the facility clears, the waiting customers are ushered to a counter to place their orders for pizza, salad bar, or sandwiches. Prices are the same as at any fast-food restaurant, but at Pizza Time Theatre food is beside the point. The main dining area is a cavernous room filled with long rows of picnic tables that can seat several hundred. At some of the tables children sit wearing party hats, holding balloons, and eating pizza. Periodically the lights dim. On a stage in front of the room large computer-operated stuffed animals begin singing and telling jokes. A quartet of guitar-playing six-foot dogs called "the Beagles" play old Beatles hits. As one human-sized animal sings "Rock and Roll Is Here to Stay," dozens of flags on the walls swing in time. Under the stage is a space about three feet high that has been divided into rooms and passageways, exciting places for young customers to run around in and explore. Very few of the several hundred children in the place are actually sitting and eating. Most are watching the animals or racing through the rest of the outlet.

Next to the stage area is a video game parlor jammed with kids sticking quarters in the slots. The darkened room, filled with the pings and clatter of video machines, is so crowded it is difficult to move through. In another room is a "general store," where people are lined up to buy stuffed Chuck E. Cheese dolls, hats, and balloons.

Children raised on a diet of such entertaining fast food have come to demand it. Youngsters might resist cleaning their plates at home or in fancy restaurants, but at McDonald's they devour the hamburgers with fervor. The powerful attraction of the chains has sharply altered the American diet. A study by the Newspaper Advertising Bureau found that the average American above the age of twelve was eating in a fast-food chain more than nine times a month. In a six-month period 93 percent of all Americans ate fast food at least once, while 60 percent patronized Kentucky Fried Chicken at least once. The Center for Science in the Public Interest reported that consumption of frozen potatoes, used mainly for french fries, rose from 6.6 pounds per person in 1960 to 36.8 pounds in 1976. Consumption of hard cheese, a prime ingredient of pizza, climbed from 8.3 to 15.9 pounds per person.

In response to critics who have questioned the nutritional value of fast food, the chains have issued reports indicating that franchised meals are nourishing. But while the chain meals do have some protein and nutrients, they hardly qualify as health food. "They are too high in saturated fats, salt and sugar," argues Bonnie Liebman, a nutritionist at the Center for Science in the Public Interest. "This kind of food can make people more susceptible to heart attacks."

Jean Mayer, professor of nutrition at Harvard's School of Public Health, told *Time* magazine that he is "nonfanatical about McDonald's." As a weekend treat it could not cause serious problems, he said. But for many people fast food is not simply an occasional treat. They have come to rely on the basic fast-food meals of hamburgers or pizza. A balanced diet must include variety, and millions of chain patrons eat the same meal over and over. Fast-food managers I interviewed mentioned loyal customers who come in nearly every day to order the same food.

Wherever they go, young people now demand menus based on fast food. At home they insist on hamburgers and french fries. In the schools, children scorn balanced cafeteria meals. Throwing up their hands in defeat, administrators now offer the fast foods kids crave. And students' tastes do not change after graduation. When the Navy became concerned about morale problems caused by dissatisfaction with food, it surveyed crew members of the U.S.S. *Saratoga*. Not surprisingly, the predominantly young sailors said they wanted fast food. They were tired of the slow-moving cafeteria lines serving traditional Navy fare of roast beef, turkey, and tuna sandwiches. As an experiment in 1978 the *Saratoga* began offering hamburgers or cheeseburgers, fries, and shakes for lunch. For supper the crew could have fast food such as pizza or fried chicken.

The Navy also borrowed fast-food-production methods. Using a system similar to Burger King's the ship increased its serving rate from four people a minute to fifteen, a figure that would do any fast-food restaurant proud. The dining areas were redecorated with bright colors, more like the fast-food restaurants the young men had known back home. The test produced immediate results. Sailors who had been skipping meals started showing up. Dinner service doubled, from 700 people to 1400. The Navy has since expanded the program to cover all its aircraft carriers.

Marketing executives argue that fast food and other franchise products have prospered because they fill needs. They say that TV ads cannot brainwash people—commercials provide information to people who freely make choices. If the product does not meet a need, it will not survive the competition of the market. The executives trot out the example of the Edsel, which was heavily marketed and failed miserably. Though companies may verbally minimize the effectiveness of advertising, they somehow place enough faith in television to spend fortunes reaching viewers. *Leading National Advertisers*, an annual volume, said that in 1981 sponsors spent $5.59 billion on network TV ads and $4.22 billion on local spots. The most heavily advertised brand name was McDonald's, which spent $136,516,200. Burger King and Kentucky Fried Chicken trailed far behind, spending $46 and $36 million each. By comparison, Exxon spent $24 million and Sears invested $23 million. Holiday Inns' figure was $16 million, while Midas spent $14 million. All these companies spent additional tens of millions on print ads.

In most cases the effects of ads for the franchises have been considerable. The mere placement of a chain's sign lures droves of customers who have been conditioned to rely on advertised brand names. Even strong regional chains face difficulties when competing with nationally advertised companies.

Carrols, the Syracuse-based hamburger chain we saw in Chapter 1, had one hundred sixty outlets in the late 1960s when McDonald's began to invade the territory. By 1974 it had become clear that Carrols was about to collapse. The company hoisted the white flag. By 1981, seventy-six of the former Carrols had been transformed by marketing sleight-of-hand into Burger Kings. The new Burger Kings were built in the Carrols buildings, and in many cases the managers and staff stayed on. "These are the same restaurants at the same locations with the same people," explained David J. Connor, president of Carrols. "All we did was change the name."

The new Burger Kings were perfectly capable of holding their own against the nearby McDonald's outlets, who were selling similar products—in many cases just across the street or down a few blocks. One ugly-duckling Carrols that had sales of $125,000 in 1975 was transformed into a Burger King swan that sold $1,000,000 in 1981.

To find out how advertising executives view the effectiveness of their services, I spoke to Dick Rich, who is surely one of the more knowledgeable authorities in the field. In the 1960s Rich helped produce a series of memorable ads for Benson and Hedges, where the long cigarettes kept bumping into things. For an ad that showed twenty-three different bouncing tummies, he wrote the line: "No matter what shape your stomach is in, when it gets out of shape take Alka-Seltzer." Along with two partners he formed Wells Rich Greene, an agency that sold its stock in 1968. At the time Rich sold 75,000 of his shares for about $1,275,000. When he left the agency several years later he still had 225,000 shares, worth $3.6 million. In 1977 Rich, working independently, produced a campaign for Wendy's. His most recent franchised client is Bojangles, a fried-chicken chain. Rich, who is fifty-two and talks with an ingratiating smile, does not suffer from modesty. "Clients don't come to me for okay advertising; they come to me for great, great advertising," he once explained to *The New York Times*. A medallion hung around his neck as he sat talking about advertising in the elegant Manhattan townhouse where he works and lives.

"Television is important for some products more than others. When tobacco was on TV they were not in the tobacco business. They were in the advertising business. The advertising and the total image was 95 percent of what determined which brand the consumers purchased. If you're going to buy a computer for an industrial application the advertising is 5 percent. With fast food the advertising is very important. It can't make a bad chain work, but it can accelerate growth. When the first fast-food ads started they had to overcome the greasy spoon image and get people to trust the places. Now people know what fast food is. Between a third and a half of all meals are eaten out. People have to decide where to eat. There are some people—I wouldn't say they're compulsive—there are some people who eat at the same place every day. But other people are going to make choices, and you want your product on the top of their minds. At that magic moment when you and I say, 'Let's go out for lunch. What do you feel like having?' I want you to say Bojangles rather than McDonald's or Burger King. Advertising keeps your name and idea before the customers."

The ads Rich produces are not terribly specific, but they are bright and funny. "Dick Rich feels that he has discovered the key to great television advertising," *The New York Times* noted. "While others are trying to create the great line, he is looking for the great picture."

The test of all Rich ads is "WIWIJ?" "Will it work in Japan?" This philosophy was apparent in Rich's Wendy's campaign. In the "Hot 'n Juicy" ads people struggle to eat the large Wendy's hamburgers while snappy music plays in the background. The hamburger customers wipe their chins as the juice drips down.

In one scene a Boy Scout hands his neckerchief to an old lady who uses it to wipe her chin. Rich's Bojangles ads open with someone dancing in front of a big mouth. Then the camera flashes to a person eating the chicken. A second customer dances in front of the mouth, then is seen eating the chicken. A lively background jingle proclaims, "Bojangles chicken makes your mouth dance." Bojangles is a regional chain based in Charlotte, North Carolina, with two hundred twenty-four outlets. Rich says that with the right breaks the chain could become as big as McDonald's. If the company fails it will not be because of a lack of slick advertising. Rich bubbles over with enthusiasm for the Bojangles product.

"It's not fast food. It's good food. I'm not saying that to be derogatory about other products. The other systems go through great pains to have food as good as they can make. But basically it's a convenience concept. When you advertise ordinary food you use the basic 'It's crispy on the outside and juicy on the inside.' What do you say when you *are* juicy on the inside, when you *are* crispy on the outside, and you *really* taste good? Do you say *really?* You can't use any virtue words. Those are the clichés of the industry. To get your attention we use a trick in the Bojangles ad. The moment you see the ad you have no idea what is going on. That is not a dishonest trick. It's not showing a naked woman and then saying now I want to sell you cars. It is, Why is that person dancing in front of that giant mouth? The viewer fills in the completion of the thought. 'Oh, the chicken makes your mouth dance.'

"When I did the 'Hot 'n Juicy' thing for Wendy's I was really capitalizing on the fact that Burger King and McDonald's were not hot and juicy. The Wendy's hamburger was served warmer and it was less chewy than the others. All my campaigns come from the product. The long cigarette was the long cigarette. When I started working for Wendy's there were different factions in the company who wanted the ads to say different things. People said, 'You've got to tell the fresh meat story. Our meat is fresh, not frozen.' Another group of franchisees said, 'We've got to get across the idea that "Have it your way" is ours and not Burger King's idea.' Someone wanted to point out that Wendy's didn't serve hamburgers under heat lamps. All of these are virtues. But that's a hamburger slinger's viewpoint. For television it's got to be much more energized. The chairman of the company suggested a nutrition campaign. To me nutrition is a fad that is not compatible with a hamburger cooked on a grill. The nutrition idea might have a great market, but it's not particularly compatible with hamburgers per se and it's not very mainstream. To me we've got much better ways to give to charity. I think people eat from hunger or enjoyment or convenience or whatever."

Since the people who produce franchise ads also sell other consumer products, it is not surprising that the chains use approaches common to many commercials. Concrete advantages are not emphasized. The ads generally try to associate the brand name with vague good feelings. Ads featuring sexy actors and titillating scenes apparently prove effective because people associate desirable qualities with the product. Millions can be persuaded that by buying a product they can purchase love or sex. If consumers spend money for the item and the miracle does not happen, still the product will remind them of the image of the people in the ad.

In an article in *Advertising Age* Dave Vadehra of Video Storyboard, a market research company, explained the approach ads must take to maximize their impact. Vadehra noted that the average viewer is exposed to more than eighty commercials a day. Since one commercial takes up only thirty seconds out of a person's day, the ad must attempt to create a strong emotional effect. "So what do viewers retain from commercials?" Vadehra wrote. "Our research shows that viewers generally retain impressions of commercials rather than specific details. In commercials facts are forgotten but feelings remain. The best a commercial can achieve is to impart an impression that is favorable to the product, faithful to the brand—but, most important, one retained by the viewers. This retained impression is all that is left of a commercial after it has been processed through human perception and memory."

Franchise ads often attempt to associate feelings of love and security with brand names. Many spots present an image of life that may have existed in America a generation ago. The family is emphasized. People are shown in rural or small-town settings surrounded by warm, caring characters. Mom shelters the kids with love. Of course, the message is that if you buy the product you can purchase feelings of love and kindness. "When my father was having problems with his eyes we went right to the Pearle Vision Center," an ad character intones. "I knew the doctor would check his eyes right. And you know that made me feel better. After years of looking to those eyes for strength, I sure couldn't trust them to just anyone." While sentimental music plays in the background, a chorus sings, "Nobody cares for eyes more than Pearle." In the ad Pearle is not attempting to persuade viewers that it sells good glasses. The message is clearly that patronizing the chain will help a customer experience the joys of fatherhood and the respect sons are supposed to feel for fathers. The image of the tight, loving family is perhaps more realistically associated with an era when optometrists knew their patients personally from the time they were children. Pearle is, in fact, a large chain owned by Searle, a major drug and health company. The franchise company's brightly colored outlets impersonally beckon speeding cars to turn in from highways.

Ads that don't promise love make even vaguer appeals. "Only 7-Eleven's got freedom of choice," a commercial claims. "Coke, Pepsi, 7-Up, or Dr Pepper—freedom's waiting for you." Of course, the whole point of 7-Eleven is to provide *less* freedom of choice. The convenience stores offering limited selections have successfully replaced thousands of corner groceries and supermarkets. The ad is apparently a dig at fast-food chains that are major competitors of 7-Eleven and are the only other food stores advertised on national TV. According to the logic of the commercial the consumer must select either a convenience store or a fast-food outlet, and the convenience store offers more brands of sugared soda water.

Some of the most convoluted advertisements are aimed at

women. Mothers find themselves pulled in a variety of directions by the ads. In the 1950s the Moms portrayed in ads were supposed to stay at home using the bright new washing machine and cleaning the floors spotless. By the 1980s Mom was still supposed to have spotless floors, but now in many ads she was encouraged to go out and make more money to buy products. Advertisers had discovered that Mom could consume even more effectively if she earned money herself. And since she already had a washing machine, the advertisers would have to sell her services she had not yet learned to rely on. It is now okay if Mom doesn't cook for the family, the ads say. In fact, buying fast food might represent a way of showing love for children. A generation ago ads for cake mixes helped mothers to overcome feeling guilty about not baking cookies for their children. Now women struggle with guilt about not cooking. The fast-food ads reduce this obstacle, to greater corporate profits.

One thing the leading chains rarely advertise is low prices. Companies such as Midas, Holiday Inns, Edie Adams' Cut & Curl, and McDonald's began by appealing to thrifty customers. As the chains established brand names and controlled their markets, they no longer needed to undersell competitors. Customers, ignoring the additional cost, patronize the famous names. The prices at the giant chains are not extravagant, since the companies are aiming at the broad middle of the market, but it is hard to find a real bargain offered by the leading chains. While H & R Block is cheaper than many certified public accountants, the chain is priced a bit higher than many independent tax preparers. Inevitably, budget muffler and motel chains have risen to challenge the leaders. Still, the national companies have maintained their firm grip on the public. Even during the recessions of the early 1980s, consumers were willing to pay higher prices for familiar brands. The cost of advertising pushes up the prices of the national companies, imposing a sort of tax on consumers. In supermarkets the same kind of surcharge exists for brand-name products such as aspirin and canned fruit. An increasing number of grocery customers avoid subsidizing ads by purchasing generic products; in the fran-

chised economy, however, there seems to be little such movement toward budget chains or independent companies.

As advertising has become a necessity for service businesses
of all kinds, chains have been formed that do little more than
offer a brand name. Local operators have come to feel their only
hope for survival is to join a chain. In the early 1970s real-estate
chains consisting of twelve to fifteen brokerage offices began
forming in Southern California. The traditional broker with
one office suddenly faced a challenge competing against chains.
In 1972 Century 21 began trying to persuade brokers to join
what the company hoped would be a national network. At first
independent agents balked at the idea of taking on the chain's
identity. After all, at the time Century 21 offered little except its
unfamiliar name. As the chain spread its tentacles around the
country, however, weaker brokers particularly began to see affiliation as a lifesaver. In a period of volatile real-estate markets, a famous name became important.

Home buyers choosing between a local person and a national
brand such as Century 21 often prefer what they have seen on
TV. "Customers respond to brand names," said Norman Young,
a former advertising man who headed Neighborhood Realty
Group. "The local name doesn't have a prayer when competing
with a brand name. The Ma-and-Pa broker is dead, like the old
candy store."

A stranger in town seeing a Century 21 office assumes that the
national affiliate will somehow be more sophisticated and
trustworthy, showing customers only the better homes in the
area. The chain's brokers do attend a cursory one-week course
in real-estate methods taught by the company, and they wear
standard green sports coats. They also can get referrals from
other outlets. But Century 21 brokers operate much as they did
before joining the chain, selling houses to local people. They use
the same buildings. Their signs still identify the owner, though
the Century 21 name appears above in larger type.

In 1979, at a time when rising interest rates were discourag-
ing real-estate sales, Century 21 increased its membership by
22 percent. To enter the Century 21 family, the broker pays an

initial fee of $8500, then sends the company 6 percent of gross sales. When the costs of advertising, signs, and other chain extras are added, the price can be steep—as much as 10 percent of gross sales. Since many brokers earn commissions of 20 percent on each transaction, the chain fees may eat up half of commission revenues. In order for chain affiliation to pay off, the broker might need to see sales double. Weak brokers have flocked to pay the price. In 1975 there were three major real-estate chains, including Century 21. By 1981 there were seven national chains and forty-eight regional operations. Large chains included Red Carpet, with 1250 members, and Electronic Realty, with 3500 outlets.

The real-estate collapse of 1981 severely hurt Century 21 along with everyone else in the industry. Dealers dropped out of the chain, hoping to save the 6 percent royalty payments. "Television advertising fees were choking me to death," a New Jersey broker trying to free himself from a contract with Realty World told *The New York Times*. But as some dropped their affiliation, others signed on. Brokers struggling in a difficult market joined chains as a last resort.

Like real-estate agencies other independent businesses have come under pressure to take on a brand name. In 1978 Emily Wight, who with her husband operated an independent campground in Sturbridge, Massachusetts, joined the Jellystone Park system. Sales immediately climbed a third. In 1979, when business was down for most of the other competing camps in the area because of gasoline problems, Jellystone's business was up 15 percent. Though the chain itself cannot afford network advertising, it benefits from association with a famous television star: Yogi Bear. All Jellystone camps feature the cartoon character. Every day someone dressed up like Yogi wanders around the campsites talking to children and pretending to steal picnic baskets. Camps have miniature golf courses with Yogi figures, and their general stores sell Yogi Bear sweatshirts and hats. All this goes over well with children, who feel comfortable with the familiar cartoon character.

Jellystone and other camp and motel chains use company

reservations systems to derive maximum benefits from their brand names. Computerized reservations programs help loyal customers find a convenient outlet of their favorite chain. Franchise motels typically obtain 20 percent or more of their business through company systems. A Holiday Inn in Van Nuys, California, reported receiving 75 percent of its customers through the corporation's toll-free 800-number lines. When franchisees occasionally drop out of the Holiday Inns chain because of disputes with the parent company, sales generally drop by 30 to 40 percent. Referrals dry up, and travelers looking for a chain outlet pass by the newly independent motel. Chains use the promise of increased sales in their efforts to attract franchisees. Some companies actively solicit independent operators. TraveLodge has signed up owners of existing motels. In some cases the newly franchised outlets were already affiliated with another chain; the motel owners, dissatisfied with their parent company, jumped to TraveLodge.

Unaffiliated hotels can quickly obtain a sophisticated image by buying a Playboy Club franchise. This magical license enables the operator to turn an ordinary restaurant and lounge space into a glittering fantasy world of computer-controlled neon lights and buxom waitresses wearing the famous bunny outfits. Visitors entering the club pass through the bunny boutique, where smiling young women in bunny suits sell Playboy membership keys as well as gift items with the company's logo. All clubs feature the Playboy Cabaret, with dining, dancing, and entertainment. Playmate bars offer seating for more than two hundred people. Couples waiting for tables can relax in Playpens, cushioned areas with soft seats.

The transition from staid hotel to swinging franchised outlet begins when the parent company assists with the waitress selection, or "bunny hunt." Hotels opening clubs lavish attention on the talent search, since it normally brings considerable publicity in local media. Before the Executive Hotel of Buffalo, New York, opened its club in 1981, the new franchisee interviewed 1500 women to choose sixty bunnies. The effort proved worthwhile. After the club opened the hotel's lunch business tripled, while dinner customers doubled. In its first eight weeks of promoting the concept, the hotel sold two thousand Playboy membership keys at twenty-five dollars each.

Franchisees must help fund the chain's national advertising program. In order to fill advertising war chests, chains have developed elaborate payment systems. In the typical franchise system the parent company and local operators all contribute a percentage of their gross to a national advertising fund. Operators pay an additional percentage to regional co-ops that purchase advertising in local media. Though advertising costs may impose a heavy burden, many franchisees expect their companies to maintain expensive media campaigns, and to recruit franchisees, companies must be able to point to a strong advertising campaign. New chains often claim they expect to have national ads in a few years.

Dunkin' Donuts franchisees contribute 4 percent of sales to purchase advertising. In 1978 80 percent of the franchisees voted to earmark an additional 2 percent of sales to begin a national television campaign, which ran for eighteen months. By 1981 the company's annual advertising fund had reached $10 million. While some operators complained about the extra expense, the wisdom of the program soon became clear. When the national television advertising began, sales at Dunkin' Donuts outlets in the New York area jumped 8 percent and stayed at the higher level for months. The advertising proved particularly effective since donuts are an impulse item. People may drive past an outlet day after day without stopping. Then after TV plants the donut idea in viewers' minds, more drivers find themselves stopping to bring a dozen home.

Before implementing a systemwide advertising campaign the parent companies usually try to sell franchisees on the merits of the program. Corporate executives introduce new approaches with elaborate presentations. It is important to win the confidence of franchisees, since they must pay for the campaign and ultimately sell the product. Holiday Inns franchisees expressed concern when the company announced plans to advertise money-back guarantees in 1982. Before the network ads appeared the company allayed operators' fears by disclosing tests that showed that only a tiny percentage of customers actually received refunds. Executives explained that under the carefully worded guarantee, franchisees could attempt to solve the problem before a customer got a free room.

While promotional efforts can build sales, chains sometimes become caught in situations where a strong brand name becomes a handicap. Holiday Inns, like many chain hotels, gained a reputation for providing clean beds and mediocre food. Franchisees who spent heavily on food and ran good restaurants were probably punished by membership in the chain. During the economic downturns of the early 1980s the chain sought to increase restaurant sales, attracting more guests as well as nearby residents. To overcome the poor image Holiday Inns decided to give their restaurants names and distinct identities, making them appear to be separate from the motel. A Holiday Inn in Roanoke, Virginia, now features Belle's. Designed to operate in only several units, the restaurant is decorated with wicker furniture and the white wooden paneling of a traditional Southern plantation mansion.

Holiday Inns' strong middle-of-the-road image also created problems for franchisees seeking to develop luxury units. A franchisee opening a resort in the Virgin Islands feared guests would refuse to pay $180 a night for a room in something called Holiday Inn St. Thomas. The resourceful operator invented the elegant-sounding name "Frenchman's Reef" and called the unit "Frenchman's Reef, a Holiday Inn Beach resort." The company objected but could not forbid the change, since the franchise contract had not anticipated the possibility that someone would seek to dilute the Holiday Inn brand. The franchisee was willing to pay royalties for the use of the Holiday Inn reservations system but did not want to be saddled with the chain's image.

Other moderately priced chains have also altered names to create luxury units. To reach the "upper-mid-priced" market Ramada developed units it calls Ramada Renaissance Hotels. The new hotels have more rooms, better decor, and price tags about 25 percent higher than typical units in the chain. Located in large metropolitan areas where their presence can help upgrade the chain's entire image, the Renaissance outlets feature health spas and what Ramada calls gourmet dining.

If a chain's image declines too badly the only solution may be a complete overhaul. In the early 1970s Howard Johnson's, with its internationally known orange roofs, began to lose its luster. Growing competition and poor maintenance in some older units caused decreases in restaurant sales. Rather than closing marginal outlets, Howard Johnson's converted them to Ground Rounds, restaurants focusing on hamburgers and featuring turn-of-the-century decor. The Ground Rounds were designed to win back local customers who had deserted the chain. By 1984 the company operated 225 Ground Rounds, most of them thriving.

Perhaps the most potent chain image-builder ever was Colonel Sanders. At his death Sanders was one of the most famous people in the country. Wherever the Colonel went people stared at the man who seemed to have stepped out of a storybook. In 1964 Sanders, then seventy-four, sold his chain of six hundred outlets to John Y. Brown, a young lawyer, and Jack Massey, a millionaire businessman. For $2 million the new owners acquired the company and the right to use the Colonel's image. They signed on the fried-chicken magnate to serve in a salaried position as a public relations man. Brown, who later became governor of Kentucky, realized that while Sanders had been pushing chicken, the real product to be sold was the Colonel himself.

In Sanders, Brown saw a trademark as memorable as Aunt Jemima or Betty Crocker. But the Colonel had the advantage of being alive and a born talker. He seemed a solid, trustworthy figure. Testifying at a Senate committee hearing on franchising in 1970, Brown explained the Colonel's native appeal: "He sells the Southern flavor and the Southern sizzle of the Southern product," Brown observed.

Brown hired a New York public relations man to make the Colonel famous. Sanders soon made his first national television appearance in 1964 on *What's My Line?*, where the panel failed to guess his occupation. Accompanied by four armed guards, the Colonel visited Johnny Carson's *Tonight Show*, where he displayed a huge fishbowl holding $2 million in cash, representing the price of his chain. The Colonel traveled a quarter-million miles a year, visiting fairs and charity events, and appearing on television shows. Even when he went out in bad weather he refused to wear a coat over his famous white outfit. Sanders delighted crowds in Tokyo and boosted the morale of his own company. "He was an electric presence," explained a franchisee whom the Colonel regularly visited to encourage the employees and present awards to good workers.

Lacking a symbol as potent as the Colonel, the hamburger chains have resorted to more conventional marketing campaigns. Over the last decade the three leading hamburger companies—Wendy's, McDonald's, and Burger King—have waged television battles trying to distinguish their products. The results of the various campaigns have been predictable. The independents and regional chains get clobbered as the giants each year gain a bigger market share. By 1983 the three leaders controlled 60 percent of all fast-food hamburger sales in the country.

Besides selling sandwiches, the advertisements have become newsmakers in their own right. Perhaps the most famous effort has been the Wendy's campaign that introduced the inquiry "Where's the beef?" to the English language. Clara Peller, the elderly actress who asked the question, became a minor celebrity. Playing a disgruntled customer at a competitor of Wendy's, Peller was unimpressed with the big bun that overwhelmed a patty, and asked querulously, "Where's the beef?" The slogan appeared on buttons and T-shirts. Walter Mondale used the ads to considerable effect in the 1984 Democratic primaries, charging that Gary Hart's political ideas offered voters no "beef." For Wendy's the ads seemed to produce an immediate payoff. The company's sales rose 19 percent in February 1984, one month after the campaign began.

Despite the successful campaign there is little chance that

Wendy's will become the leading hamburger chain soon. The title is firmly held by McDonald's. Ray Kroc's finely tuned creation sells 19 percent of all fast food. It is the largest, richest food-service company in the world. In 1982 the McDonald's system registered sales of $7.8 billion. In that recession year the number of its outlets expanded from 6739 to 7259. Burger King achieved sales of $2.6 billion from 3400 units, while Wendy's total was $1.6 billion at 2400 stores. McDonald's spent $368 million on advertising, a figure that exceeded the sales of all but a handful of franchise companies. Burger King, the second heaviest advertiser, spent $125 million. It is no accident that when infants barely able to speak toddle into a McDonald's, they immediately gurgle the name "Ronald McDonald" and hum the chain's current theme song.

McDonald's is able to spend so much money partly because of the company's unique franchise contract. In the early days of the chain, Ray Kroc made a crucial gamble. He decided that McDonald's would own its restaurants and lease them to franchisees. While other companies relied on local operators to pay for construction of outlets, Kroc's fledgling parent operation assumed the financial burden itself. The strategy slowed McDonald's initial growth, but it has paid enormous dividends since then. Other franchise chains only skim off royalties of 3 or 4 percent from the sales of franchisees; McDonald's takes a whopping 11.5 percent, since part of the fee covers rent. Kroc's company might sell hamburgers, but an important source of profits for the parent is real estate. Franchisees also make additional payments for local and national ads. As the chain has expanded, huge amounts of money have flowed into the parent company's coffers, enabling it to sponsor so much television advertising that children begin to believe McDonald's is synonymous with the hamburger.

McDonald's faces the problem of what to do with all the money the system produces. "It becomes hard when you have that much money generated by a formula," an advertising executive for a competing company said. "How do you get rid of it? You have to spend it. But you can only put on so many ads without irritating people." Competitors, properly awed by the McDonald's campaigns, concede they face an uphill battle against the number-one chain. "We believe we can build our average store volumes over the next three or four years to be as large as McDonald's," Burger King executive vice president Kyle Craig told *Restaurants and Institutions.* "Do we expect to develop enough units to overtake them in total sales in anywhere near that time? No, we don't."

The McDonald's ads have aimed to present the All-American image Ray Kroc originally conceived for the company. In 1967 the chain plunged into national advertising with a $5 million budget, an enormous expenditure at the time. The figure increased to $15 million two years later and then $60 million in 1974. Early spots showed freckle-faced children in suburban settings. In 1970 the company began a series of consistently powerful campaigns that helped to shape the nation's eating habits. "You Deserve a Break Today" was a theme song that became imprinted on the memories of millions. A later commercial personalized the chain's service, claiming, "You, you're the one . . . we do it all for you." The television campaigns shifted attention away from the food to the experience.

Whatever techniques are used, McDonald's promotional campaigns sweep over the marketplace like tidal waves, altering whole industries. The hot dog, once a national symbol, was annihilated as children were educated in the virtues of hamburgers. Egg farmers, who suffered declining sales because of health concerns, received a big boost from the Egg McMuffin, a product that benefited from an expensive ad campaign.

Some of McDonald's most effective advertising is done at the local or regional levels. In areas with concentrations of stores, local groups conduct strong promotional campaigns. In 1981 McDonald's Kentuckiana Advertising Cooperative gave away a house worth $100,000. The co-op, consisting of thirty-five units in Louisville and neighboring Indiana, received 3.5 million entries before a seventeen-year-old high school student won the prize. All told the stores spent $300,000 on prizes and advertisements for the contest. Even though no purchase was required to enter, sales in the stores were up 3 percent over the previous year, and the franchisees believe the contest is largely responsible. The entries were mixed in the bin of a concrete truck mixer and poured into a Plexiglas box; Ronald McDonald selected the winner.

The promotional campaigns are supplemented by public relations efforts aimed at making McDonald's seem like a wholesome member of the community. Many companies do good deeds to improve their image; few use charity dollars as effectively as McDonald's. Franchisees serve as soldiers in the chain's public relations army. When a flood or fire strikes, franchisees rush to the scene, passing out free hamburgers just when media from all over the country can easily note the generous contribution. Franchisees cooperate with the Salvation Army to feed needy people a McDonald's meal. One Wisconsin outlet presented free hamburgers to students who had A's on their report cards. Because the company lavishes so much money on what are often shrewd ideas, public relations ploys take on the appearance of being national institutions. McDonald's All-American Basketball Team recognizes top players. The company's All-American Band brings two high school musicians from each state to play at the Macy's Thanksgiving Day parade and at the Rose Bowl parade.

The chain's most heartrending projects—as television viewers well know—are the Ronald McDonald houses. Supported by franchisees the facilities house families while their children are being treated at nearby hospitals. Exploiting the condition of desperately sick children, McDonald's advertises the houses to project a tender-hearted image. At a time when the corporation has been attacked by consumer groups and environmentalists, the Ronald McDonald houses have proved a cheap way to win bountiful good publicity. The houses make natural subjects for the soap-opera features local television news directors love. Newspaper reporters have eagerly carried the public relations ball for the company. In 1981 the *Philadelphia Bulletin* ran a typical article that began, "There isn't much you can say or do to cheer a family when cancer strikes one of its children."

Adults are moved by these reports, while children learn early that the hamburger company is their friend.

The effort to polish McDonald's image began in 1957, when Kroc hired a small public relations firm named Cooper and Golin for five hundred dollars a month. Though the expense seemed excessive to some of the young chain's executives, it soon became clear that the firm would more than earn its keep. A campaign the first year sought to identify McDonald's with Christmas. Observing one company project, the *Chicago Sun-Times* wrote that "Ray (McDonald's Drive-Ins) Kroc" served coffee and hamburgers to Salvation Army kettle workers. The public relations firm circulated a story about a child who was asked where Santa met Mrs. Santa. At McDonald's, the child replied. The story was carried by wire services and featured prominently in small-town newspapers. In 1963, Ronald McDonald was introduced as spokesman for the chain. Several years later the public relations firm discovered that 96 percent of American children could identify Ronald, making the clown the second-best-known figure among youngsters after Santa Claus. This statistic, produced by a "Ronald McDonald Awareness study," was treated by the news media as if it were scientific fact; *Time* magazine dutifully reported it in an article about the company.

In 1966, when McDonald's shares were listed on the New York Stock Exchange, company representatives ate hamburgers on the floor of the stock exchange, a meal mentioned in numerous press accounts. Perhaps the company's most famous attention-grabbing device has been the famous signs listing how many billion hamburgers have been sold. In 1966 the figure was 2 billion. By 1984 the total had climbed to 45 billion.

Early on, Ray Kroc realized that the McDonald's name was becoming a valuable possession. It conjured up images of the old farmer in the song, something that would appeal to children. Since then the company has guarded its name carefully, stamping out the smallest stand that might try to use the trademark. When pirated McDonald's outlets were reported in Quito, Ecuador, the chain quickly investigated. The company is equally vigilant about its product names. Trademarked names such as Big Mac, Egg McMuffin, and Filet-O-Fish are carefully protected. Franchisees are taught to be on the alert for offenders. When United Airlines jokingly used "Big Mac" in a promotion, the McDonald's legal staff leaped into action.

The chain fears it could lose exclusive rights to its brands, as has happened to the unprotected names of cellophane, escalator, and aspirin. McDonald's has maintained firm control of all its trademarks, despite challenges to the use of "Quarter-Pounder." The greatest danger may come if McDonald's is *too* successful promoting its brands, making the names truly synonymous with the products. Xerox and 3M's Scotch Tape, facing the problem, have fought to prevent cancellations of their trademarks, which have moved into the language as generic terms.

Franchise companies with lesser-known names, hoping to establish their identities, have emulated McDonald's techniques. Bonanza International steak houses came up with ingenious outdoor advertising, proclaiming, "You deserve a steak today." Burger King, though unable to match McDonald's expenditures, has managed to support memorable advertising counterattacks against the leading chain. When McDonald's introduced its Quarter-Pounder, the second-place hamburger chain emphasized the size of its own large sandwich with ads noting, "It takes two hands to handle a Whopper."

To distinguish itself from the fast-food leader, which is known for uniformity, Burger King developed its "Have it your way" campaign. Introduced in 1973, the Burger King campaign attempted to take advantage of the company's own weakness. Burger King has always lacked the efficiency of McDonald's. According to surveys, customers were impatient with the smaller chain and felt McDonald's offered faster service. "Have it your way" provided a convenient explanation for why people had to wait.

Despite the "Have it your way" theme, Burger King was frustrated in its efforts to overtake McDonald's. In 1976 Burger King joined the battle for the loyalty of children. The company introduced the Magic Burger King, a cheery ruler who has red hair and royal clothing. He appeared on television and at stores, announcing games and prizes. The advertising budget was increased sharply, with a quarter of the funds earmarked for the children's campaign. Franchisees pitched in 4 percent of their sales volume to support the effort, and for a time the company narrowed McDonald's lead.

By the early 1960s advertisers had learned that children could be lucrative targets. Mattel, the toy company, spent heavily promoting the Barbie doll, and the investment paid handsome dividends. Children could be taught to lobby strenuously for products they had seen on TV. Just as effectively they could silently boycott unfamiliar names. In one study Helizter Advertising discovered that "parents will pay 20 percent more for an advertised product with child appeal—even when a less expensive, nonadvertised product is no different."

Since they did not understand that commercials were trying to sell them something, youngsters would become obedient servants of the ads. "To children, normally impulsive, advertisements for appealing things demand immediate gratification," said Richard Feinbloom of the Harvard Medical School, in a statement presented during hearings on advertising held by the House Committee on Interstate and Foreign Commerce in 1975. "The child lacks the ability to set priorities, to determine relative importance, and to reject some directives as inappropriate."

While children could be easily persuaded, their loyalties were often short-lived. In an article in the *Journal of Advertising Research*, William Wells points out, "Some commercials make children want the specific object advertised, while others evoke a more generalized need which can be satisfied in a variety of ways. At one end of this scale are commercials for toys, movies, and TV shows, which almost invariably make children want the specific toy or the specific entertainment. . . . At the other end of the scale are commercials for ice cream and peanut butter, which do little to create preference for the advertised brand."

Industry executives agree that McDonald's flood of advertising won over children for the entire fast-food industry. With its TV ads the company introduced fast food to a generation of consumers. Customers lined up at regional chains because they had seen McDonald's on TV and learned about the attraction of fast food. For the largest chain this produced a certain inefficiency. McDonald's was spending money to sell other people's hamburgers. The problem is a common issue in advertising. Companies must work particularly hard to teach youngsters brand loyalty. McDonald's began making special efforts to reach children.

Advertisements—like the small hamburger patties—were designed to please young consumers. Ronald McDonald, the red-haired clown, became the company's special ambassador to youngsters, a symbol that would draw people to McDonald's and not other chains. A benevolent, fun-loving figure, Ronald is a perennial star during Saturday-morning children's programming periods. To reinforce the brief televised appearances, fifty Ronalds visit restaurants around the country, skating, performing magic tricks, appearing at children's birthday parties, and always eating hamburgers. A trainer overseeing the clowns makes sure they maintain a standard image. "Ronald McDonald has been a damned Pied Piper," a Burger King executive groused to *Restaurants and Institutions* magazine. "He's brought millions of kids into McDonald's."

In the early 1970s parent groups began to express concern that TV ads such as the Ronald McDonald spots were manipulating children and placing unfair burdens on families. Peggy Charren of Action for Children's Television argued that the effect was greatest on the poor. "The dilemma of the low-income parent is particularly cruel, because he must divert his limited resources to buy an undesired product, or risk being considered less generous or less successful than other children's parents. To him, the middle-class compromise of 'giving in' on expensive items is unavailable. The result is likely to be feelings of deprivation and inferiority."

In recent years the Federal Trade Commission and other regulators have issued guidelines that have weakened some of the power advertisers have over children. It is no longer permitted for advertisers to urge children to "be the first kid on your block," a phrase that plays on their need for prestige. Hosts of children's shows—powerful authority figures for young viewers—are no longer permitted to push products. Advertisers have easily skirted these barriers. Ronald McDonald is a more powerful authority figure than any real TV adult ever has been. Mothers who take children to supermarkets or fast-food rows must still endure the pleadings of young consumers.

In 1982, facing a powerful Ronald McDonald, Burger King came out swinging hard. The chain introduced ads that claimed consumers preferred its hamburgers over McDonald's and Wendy's. The campaign proved highly effective, generating publicity and probably increasing sales. In its annual summary of top television spots, *Advertising Age*, a leading trade publication, summed up the hamburger bout. "If one advertising campaign captured the attention of the public—and the media—in 1982, it was the noisy Burger King comparative campaign. The 'battle of the burgers' turned into a month-long sparring match between the Miami-based chain, category leader McDonald's, and number-three Wendy's International."

Burger King had been running a campaign around the theme of "Aren't you hungry?" The chain's advertising agency, J. Walter Thompson, designed the comparative spots as a "mini-campaign" to run for six to eight weeks within the larger program. Franchisees welcomed stronger advertising. They believed that their product was better than McDonald's and that the ads should make that clear. Pepsi-Cola had run a successful campaign comparing its product to Coke. The franchisees believed Burger King could achieve similar results. Burger King raised its advertising expenditures for the last quarter of 1982 by 25 percent over the year before, investing $18 million on the battle-of-the-burgers ads.

In September the campaign began with a spot featuring a Burger King employee offering condolences to the other chains. "Y'see the Whopper beat the Big Mac for best taste overall among consumers of both burgers," she said. "In a similar test we beat Wendy's single. Now that may have surprised McDonald's and Wendy's, so we just wanted to say it's okay, guys. Winning isn't everything. But it sure is fun." The ad asserted that the "broiled" Burger King product was preferred over the "fried" McDonald's burger by three to one.

Newspapers and television news picked up on the battle of the burgers, providing fast food with free publicity. The competition was treated humorously. The two "losing" chains were not amused. McDonald's sued to block the campaign, charging the ads were "false and misleading." Wendy's asked for $25 million in damages in another suit and confidently challenged the other two chains to a taste test run by an independent testing service. The two chains pointedly ignored Wendy's offer, and the stinging Burger King spots continued running throughout October.

On November 1 *Advertising Age* reported the companies reached an out-of-court settlement, in which Burger King agreed to phase out the ads. It was not clear why the chain had compromised. The campaign seemed effective, and franchisees were enthusiastic. The three hamburger companies refused to talk about their secret agreement. In the advertising industry the campaign was widely admired. At first there had been speculation the campaign could backfire. Viewers might resent seeing McDonald's attacked. Burger King's advertising agency had been careful to use a light touch, Burton J. Manning, chairman of J. Walter Thompson, explained to *Madison Avenue* magazine. "If you have the wrong tonality people won't believe you," Manning said. "The style, tonality, and executional nuances are critically important to the success of this campaign. After all, McDonald's is an American institution. You don't play fast and loose with that. You've got to really handle your comparison in a way that Americans get a kick out of."

As the agency hoped, consumers were enjoying—and remembering—the ads. *Advertising Age* conducts polls it calls Ad-Watch, randomly phoning 1250 adults and asking, "Of all the advertising for fast-food products you've seen, read, or heard in the past month, which comes first to mind?" While hardly a precise measure, the poll does provide a rough gauge that is closely watched by advertising officials. In August 1982, 39.9 percent of those polled said the first fast-food advertising that came to mind was McDonald's. This was down from 49.2 percent in June but far ahead of Burger King's August score of 7.4 percent. By late November, after the comparison campaign had been running, Burger King's awareness score soared to 24.1 percent. McDonald's, while still leading, had dipped to 35.6 percent. In a poll of all products, not just fast food, Burger King climbed to number three behind Coca-Cola and Miller beer. It was the chain's first appearance in the Top Ten. McDonald's, which had been number three in the rating, dropped to six.

In the rating category that matters ultimately—sales figures—Burger King showed healthy results. In September the chain's sales were running 7 percent ahead of the previous year. With the campaign in full swing, sales jumped 13 percent in October, then 7 percent in November, 12 percent in December, and 17 percent in January. In September 1983 the parent company of Burger King, Pillsbury, predicted that its earnings would rise 35 percent for the first quarter of 1984 largely because of the hamburger company's strong showing.

The fall treaty between the companies ending the comparative ads proved short-lived. In February 1984 Burger King introduced new spots noting that customers preferred flame-broiled burgers to the fried version. McDonald's countered by spending heavily on its "McDonald's and You" ads, with which they inundated the airwaves.

In May 1983, when most of the burger-battle smoke had cleared, I interviewed James Patterson, a senior vice president at J. Walter Thompson who had worked on the Burger King campaign. A novelist, whose most recent work, *Virgin*, was a big seller, Patterson explained why the comparative advertising was effective. "People who prefer Burger King were automatically going to McDonald's. In our surveys you would hear people saying over and over again, 'I think Burger King has a better hamburger.' So you ask them, 'Where do you go?' And they would say, 'Well, I go to McDonald's.' What we were trying to do with the ads was make customers think about what they really wanted. They didn't think. They just acted automatically. What we were trying to do was bring to the top of their minds that preference that they already had."

Patterson's survey did not produce much of a surprise in the fast-food industry. McDonald's "quality problem" is much discussed among chain executives. In my own informal surveys more people had negative feelings about McDonald's than the other chains, and a study by *Restaurants and Institutions* confirmed this. The magazine polled fast-food customers, asking people whether they liked a particular chain "a great deal" or "somewhat." They could also say they "don't like it." Wendy's led the race, with 40 percent of its customers saying they liked the chain a great deal. Burger King was second at 35 percent and McDonald's trailed with 34 percent. More than 15 percent of McDonald's customers said they didn't like the chain. Only 10 percent didn't like Burger King. Most people fell in the lukewarm category. These figures raise some peculiar questions. What are millions of people doing buying something they don't like? Why are they going to McDonald's if they prefer Burger King? The answer is that people make their purchases based on advertising, packaging, and vague factors such as the "ambiance" of the outlet. Having watched hundreds of McDonald's ads day after day they "automatically" go to the leading chain.

While Burger King's ads probably helped to increase its sales, the comparative campaign may prove to be a subversive exercise that hurts the fast-food industry. The ads, in effect, said to consumers, "You have been fooled. McDonald's has tricked you into buying a product you don't like. You are buying a product because of its brand name. But you cannot trust brand names." If consumers take the ads seriously and begin questioning the reliability of brand names as guides to purchase, Burger King and all franchise chains will be in trouble. McDonald's vice-chairman, Edward Schmitt, indirectly acknowledged this in an interview with *Restaurants and Institutions,* in which he discussed the impact of the Burger King campaign. "Business today involves a very sensitive relationship between the consumer and the industry," he said. "Anything that shakes consumers' confidence in the industry undermines that relationship. To me, that's the bad thing that Burger King has done."

7

New and Improved: Franchised Research and Development

Louis Groen, the McDonald's franchisee in Cincinnati, had begun to grow desperate. In the early 1960s he was challenging the Big Boy chain that dominated his area, and it appeared he was losing. Groen could struggle along during most of the week but on Fridays his sales vanished. In heavily Catholic Cincinnati customers turned faithfully to the Big Boys on Fridays because they served fish sandwiches. To the franchisee the choice was clear: He would have to add fish or close the store. When Groen approached Ray Kroc with the idea, the chairman of the young hamburger chain was mortified. McDonald's was dedicated to selling only one product. "I don't care if the Pope himself comes to Cincinnati," he told the franchisee. "He can eat hamburgers like everybody else."

The franchisee presented his case to other executives of the company, who proved more sympathetic. They prevailed on the stubborn chairman to try fish. After Kroc reluctantly approved the experiment, the company began what would be a two-year process to develop the product. The first step was to choose the right kind of fish. Food technicians experimented with cod and halibut; cod emerged the winner. This displeased Kroc, who felt the name carried childhood associations with cod liver oil. After an executive discovered it was legal to call the species North Atlantic whitefish, the chairman was mollified. A considerable number of tests followed to determine how to bread the fish and make the tartar sauce. At the suggestion of a young crew member in Cincinnati Kroc topped the fish with a half-slice of cheese and was delighted with the results. Having resolved the production problems, McDonald's began selling its new Filet-O-Fish on Fridays in selected areas. By 1965 so many franchisees requested the sandwich that the company made it a permanent menu item in stores around the country.

Encouraged by the success of fish, Kroc decided to try other additions. Confident of his ability to discern what the public wanted, McDonald's chairman felt certain he had a winning product in the Hulaburger. The sandwich consisted of two slices of cheese with a slice of grilled pineapple on a toasted bun. Kroc believed it would be even more popular than Filet-O-Fish. Customers, however, carefully avoided the new product. "I like the hula but where is the burger?" one consumer wondered.

Fast-food chains quickly learned that predicting the American public's taste was a chancy business. And as the fast-food market grew more crowded, it proved helpful to tinker with the menu. The chains found they could not maintain the same limited selections indefinitely. Patrons who visited fast-food outlets several times a week grew tired of eating the same hamburgers day after day. Loyal McDonald's customers would occasionally abandon their favorite chain for a meal of chicken or pizza. To keep the troops from deserting, the chains began to spice up their offerings periodically. Like soap manufacturers advertising "new and improved" products, fast-food outlets constantly added new pizzazz to their menu boards.

The idea of slightly altering a line of products is a time-tested marketing device. In the 1950s automobile companies elevated the practice to a subtle art, bringing out new cars annually that looked distinct from the previous year's batch. A change of tailfins or an addition of chrome would make the new line seem more exciting, the year-old models seem shabby. The car companies spent millions redesigning and advertising, even though their basic vehicle remained unimproved. The cost of model changes was, of course, passed to the consumers. As much as 20 percent of the price of a car could be attributed to styling changes.

Like the car companies, Holiday Inns found itself financing expensive styling changes. The chain's original success came from offering a jazzier model; older, independent motels seemed out-of-date compared to the shiny new franchised units. However, other companies quickly learned the motel styling game. If Holiday Inns offered bigger motels, Ramada would offer bigger motels, and so would most independent operators. Customers who had been conditioned to want what was bigger and shinier could choose among the rivals.

Holiday Inns has therefore constantly come up with new features its franchisees must introduce. Older motels with small front desks and restaurants were required to build large reception areas and bigger coffee shops. Units were told to add a canopy that would shelter drivers as they left their cars to register. In 1980 Holiday Inns franchisees spent about $300 million making such improvements, and all this cost was passed on to customers. Individual improvements that may be of little value carry large price tags. In 1981 a franchisee in Alexandria, Virginia, was forced to install a new temperature-control system, allowing each guest to decide whether to have hot or cold air. The unit had previously been providing all rooms with heat in the winter and air conditioning in the summer from a central control. With the improvement, guests could select air conditioning in the winter. The change cost the franchisee about $175,000.

Franchisees are given a number of years to add the latest features. Since all hotels built the same year must meet the same standards, Holiday Inns veterans can look at an unrenovated unit and tell whether it is a vintage 1965 model or a 1967. The company believes that all this remodeling is important to maintain profits. Customers will not go to a motel that looks outdated, even if it is clean and comfortable.

To spruce up their "models," fast-food chains have resorted to a range of superficial changes. In the recession of the middle 1970s Kentucky Fried Chicken suffered from weak sales. Management naively responded by lowering prices; naturally the tactic failed. Had the chain consulted with any 1950s automobile marketing executive it would have picked up an important principle: The fastest way to destroy a weak name-brand product is to cut its price. The goal of marketing, after all, is to make a product seem more valuable, not cheaper. In 1977, recognizing its error, Kentucky Fried Chicken made a move that *Restaurants and Institutions* magazine called "gutsy." The chain had been charging the same price for "Original Recipe" chicken as "Extra Crispy." To make the Original seem more desirable the company raised its price. "All the research told us that loyal users bought Original Recipe," Donald Doyle, vice president of marketing, told *Restaurants and Institutions*. "We decided to leverage this by setting up a two-tier pricing system under which we charge a little more for Original Recipe. The idea was to set up Original Recipe as the premier brand and then support this with all advertising and merchandising programs."

By 1980 the pricing ruse had proved effective. The marketing executive seemed slightly amazed at the suggestibility of customers. "The damn thing worked," a relieved Doyle told the magazine. "Sales of Original Recipe climbed dramatically, and because of the premium pricing, the margins were better."

Some of Kentucky Fried Chicken's most successful marketing campaigns have centered on the Colonel's secret recipe. The company has boasted that the recipe is a magical formula known only to a few insiders. The recipe is locked away in a safe in Louisville, company publicity releases observe. Security precautions protecting the "multi-million-dollar recipe" would make "even James Bond proud."

Ordinary customers reading such claims might wonder why

rival chicken chains don't hire chemists to buy some of the Colonel's chicken and determine what the eleven herbs and spices are. In fact, corporate scientists who use elaborate procedures to duplicate the Kentucky Fried Chicken formula might be disappointed. William Poundstone, in his book *Big Secrets*, reveals to all that the mysterious recipe consists mainly of salt, pepper, and monosodium glutamate.

Special formulas and innovations developed by chains are often attributed by the companies to "Research and Development" departments. The term "research" conjures up images of Thomas Alva Edison inventing the light bulb or teams of scientists building moon rockets. Chains like to give franchisees the impression that corporate facilities staffed by white-coated Ph.D.s are pushing back the frontiers of science. In fact, the programs have modest goals. Chemists for CutCo Industries strive to produce refined hair preparations. A Blimpie vice president who oversees research recently reshaped the company's kitchen tables. Burger Chef proudly announced that research on its simple sandwiches was being overseen by an experienced chef who had presided over the kitchens of elegant hotels. Small companies with limited resources often confine their research operations to stealing ideas from the big chains.

Thanks to expanding research divisions, the hamburger has come to be probably the most heavily studied food in the world. Hamburgers, little known before 1930, are said to have been invented at the 1904 St. Louis World's Fair when an overworked cook slapped a patty on a bun. Over the years hundreds of people have come to examine this simple sandwich, trying to improve it. The researchers study such monumental questions as whether the patty should be broiled or grilled, whether the bun should have poppy seeds or caraway, whether lettuce should be shredded or leaf.

In 1961 Louis Martino, husband of Ray Kroc's secretary-treasurer, set up McDonald's first research and development laboratories. An electrical engineer, Martino gave up his career to buy a McDonald's franchise in 1959. Under Kroc's urging, Martino took charge of refining McDonald's production. Along with a group of equipment suppliers, Martino's lab produced a steady supply of gadgetry that would dazzle customers. The engineer brought forth a dispenser that squirted exactly the right amount of catsup and mustard onto the patties, an electronic computer to measure the moisture of fish while cooking, warning lights to tell countermen when to flip burgers, and devices to test the fluffiness of shakes. To determine if hamburger meat was 19 percent fat, as the company specified, the labs produced the Fatilyzer, a machine that allowed the franchisee to check his meat quickly and return inferior grades to the supplier.

The company's kitchen labs tested a steady stream of new food products. Early on, the company began a long search to find the right kind of dessert. Strawberry shortcake sold well for a time, then sales evaporated. Pound cake was rejected since it did not seem to have glamour. Hot apple pies finally fit the bill, increasing overall sales and enhancing the company's wholesome image. Other wildly successful products included the Big Mac, which was introduced in 1968, and the Quarter-Pounder, which came in 1972.

After developing a new item in its test kitchens, McDonald's tries the product on preference panels of seventy-five people. Despite such elaborate precautions, few menu additions win permanent places on the chain's menu. McDonald's has tested unsuccessfully cheeseburgers QLT (quality, lettuce, and tomato, as a slogan had it), roast beef sandwiches, Tripple Ripple ice cream cones, and fish and chips. Such tests may offer the public temporary bargains, since companies provide huge discounts to see if customers will accept the product and if the stores are capable of turning out the dish fast enough.

Perhaps the most profitable fast-food menu addition came with McDonald's Egg McMuffin. For the chain, breakfast seemed a way to squeeze more sales out of outlets that were sitting idle during morning hours. However, the company faced considerable obstacles in implementing its strategy. Customers would have to be taught that what had been fast-food hamburger outlets were now also good places for breakfast. Franchisees had to be persuaded that they would make money staying open longer hours. More crew members would have to be hired and trained to prepare the egg sandwiches.

McDonald's proved capable of handling the considerable task. By 1977 the chain had introduced a full breakfast menu, consisting of Egg McMuffins, eggs, pancakes, bacon, and sausage. In 1981 breakfast accounted for more than 15 percent of the company's sales, or about $1 billion. Preceded by four years of testing and backed by a mammoth advertising effort, McDonald's breakfast campaign converted new customers to fast food. People who had always eaten breakfast at home were stopping for Egg McMuffins on the way to work. For the public, the role of fast food had been expanded.

Other chains sought to take advantage of the new ground broken by McDonald's. Burger Chef and Wendy's tried entering the morning field. For Burger King, adding breakfast was necessary in order to prevent McDonald's from widening its sales lead. But the second-place hamburger chain faced a problem. McDonald's could fry eggs on the grills it used to cook hamburgers. Burger King did not have grills; it cooked burgers in broilers. To solve the equipment problem, Burger King found it could place a flat pan above the french friers. Heat from the grease that is used to cook fries could be used to scramble eggs. The breakfast delay has been costly for Burger King. Hardee's, a hamburger chain that uses a broiler, solved the breakfast problem by adding a special grill on wheels. Used only during the breakfast serving period, the grill is moved aside after ten-thirty a.m., when the restaurant switches to its regular menu. The breakfast equipment costs franchisees $10,000, an expense they now feel is worthwhile.

The trade press spawned by the restaurant and motel chains faithfully reported the great breakfast breakout. In 1981 *Restaurant Business* quoted Hardee's president as saying that new products were made possible because the chain was now spending $1 million on research, compared to $40,000 spent in 1973. *Fast Service* reported that companies were "creatively repackaging" breakfast items. "McDonald's combined eggs, cheese, and Canadian bacon with an English muffin. Now Burger Chef puts its eggs and bacon on a bun, calling it a Sunrise sandwich. Hardee's uses muffins with different breakfast items." *Restaurants and Institutions*, heralding the originality of Hardee's "successful new product," noted the chain's "breakfast program is based on sandwiches made with baking-soda biscuits baked fresh daily and filled with combinations of egg, sausage, ham, cheese, and jelly. Wrapped in foil, the product makes an excellent takeout item."

In the 1970s the flow of new fast-food products accelerated. Established companies, faced with hordes of imitators, added dishes to stay ahead of the competition. In addition, as more outlets opened, the public's preferences shifted whimsically. During the 1970s Americans consumed less beef and more fish and chicken. Pizza and Mexican food, products many adults had never tasted as children, became more popular. To increase sales, chains offered items that would have seemed incongruous a decade earlier. Burger King added a veal parmigiana listing, while Pizza Hut offered sandwiches. Arby's, the roast beef sandwich chain, added ham-and-cheese subs. Dairy Queen experimented with hard ice cream. Hardee's expanded its development efforts so that it was always trying out five or six new items. Chains constantly juggled prices, and weak-selling items quickly vanished from menu boards.

At Burger King and other hamburger chains, sales dropped sharply in the face of higher beef prices in the late 1970s. Wendy's was hit particularly hard by the rise in beef prices. To make itself less dependent on volatile beef the company introduced salad bars. Salads seemed a good bet to attract growing crowds of working women as well as the health-conscious, who were growing wary of red meat. By altering the limited hamburger menu Wendy's risked blurring its skillfully shaped image and slowing its service. Aware of the potential problems, the company carefully refined its new salad bars and introduced them slowly in prime suburban outlets. The gamble paid off. Salad bars became a main attraction at many of the restaurants.

As more products come on the market the distinctions between fast-food chains have become blurred. It is no longer possible to say a chain is purely a chicken or hamburger outfit. Industry observers worry that in their quest for greater variety companies may be losing efficiency. As new items are added, service tends to slow down. With the introduction of more expensive sandwiches, the price advantage that fast food had over coffee shops is disappearing. Indeed, some observers say, now that fast-food restaurants are serving breakfast and a wider range of sandwiches, they are beginning to seem like coffee shops. One manager even believes there is room in the market for a drive-in resembling the McDonald's of the 1950s. "It's inevitable," he sighed. "Someone will come out with a cheap one-item menu and they'll make a bundle."

While McDonald's and other giant chains have managed to publicize their new menus, smaller companies have become concerned that they may be confusing customers. By adding items, Burger Queen, a chain of one hundred sixty units, moved away from its original image. Now 70 percent of its revenues comes from such nonhamburger products as fried chicken, deep-fried fish, and breakfasts. To announce this development the company started an advertising campaign in 1980 that said, "Something big's cooking at Burger Queen. Don't let the name fool you."

Unfortunately customers continued holding illusions about the chain's menu, so the company switched its name to Druther's in 1981. "Our research told us that customers perceived more menu variety in some of our single-item competitors than in BQ," Mark Hughes, director of advertising, told *Restaurants and Institutions*. "And we know that every time we use the name Burger Queen, we're telling customers we sell burgers but not chicken, fish, breakfast, or complete meals."

Pizza Hut has struggled to develop a menu mix that will enhance its image. Starting in Kansas, the chain grew rapidly throughout the 1960s in the Midwest, an area of small Italian populations where few people had tried the product before. When the company invaded the East and West coasts in the middle 1970s it suffered severe setbacks. Customers used to the tangy pizza of local independents scoffed at the bland chain pie with its thin crust. To overcome this resistance the company offered "Thick 'n Chewy" pizza, a more substantial product at a higher price. Pizza Hut spent $400,000 testing its new pie over two years before introducing it systemwide. It also added sandwiches, salads, and pasta, hoping to attract more families and people who don't like pizza. Advertisements boosted the theme of "Hometown Pizza Hut," a campaign designed to argue that the chain pizza was made as carefully as local products.

Experimenting with new recipes, Pizza Hut soon discovered it would be difficult to produce one standardized formula that could satisfy the tastes of fussy consumers around the country. Customers in Boston favored Greek-style pies with white natural cheddar cheese, while people in Chicago were dedicated to deep-dish pizza. Tastes differed widely even within one region: In upstate New York Pizza Hut enjoyed success with its original Midwestern product, but on Long Island people wanted a spicier flavor; just one hundred miles away in Connecticut, customers demanded a totally different taste. The company bowed to these preferences, permitting local variations on standard recipes. Pizza Hut did manage to gain ground against the independents, though part of the reason may have been the company's clean-cut image. The chain outlets, with their wholesome atmosphere and limited alcohol sales, provide a safe place to take children.

One of the more radical product changes was executed by Church's Fried Chicken. In an unusual move for a fast-food chain the company offered larger portions. Trying to overtake Kentucky Fried Chicken, Church's deliberately selected slightly larger chickens and cut them into one less piece than did its giant rival. The portions were then priced about the same as the Colonel's. Although this made food costs higher, Church's management said it had achieved greater sales volume, which offset the extra cost. Indeed, the company grew quickly in the late 1970s, making it the second-largest chicken chain. The best indication that Church's may have found a strong formula is that

Kentucky Fried Chicken tried the large birds in some markets and, reportedly, its sales increased.

Many expensive product introductions fail badly. After considerable testing and great advertising fanfare, Kentucky Fried Chicken introduced "Country Style Ribs." The idea seemed well designed to enhance the chain's Southern image while drawing more customers. Unveiled in 1975, the breaded spare-ribs at first seemed to be little short of sensational. Stores in San Antonio, Texas, reported total sales increases of 50 percent the first six weeks they carried the new product. But as the novelty of the ribs wore off it became clear that, for reasons that are still unclear, customers were not coming back for seconds. And because of the huge purchases of pork by the giant chain, prices began to rise. When Kentucky Fried Chicken began buying ribs in 1974 they cost eighty cents a pound. Soon the chain's buying pushed up the price to a dollar and forty cents. The company had created a shortage of the product, forcing prices up and cutting its own profits. In 1976 the ribs were dropped.

Sometimes parent companies hire outside firms to conduct what appear to be objective studies. If the franchisor produces a survey indicating that all units should spend $10,000 to install breakfast equipment, franchisees may grumble. If an outside consultant signs the report, the idea will carry more weight. In June 1980 *Fast Service* reported that Burger King had hired Behavioral Science Research Corporation to determine why customers chose to patronize Burger King or McDonald's. Interviewing customers and analyzing their views cost more than $125,000 a year. The research firm, which is headed by Robert Ladner, who holds a Ph.D. in sociology, found that of the customers who chose Burger King, 35 percent selected the restaurant because they liked the chain most, 29 percent because it had the most convenient location, 12 percent because it had the best-tasting sandwiches, 12 percent because it had the fastest service, and 12 percent because it offered the best snacks. The results for McDonald's customers were very similar to the Burger King statistics. Ever the astute social scientist, Ladner conceded, "The findings would have been a lot more useful if they had looked further at what went into 'liking the product.' We tried to convince them that the analysis was only half-completed, but they were only interested in seeing how they stacked up against their competition."

Burger King constantly tinkers with its restaurant operations. The company points with pride to its increasing use of computers in designing restaurants. However, for all its research efforts, Burger King units remain very similar to the restaurants of all the major fast-food chains. The number-two hamburger chain began looking for new applications of computer technology in the late 1970s, a time when the company was being overwhelmed by changes it had made. During the five-year period ending in 1977, Burger King expanded its menu, began offering drive-through window service, and completely altered its cafeteria-style serving lines. This created serious problems for store managers, who were uncertain how to operate the restructured stores. "All of a sudden management was not familiar with the system," explained William Swart, Burger King's director of industrial engineering.

Managers could no longer be sure if their crews were working fast enough, since in a changing system it was not clear what "fast" was. How many workers should operate a drive-through window, managers wondered? In the changed environment past experience could provide little guidance. The fast-food machinery was clanking out of control. To find out how restaurants should be operating, the company studied forty stores in ten regions of the country. It found wildly varying performances. Some stores took twenty seconds to prepare a Whopper, while in others workers required a full minute. Using the data, the research staff developed what it felt were optimal standards for various restaurants, depending on size and volume. For example, a Whopper prepared in a small restaurant by one person should be done in thirty-two seconds.

The information was used to prepare a computer simulation of how a Burger King should operate. After the number of customers and items ordered were determined, the model could suggest ideal staffing and equipment. Franchisees could tell whether they were operating at peak efficiency. In 1980 Mike Simmonds took over a Burger King in Omaha that had poor sales. The location had strong potential since a nearby competitor was doing outstanding business. The problem seemed to stem from inefficient operations. The planning process began with the owner setting a goal of increasing sales during lunch from three hundred dollars a day to seven hundred. After analyzing the store's sales pattern, the Burger King staff recognized that customers were waiting in line too long. Consulting the computer model the staff suggested installing another cash register, increasing the crew from eight to fifteen members, and adding two new microwave ovens. The franchisee reported increased profits.

New products developed in Burger King's test kitchens are examined in computer simulations. The computers predict how many staff members will be needed to prepare the new items and what this will cost. If the dish is too expensive the research staff will send it back to the test kitchen for more refining. If the new product seems like it can be sold profitably, it will be sold in one of the company's five test restaurants in Miami. In the working test restaurants, which have sales of about $5 million a year, unsuspecting customers "benefit" from the latest developments coming from the company labs.

Burger King is constantly trying to speed up its procedures. Most of the chain's restaurants can increase their profits by serving food faster, executives say. During lunch hours most stores have a period when they are operating at peak capacity, selling as much as they can produce. If the units could make more hamburgers, they would sell them. "You are in effect turning away people," William Swart of Burger King noted. "Either they actually go away or they come less frequently because of the negative experience."

To speed service the company moved its drink stations to positions on the counters separating the cashiers from the cooking areas. In the past workers preparing food also poured the drinks; in the new system either the cooks or cashiers can pour the drinks, depending on who is busier. Suggestions to save seconds and pennies are developed by task forces of about a dozen people that are formed periodically. Consisting of franchisees and company officials, they come up with recommendations that are reviewed by the company's research staff. Those that prove feasible are adopted as requirements for the whole chain.

In the late 1970s Burger King formed a task force to study its drive-through windows. The windows, which enable a customer to pick up a meal without leaving his car, had recently been rediscovered. In the 1950s most fast-food outlets had drive-up service, and a few had drive-through windows. The windows had been abandoned by chains who considered the drive-through less impressive than restaurant seating. In the mid-1970s Wendy's returned to the windows and achieved strong sales. Burger King, McDonald's, and many lesser chains followed Wendy's lead.

Burger King hoped to speed its window service. In the system a bell in the store rang when a car drove over a hose located under the drive-through window. Hearing the bell, a worker would go to the window. The task force, after intense study, reached the monumental conclusion that it took the order taker eleven seconds to react to the bell and come to the window. To speed the procedure researchers decided to move the hose back ten feet so that by the time the car reached the window the worker would be ready.

Like Burger King, Holiday Inns uses computer-aided research in its effort to please customers. The company spends $1 million a year maintaining a staff of twenty-two to review all aspects of the business. The company knows the soap its guests prefer, how many hours of television they watch, and where they put their luggage. Such information has led to expensive redesigning of rooms. The original Holiday Inns room featured two double beds, an innovative concept designed to serve the standard suburban family of the 1950s. For two decades this approach went unchanged. In the 1970s, as Holiday Inns grew to the size of a large corporation, it began to review its operations systematically. The company set up a department of market research under a vice president who started carefully examining customer preferences in 1975.

It soon became clear that while the motel rooms had stayed the same, the guests had changed. Gone were the station wagons filled with children. People who once stayed in downtown hotels were coming to Holiday Inns. In most cases guests were solitary business people or couples without children. The second double bed was now mainly serving as a luggage rack. To satisfy this new breed of customer, the company developed a new standard room that features a king-sized bed. Instead of a second bed there is a work area, with easy chairs, small tables, and a desk. Customers, when asked how they felt about the altered rooms, voted nine to one in favor of the new design.

Other company surveys identified two hundred fifty different problems that guests experienced in hotels. Noise and dirt figured high on the list. A major complaint, surprisingly, was pillows. More than 15 percent of the subjects interviewed said they brought along their own pillows because they disliked the ones supplied by hotels. Based on these surveys the company began offering more amenities, such as pulsating showerheads, larger bars of soap, and clock radios.

Holiday Inns, like most chains, introduces new ideas gradually. After the concept has been refined it will be tested in a few select outlets. If the innovation seems profitable the number of units testing the idea will be increased until the entire system has been altered. Holiday Inns tests new ideas at its 240 company-owned units before urging them on the 1500 franchised outlets.

Most of the exploration work done by chains like Holiday Inns and Burger King can best be categorized as market research. The research and development departments focus on learning more about customers so that competing chains will not lure business away. With this approach it is unlikely that the corporate departments will produce any bold innovations that will fundamentally alter the service industries or achieve the productivity increases the nation needs. In recent years discussion of U.S. economic ills has focused on research and development. In 1964 R&D expenditures reached a peak of 3 percent of Gross National Product. The figure dipped steadily to 2.2 percent in 1977, and in 1982 it was back to 2.7 percent. (The Japanese spent 2 percent.) But as John Kenneth Galbraith has noted, most R&D money in the United States goes for defense, with much of the remainder spent by a few large companies in oil, chemicals, and in recent years, computers. There is virtually no research and development being done in such enormous areas of the economy as housing construction and the service industries. This helps to explain why productivity in these fields has shown little increase and why most businesses operate in much the way they did a generation ago.

It may be argued that there are simply no great innovations possible that could revolutionize the muffler replacement outlet or the chain motel. But there is no way to tell as long as businesses pour development money into marketing efforts and not the search for basic improvements. As Galbraith points out, it is easy to overlook a lack of advances in an industry. Inventions that are not made are not missed. A lack of imagination is not a new trait of the chains. In the restaurant industry most of the important developments were achieved by small operators like Howard Johnson, who came up with a better brand of ice cream and a new way to sell it. Corporate research has done little but add new wrinkles to the old concept.

Jane Jacobs, in *The Economy of Cities*, argues that most original concepts come from small businesses. New ideas are developed in haphazard, unpredictable ways, she argues. They must be tested in the marketplace and allowed to develop. Giant corporations do not have the patience to nurse along fledgling businesses. And new business ideas often conflict with the existing interests of a corporate bureaucracy. Old products lose sales to the new. An innovation creates problems for managers who must hire and supervise the people to implement it. New ideas are always risky. Consequently, large companies prefer to obtain new business ideas by buying smaller companies. Small business experiments and assumes risk; then if the product succeeds, a large company buys out the owner to market the product on a large scale. General Electric and other large companies, recognizing their own limited capacity to implement new business ideas, have set up venture capital funds for the corporations to invest in small companies and share in the new knowledge generated by risk-taking entrepreneurs.

As more small businesses are overwhelmed by franchise chains and entrepreneurs are forced to become franchisees, the amount of business experimentation is reduced. The franchisee cannot test any ideas—he simply implements what is handed down from corporate headquarters. If, like Colonel Sanders, a franchisee developed a markedly faster way to cook chicken, a large chain would certainly be slow to adopt it. Whole expensive kitchen procedures would have to be revised. Making even a minor alteration involves months of preparation by hundreds of people. While an independent operator may act on instinct, the large chain employs task forces analyzing reams of data. The new product must be refined, tested on consumers, and advertised. Hundreds of outlets may have to be re-equipped, franchisees must be called into district headquarters to be trained, suppliers must be found, and distribution must be streamlined to permit steady flow of the product.

Any change, however seemingly small, cannot be made lightly. The kind of bold transformations that would increase productivity are avoided. For the chains this cautious strategy has worked admirably. For while productivity has stagnated, profits have climbed. The key to this approach has been low wages.

8

Help Wanted

One morning in April 1981, a crowd of about twenty young people disrupted the careful routine of a Burger King in Detroit. Some wearing Burger King uniforms, others in street clothes, they congregated outside the office of the store manager, Peggy Amato, and began chanting, "Sign it, Peggy. Sign it." The demonstrators, employees of the store, were urging their boss to sign papers recognizing the Detroit Fastfood Workers as bargaining agent for the outlet. While the surprised manager watched the employees, an assistant manager hustled customers out the door and locked the restaurant. In a few minutes police arrived, who moved the demonstrators outside where they picketed. To the tune of the company's theme song they sang, "Make it special, a *union* at Burger King."

In recent years such demonstrations have not been uncommon sights in Detroit; labor organizers chose the heavily unionized, depressed auto capital as a likely area to recruit members. But despite support from some members of the United Auto

Workers, the new union has enjoyed little success. The fast-food workers apparently won an election in 1980 at a Burger King owned by Greyhound in the Detroit bus station. However, the company tied up certification procedures in a series of court challenges that were still not resolved two years later. In Detroit, as in the rest of the country, all franchised fast-food restaurants are still nonunion.

The Detroit workers include teenagers and students attending community colleges or four-year institutions. Like fast-food employees around the country they are paid the minimum wage of $3.35 an hour. While the companies spend little on paychecks, they have made substantial investments to prevent workers from rebelling against unsatisfying jobs. McDonald's trains franchisees to use the soft approach in labor relations, holding "rap sessions" in which workers discuss problems. The sessions give workers the feeling they are being heard and allow managers to pinpoint possible dissidents. If union organizers appear, the company showers employees with kindness. "The unions haven't been able to touch us with a ten-foot pole," McDonald's founder Ray Kroc is quoted in *Big Mac* by Max Boas and Steve Chain. "Hell, we got employees going to football games, basketball games, track events, hockey games. We have picnics for them."

When an organizing campaign heated up in Detroit the company invited workers to play "McBingo," a game where everyone won sums of five dollars to one hundred dollars. The week before the union election McDonald's brought in Earl Campbell, a star running back for the Houston Oilers, who signed autographs and encouraged workers while management officials spoke against the union. The National Football League Players Association criticized Campbell for appearing on behalf of the company and urged workers to vote for the union.

The fate of the Detroit fast-food workers is of considerable significance for the overall economy. These young people labor in one of the fastest-growing employment categories in the country. While jobs in automobile and steel plants were declining, work in fast food was growing rapidly. From 1970 to 1982 there was an increase of more than two million jobs in the Labor Department's category of eating and drinking places, with much of that growth in fast food. This *increase* was greater than the *total number of jobs* in the steel and automobile industries combined. The rise in fast-food jobs is part of the overall shift in the economy toward the service sector.

In the 1970s, while employment stagnated in Germany and grew slowly in Japan, the number of people employed in the United States increased steadily. Most of the new jobs were in service industries. As we saw earlier, the service sector began outpacing agriculture and production of goods before World War II. Beginning in the 1950s the difference in growth rates between sectors became especially pronounced. In 1948, 48.1 million people were employed in the United States, with 20.9 million in production of goods and 27.2 million in services. By 1982 total employment had nearly doubled to 89.6 million. Almost all the increase was in services, which accounted for 65.7 million jobs. Production jobs totaled 23.8 million.

Several factors contributed to the shift. Output of both goods and services was rising, but as productivity increased in the goods sector, the same number of workers could turn out more. A greater output could be achieved with the same number of workers. In order to increase output in services, payrolls had to be expanded. If a factory wanted to build more aluminum doors it would add more efficient machinery. The accounting firm providing support for the factory, instead of buying machines, would hire more clerks and messengers. Besides the productivity factor, certain areas of the service economy grew because of sharp increases in demand. The number of teachers climbed dramatically as baby-boom youngsters entered school and then stayed there longer than their parents had. Jobs in nursing homes, dental offices, and hospitals increased as insurance policies and government programs supported mounting health-care expenditures.

To a large extent the shift in the economy represented a revolution in the roles of women. Fifty-four percent of the new jobs went to women, and the service positions often consisted of what had traditionally been "women's work": nursing the sick and the elderly, cooking, teaching, working as secretaries or store clerks. The Department of Commerce reported that in 1950 33.9 percent of women were employed. In 1982 the figure was 52.7 percent. It was not entirely clear how much real additional economic activity was being accomplished by the move of women out of the home. If a woman cooked for her family she was not paid, and her output was not measured by the Bureau of Labor Statistics. If she cooked in a restaurant her output was said to enlarge the Gross National Product.

Some observers, such as John Naisbitt, author of *Megatrends*, see a bright future for the service sector. In making the transition to services, some argue, the economy will offer lucrative positions for computer programmers, financial analysts, and corporate lawyers. So far this promise has not been fulfilled, since the vast majority of new service jobs are low-paying, low-skilled positions. In 1982 the Labor Department announced that the leading categories of job openings in 1980 included retail salesclerks, cashiers, secretaries, waiters, cooks, and nursing aides. The Labor Department predicted more of the same to come. In the decade of the 1980s there were expected to be openings for only 120,000 computer programmers, but three million secretaries and office clerks. Other growth areas are nurses' aides and fast-food workers.

Robert Samuelson, writing in *Newsweek*, has pointed out that manufacturing jobs are not necessarily high paying. States with high concentrations of manufacturing jobs, such as North Carolina and Indiana, have lower-than-average per capita incomes. But on average, service jobs pay less.

In 1983 the average hourly earnings in the United States were $7.90. The average hourly figure for wholesale and retail trade was $6.44. Eating and drinking places paid $4.21, while hotels and motels offered $5.23. Besides paying lower hourly wages, in many cases the services offered their employees fewer hours per week. Companies such as franchise chains were discovering it was cheaper to use part-time employees. The average hours worked in wholesale and retail trade dropped from 38.2 in 1962 to 31.5 in 1983. While the average weekly salary in 1983 was $273, the figure was $106 for eating and drinking places, the poorest-paid industry in the country. Drugstores offered $148, and hotels and motels paid $153. Earnings in many service jobs did not keep pace with inflation. In 1972 dollars, hourly earnings in eating and drinking places declined from $3.16 in 1973 to $3.08 in 1979.

As the service jobs expand, the well-paid goods-producing jobs vanish. In the recessions of the early 1980s hundreds of thousands of factory positions disappeared forever. These were the jobs in the auto plants and steel mills that had helped create a blue-collar middle class. Factory workers had bought the houses and washing machines that enabled the economy to prosper. Because of the shift to services, most of the laid-off workers can expect a permanently lower standard of living. People who assumed their children would enjoy middle-class prosperity now face a new reality. Journalists have begun discussing "downward mobility." The Bureau of Labor Statistics studied the twenty fastest-growing occupations and the twenty declining most sharply. Workers in the fastest-growing jobs earn on average five thousand dollars a year *less* than those in the declining categories. High school graduates of the 1950s and 1960s could find high-paying jobs in manufacturing or government. For the current crop of young people there are few such opportunities.

Entry-level positions in the services pay little and offer few opportunities for promotion. The maid in the motel, the cook at the fast-food restaurant, the haircutter in the beauty salon—all have little chance to move up. Pay scales in a traditional factory could be plotted on a bell curve. There were a few high-paying positions at the top and a few low salaries at the bottom. Most workers fell in the middle. In the service businesses, whether banking or motels, most jobs are low-paying.

To be sure, the services are not monolithic. In *Services: The New Economy*, a book published in 1981, Thomas Stanback observes that while services as a whole pay lower than manufacturing there are low-paying factory jobs and high-wage service positions. But most service fields offer concentrations of low-wage jobs. Using 1975 figures from the Department of Labor, Stanback notes that 26.2 percent of manufacturing jobs paid $12,000 or more while 55.7 percent paid $9500 to $7000 and 18.1 percent paid less than $7000. In producer services—relatively high-wage areas such as accounting, advertising, and insurance—30.8 percent of workers earned over $12,000, but only 23.5 percent earned $9500 to $7000 while 45.8 percent earned less than $7000. The service areas offering the lowest salaries are the fast-growing fields where franchises are concentrated. In retail services, Stanback notes, 60.1 percent of workers earned less than $7000. In consumer services—including muffler shops and beauty salons—82.7 percent earned less than $7000.

In franchise companies the gap between income classes is particularly stark. At the top are the wealthy franchisees and executives who earn salaries comparable to the highest paid in any industry. In 1982 Michael Rose, president of Holiday Inns, received a salary of $907,410. Dairy Queen president Harris Cooper was paid $397,726. In contrast, most workers at motels and fast-food outlets are paid little more than the minimum wage.

The wage pattern can be seen clearly at CutCo Industries, the haircutting chain. The median sales of franchised outlets is $250,000. The company is reluctant to give out franchisee earnings, but prosperous operations in the industry can be expected to produce annual incomes of $30,000 to $70,000. A busy outlet is staffed by a manager, an assistant manager, ten operators, and two assistants. The managers and assistant managers usually receive $18,000 to $25,000. Operators, the people who actually fix the hair, earn the minimum wage plus tips. At an outlet I visited on Long Island, New York, the extra income from tips amounted to $300 to $500 a month. Total earnings averaged about $220 a week. Assistant operators, who do all the shampooing and help with permanents, earned less.

The growing importance of such service businesses threatens the American ideal of an egalitarian society. Over the last two decades the differences in income have been increasing. The number of people below the poverty line increased from 23 million in 1974 to 35 million in 1983, according to the Census Bureau. In 1983 a family of four was classified as poor if it had a cash income of less than $10,178. In 1971, 36.5 percent of households had annual incomes of less than $15,000 in 1981 dollars, according to the Census Bureau. By 1981 the figure had climbed to 39.8 percent. Those with incomes of $15,000 to less than $35,000—what may be called the middle class—declined from 47.6 percent of the total to 40.9 percent. Those families with more than $35,000 grew from 15.9 to 19.3 percent. The top 20 percent of families, those making more than $34,300, received 44 percent of earnings. The lowest 20 percent, making less than about $8,000, got only 3.9 percent of payrolls.

The franchise chains have faced few problems finding people to accept low-paying jobs. Since the baby-boom generation entered the work force in the 1970s, there has been an oversupply of young laborers—people ranging in age from their teens to mid-twenties. And as production jobs have migrated overseas in search of lower-paid workers, millions of Americans have been thrown on the job market. With high unemployment, companies come under little pressure to raise wages. In many cases unionized restaurants and hotels have been replaced by franchise outlets where unions have been blocked, with the full-time union jobs of adult waiters and cooks being replaced by part-time minimum wage positions for young people.

In the 1960s, as the chains expanded, they discovered a huge untapped source of labor: young people. Today half of all high school juniors and seniors work part-time. There is a fivefold increase of boys aged fourteen to sixteen working compared to forty years ago, while girls have experienced an elevenfold rise. Part of the reason for the increased work participation is that young people stay in school longer; instead of quitting school to work, they continue their education and work part-time. In addition, with the rise of the service sector there are more positions open for students. Some educators have hailed the growing entry of young people into the world of work. In 1973 the National Commission on the Reform of Secondary Education argued that early work experience might help young people make the transition to adulthood. Youth unemployment might be reduced as students acquired skills and learned how to accept responsibility for performing a task.

Some jobs may indeed stimulate young people and help them mature. But for millions of youngsters work means toiling in the stifling atmosphere of the franchise restaurant or store. McDonald's alone employs about a million young people a year in its operations, most of them working part-time for brief periods. Fast-food companies prefer young employees, since the work must be done quickly and the pay is low. Workers perform jobs that range from boring to completely odious. Cooks must function like robots, quickly completing routine tasks over and over. In this environment there is little time to take a break or talk to customers. "It's hot, noisy, and dirty work," said Laurence Steinberg, an assistant professor at the University of California at Irvine, who has studied young people working at various jobs. "They're under a lot of time pressure."

Steinberg and his colleague Ellen Greenberger found that the benefits of young people working may be overestimated. The researchers reported that "adolescents do not typically learn new skills on the job, practice school-taught skills, form meaningful relationships with adults, nor engage in high levels of responsibility-taking or social cooperation." Work also detracts from many youngsters' educations. Working students spent less time on schooling and enjoyed class less. They were absent from school more and showed poorer grades. Though the companies claim they show young people the value of work, the fast-food jobs may only instill cynicism. "If you were trying to teach young people responsibility you would not design the kind of jobs there are in fast food," Steinberg says.

In one survey Steinberg presented fast-food workers with this statement: "Anyone who works harder than he has to must be crazy." The longer the young people had been employed, the more they agreed with the assertion. About 60 percent of the first-time workers told the researchers they had committed some form of theft or irresponsibility within the first nine months of employment. They gave away goods or services, falsely claimed to be sick, stole, or worked while intoxicated. For many young people the workplace serves more as an extension of adolescence than as a bridge to adulthood. Most youngsters work in the company of their peers and have little contact with adults. Most income is spent on items that are important in the teenage culture: cars, records, extra clothes, cigarettes, alcohol, and marijuana. Few workers save for long-term objectives.

Fast-food employees complain of supervision by poorly trained managers. Most restaurants are headed by managers who are only a year or two older than the teenage workforce. Usually paid around $15,000 for what may be a sixty-hour week, the inexperienced supervisors are often abusive and arbitrary in their efforts to meet sales goals. They take advantage of young employees, who have few protections on the job. *The Wall Street Journal* reported in 1979 that one suburban McDonald's ordered part-time employees to report an hour ahead of time and then punch in only when the manager gave permission. At other restaurants workers complain of abusive language and sudden schedule changes. Industry officials concede there is a problem in finding competent managers. A Burger King executive told *The Wall Street Journal* that the companies had been "putting young men or women in their early twenties in charge of a $1 million restaurant with forty employees under age eighteen and expecting them [the managers] to function."

One employee caused Wendy's special embarrassment when she quit in disgust. When the chain hired a seventeen-year-old named Wendy Hamburger for a suburban store near Chicago the company proudly informed newspapers of the memorable name. Chairman David Thomas mailed the teenager an autographed picture. Despite the fanfare the high school senior lasted only three months on a job where she earned about forty dollars for a fifteen-hour week. During her brief tenure the store went through three managers, all of whom made life difficult for workers. When a manager threatened to fire Wendy if she refused to work an extra shift on a holiday, she quit.

Wendy Hamburger's problems are typical of what fast-food workers experience. Most of the young employees I interviewed encountered similar difficulties. An eighteen-year-old McDonald's employee from Bethlehem, Pennsylvania, who was a student at a junior college, said he worked for gas money. Most of the other workers at his store were sixteen to nineteen, he said. During the day some workers were older women in their thirties, many of them married. "I've been working there for two years," the young man explained. "There are five or six of us who have been there for a while. The rest of the people come and go. I started at $3.35 an hour. After a year and a half I was raised to $3.40. I don't like the job, but it's the only place I can work every Saturday. It gets tedious when you're doing the same thing over and over. You have to stay in your place. If you go to the back room you have to have a reason, and you aren't supposed to move around.

"All the managers are ladies. One I have is about forty-five or forty-six and the other is twenty. One of them I think has a problem. If you do anything she blows up. I've seen their supervisors yell at them and then they take it out on us. They have an evaluation of how you are dressed, your personal behavior, if you talk back. You are supposed to get a raise every six months if you have a good evaluation. In the first evaluation I was rated fair, then I was rated good, but I didn't get a raise. I got yelled at once for not being neat. My hat was set back on my head instead of being straight. They don't let you have any mustaches or beards. At first I tried to be friendly to the managers, but after a while I learned the best thing you could do is just keep to yourself and do your job."

The problems of attracting and using managers effectively are of much concern to the fast-food industry. A poor manager can disrupt the operation of an outlet and hurt profits. Harris Cooper, president of Dairy Queen, discussed the issue at a forum described in an article in *Restaurant Business* in the May 1, 1981, issue. "The key vulnerability of the industry at this time is our inability to attract the manager who can come away from our experience feeling that he or she is a better, knowledgeable, competent, developed person," Cooper said. "This is sad, but it is true. Here we have failed. Managers think of us in this industry as ogres, basically because we neither understand their needs nor have the capability of dealing with their thoughts and problems."

Robert Emerson, a fast-food analyst for Fred Alger & Company, argued that managers are crucial for success in fast food. Since they are poorly paid for sixty- to seventy-hour work weeks, the main reason the managers stay is the hope of promotions. In a growing chain there is room for managers to become district supervisors. But when the chain stops growing the manager is left without any motivation.

The low wages and hostile working conditions have discouraged college graduates from seeking jobs as restaurant managers. Students at hotel- and restaurant-administration schools have been notably unenthusiastic about careers in fast food. Donald Bell, an instructor at Michigan State, and John Stefanelli, assistant professor at the University of Nevada at Las Vegas, began surveying hotel and restaurant students around the country in 1977. In several studies they found that only about 10 percent of the students had any interest in fast food, even though the industry is the fastest-growing segment of food service and would seem to offer opportunities for striking it rich. The franchised chains, with their sophisticated market research and production facilities, might be expected to appeal to ambitious college students. In fact, the would-be restaurant managers are most interested in positions with quality outlets featuring more expensive prices and higher-paid workers.

A former Pizza Hut manager, who worked for the chain for three years in the late 1970s, told me he quit the job because it was so grueling. He joined the company as an assistant manager in an outlet near Albany, New York. "I had recently graduated from college and I started because it looked like a good career. At first I enjoyed it. I was brand new to the working world, and all the sudden I felt like I was in a position of authority. I was handling money. After a while it begins to be a grind. Suddenly the glow of being a manager and being in charge fades as you're mopping the floor at two o'clock in the morning. The restaurant opened at noon and closed at midnight. On Fridays and Saturdays it closed at one. So you would be there till two.

"As an assistant manager I was on a salary of $175. The cooks were paid by the hour. You had a manager who scheduled you. He had a profit line to work out with his district manager. He could either put on the cook and pay him the minimum wage plus overtime, or he could schedule the assistant manager who had to work all those crazy hours without any overtime. I usually worked about fifty hours, but there were people working sixty or seventy hours because their manager scheduled them that way. The assistant managers were making less than the minimum wage. The Labor Department investigated, and now I understand it isn't as bad. As an assistant manager I generally spent the whole shift cooking. Late at night you generally just had a cook and a waitress. Somebody would have to mop the floor so I would do it. After about seven months I was offered a job of manager of my own Pizza Hut. I was really pleased. The money was about $10,500. Take-home pay was a hundred fifty a week. I was twenty-four and living a student's existence. I was sharing an apartment with two other guys so I could live well on the money.

"As manager I was doing exactly the same stuff as before, except now I was doing the scheduling. The restaurant required that certain pieces of work get done. Somebody had to make salad, somebody had to make the dough. Somebody had to sweep and mop the floors. It didn't matter who did it. The manager's job was to assign someone to do it, including himself. When you're young you have this concept of a manager. You sort of see him as a miniature Lee Iacocca, walking through the plant with his suit and tie on, directing people. After a while you realized you were a glorified cook.

"You had an incentive for earning higher profits. The less

hours you had employees work, the more hours you worked yourself, the higher the profits, and the higher your bonus. My store always made very good profits because I was working so many hours myself. I was working sixty or sixty-five hours. I was single and I chose to make more money in bonuses by working more hours than most people who had a family would be willing to do. My first year as manager I made twelve or thirteen thousand. To me that was pretty good. At first I thought, Gee, I don't mind this. I couldn't make this much money anywhere else.

"There was a high turnover of workers. The people I hired tended to be college students or recent high school graduates. They were not people looking for a career with the company. It was very difficult to find the right people. I made all sorts of mistakes in hiring people. You're hiring someone with the expectation that with several weeks of training he can run the restaurant and he can close it up. So you have this nineteen- or twenty-year-old guy. You show him how to make the pizzas. You leave the place and you cross your fingers and you hope that when you come in the next day everything will be all right. They were always asking you how to do this or that. They would say, 'This happened. What should I do?'

"The work was fast-paced. You were on your feet and you were checking the oven and you were running here and running there. It got to be a grind. All of the sudden it would be one o'clock in the morning and you were exhausted. I began to hate it. I began to dread going in to work. Finally the area manager sat down with me and said, 'You look like you're unhappy. We can see that your performance is not up to par. Why don't we come to a parting of the ways.' That's how I felt too. I was burned out. That happened to most people who started as manager when I did. They got burned out and left or were fired. You just can't last as manager very long."

The chains are fully aware of the discontent of workers. The average worker quits after four months. With a turnover rate of 300 percent a year, fast food has the highest turnover of any industry. Most businesses would go bankrupt if their employees left so quickly. Still, the franchise companies have not taken steps to improve working conditions. By keeping hours and wages unappealing the companies ensure that employees will leave before they become entitled to raises or benefits. High turnover also makes it difficult for unions to organize workers. The policy has a price. The ineffective use of people may be a major reason why productivity in the industry does not increase, observes Richard Carnes, an economist at the Bureau of Labor Statistics. Workers become more productive the longer they are on the job. When there is constant turnover, new people must be introduced and trained. During the several days it takes to train a person, the new worker is not fully productive, and a supervisor must spend time breaking in the novice. Equipment introduced by the chains has failed to offset productivity lost through ineffective personnel policies. "The idea that better equipment will replace people is a gross exaggeration," Harris Cooper, president of Dairy Queen, told *Restaurant Business*. "As in the computer field, there is still truth to the maxim: 'Garbage in, garbage out.' It is still a people business."

Jim Newman of SHR International, a management consulting firm, has advised fast-food clients to attempt to reduce their turnover. He suggests that companies seek to hire older, more stable managers. However, most chains have been reluctant to alter traditional policies. "They don't realize how much turnover costs them," he said. "It can cost five hundred dollars to hire someone in paperwork and supervisor time."

In establishing their personnel policies, the fast-food chains faced a choice. One option was to pursue higher productivity growth by investing more on capital and labor. They could spend more on training and wages, developing a higher-paid, relatively small work force. But the companies chose a different course. They came to rely on a large force of low-paid, low-productivity workers. In opting for low productivity growth, the chains were following a course taken by the automobile makers in the 1950s and 1960s. Detroit, as we observed earlier, focused on marketing and allowed productivity to grow slowly. When unions demanded high wages, the companies passed the extra costs on to consumers. The car makers' bubble burst when consumers refused to pay higher prices and high-productivity foreign competitors appeared. So far the franchise low-productivity strategy has not faced a crisis. No foreign competitors have emerged. By keeping unions out, chains have held down wages and prices. The low wages of workers have financed expensive marketing campaigns, high salaries for executives, and healthy profits for shareholders.

In recent years chains have raised executive salaries and begun competing with other corporations to hire top administrators. In the past franchise companies attracted bright young people by rewarding loyal managers with franchise licenses or promoting them to corporate staff jobs. But as the value of an outlet topped two hundred thousand dollars, companies became reluctant to give them away. Corporate executives have increasingly come from business schools or other companies. While Harlan Sanders never finished high school, in recent years Kentucky Fried Chicken has looked to experienced marketing executives for leadership. In 1977 the company appointed Michael Miles chief executive. Miles, who studied journalism at Northwestern University, served the ideal apprenticeship for the fried-chicken magnate of the 1980s. He worked for ten years at the Leo Burnett advertising agency, laboring on behalf of Procter & Gamble, the giant maker of brand-name household products such as Tide laundry detergent and Crest toothpaste. In 1970 he became supervisor of the fried-chicken account. The Kentucky chain hired him in 1971 to be senior vice president for marketing. As chief executive, Miles moved to recruit graduates of the same business schools that staff major industrial corporations. After a distinguished stint at the chicken chain, Miles went on to serve as president of Kraft, the cheesemaker.

Chains whose franchisees include wealthy investors may persuade owner-operators to join the corporate staff. Before founding Wendy's, David Thomas jumped from being a franchisee of Kentucky Fried Chicken to serving as vice president of the chain. Ronald Fay, executive vice president of Wendy's, began as a franchisee. Roy Winegardner, a Holiday Inns franchisee in Cincinnati, is said to have criticized the chain loudly after the 1973 Arab oil embargo hurt sales. Holiday Inns then hired the disaffected operator, telling him to try his hand. David Lewis, who owned eighteen Holiday Inns in South Africa, was selected in 1974 to head the company's European operations. Sometimes the career paths in franchise chains work in the reverse direction as executives quit to become franchisees, a step that may increase their incomes. Leonard Rawls, chairman of Hardee's, stepped down to take a franchise of the company.

For fast-food companies unable to develop their own management talent, one sure source of experienced people is McDonald's. Stealing top executives apparently seems the fastest route to duplicating the hamburger giant's success. Edward Lifman, a former McDonald's vice president, became chairman of Arthur Treacher's. In a move that shocked the industry in 1977, Burger King snapped up Donald Smith, the McDonald's senior vice president who was considered the likely heir to the company's top position. For three years Smith headed the number-two hamburger chain, using McDonald's techniques to improve sharply the company's lackluster sales. Having turned around Burger King, Smith took his franchise expertise to Pizza Hut, another troubled chain. In 1978 Burger Chef landed Terrance Collins, a McDonald's vice president. Collins then took over the Victoria Station restaurant chain in 1981.

Few chains can completely staff their ranks by raiding other companies. Early in the life of a chain it is usually necessary to begin a training program that can develop employees and franchisees. As the H & R Block chain expanded in the 1950s more quickly than its founders ever hoped, the company began to face a serious roadblock: There were simply not enough tax preparers. During the three-month tax season the offices needed a small army of people knowledgeable in the mysterious ways of the Internal Revenue Service. After April 15 the company required only a skeleton staff. Since the chain could not afford to hire expensive tax accountants, Block turned to part-timers.

The new Block employees were either moonlighters or those

without jobs—schoolteachers, housewives, retired people. Block trained these fiscal amateurs in the basics of filling out tax forms. Working with franchisees the company developed a standard federal tax course and program for individual states. As television spread the name of H & R Block, more people became interested in attending the company's schools. Some only wanted to learn to fill out their own returns. Recognizing a new market for its services, Block opened its schools to the public, charging a fee. Top graduates were eligible for jobs with the company. By 1980, 500,000 people had taken the Block course, which now runs twelve weeks and costs $99.50. In 1981, 85,000 signed up, an increase from 70,000 the year before, as taxpayers rushed to learn about the new regulations promoted by the Reagan administration.

Thanks to its training program, Block now has an ample pool of workers to staff its more than eight thousand storefront offices. The company employs a year-round force of 2245 that swells to 43,000 during the busy season. Corporate headquarters maintains a staff of five to monitor tax laws and update the course each year. Besides training employees and franchisees, the Block program earns the company healthy profits.

While it is unusual for a franchise company to make money by offering training, most major chains—like Block—do pay attention to developing the skills of franchisees and workers. Providing standardized knowledge is necessary in order to open outlets around the country. And training can be a major reason for a franchisee to join a chain. The parent company, claiming vast expertise in its field, promises to teach the novice muffler merchant the secrets of succeeding in a strange business.

As the chains have grown larger and their equipment has become more complicated, the franchise schools have grown more elaborate. Frequently called "universities," the training centers offer courses to hundreds of students. At Holiday Inn University managers from around the country learn the basics of the motel business. Special courses are developed to introduce new technology, such as the computerized reservations system. The motel school supplies franchisees with training films that can be used to teach workers everything from making beds to managing restaurants.

Minuteman Press requires all its franchisees to attend a two-week training session at company headquarters, where they are taught to run a printing operation. Franchisees learn to use presses in a room filled with printing equipment. In a classroom next door they review the company's system of bookkeeping. At the end of the course the new operators will not have mastered the printing business, but they will know enough to hire skilled pressmen and then learn on the job.

Most franchise universities stress that the company's methods are the only ways to run the business. Instructors inculcate the idea that the parent company is all-knowing, and the franchisee will face certain ruin if he deviates from the standardized techniques. In the universities the parent begins its efforts to control the operators. Lessons on the importance of uniformity are particularly emphasized at fast-food universities. Franchisees and their staff must master all procedures.

McDonald's points with pride to its training program. Each year more than two thousand franchisees and managers study at Hamburger University, McDonald's training center at Elk Grove Village, Illinois. More than twenty thousand participants have earned the bachelor of hamburgerology degree, with its golden arches appearing at the bottom of the certificate. The school is headed by a "dean" and offers eighteen courses such as "Beverage Electives" and "Market Evaluation." Alumni of the basic program can return for graduate seminars. The elaborate facilities include closed-circuit television and rooms full of equipment used to make hamburgers and french fries. In each class one student receives a golden chef hat for making the most significant contribution to class discussion, while another wins a ceramic hamburger model for academic achievement.

Instilling pride is important, because the positions awaiting graduates are generally tedious jobs requiring faithful attention to detail. Courses are designed to prepare graduates for the routine tasks of preparing food and hiring crew members. The difficult problems requiring creative intelligence are resolved by the researchers and executives at corporate headquarters. What remains to be taught to field managers is how to survive the maddening quirks of everyday restaurant life. Courses emphasize what to do when a griddle fails or a milk shake machine refuses to cooperate. "We learn how to handle situations such as when you're taking it easy at around three p.m., and a big bus pulls into the parking lot," Gary Rose, a franchisee, told *The New York Times.*

Admission to Hamburger U. does not require distinguished academic credentials. Students include franchisees who have passed through the ordeal of performing menial labor at a McDonald's and appear willing to oversee a crew of eighty bored teenagers according to company dictates. Other Hamburger University participants are managers, most of them veterans of at least six months of working in a store. Caught in a tight job market with limited education credentials, they took jobs at McDonald's and enrolled in the university hoping to move up in the company—a prospect dimmed by the slowing economy.

Kentucky Fried Chicken's National Training Center boasts six modern classrooms, three model kitchens, and a staff of eight. The school has greatly evolved from Colonel Sanders' first efforts to teach his recipe to franchisees. After selling a franchise the Colonel would spend about three days teaching the new licensee how to prepare the chicken. When Sanders was satisfied the operator had mastered the cooking procedures, he moved on to sell more licenses, leaving copies of the recipe behind. By 1964 the chain had grown so large it was no longer possible for the Colonel to teach everyone personally. The company was forced to establish its first formal training center at a store in Louisville. Franchisees arrived on a Sunday night in groups of fourteen. For four and a half days they labored to master company techniques, working in a classroom and a special kitchen in the basement of the store. On Thursday the Colonel would speak, inspiring the new operators. On Friday at noon the franchisees would be sent on their way to practice what they had learned. Over the years the facilities were expanded and the training manual grew from a forty-page pamphlet containing recipes to a 382-page book covering all aspects of the company.

In 1977, when sales at Kentucky Fried Chicken stores dropped more than 12 percent, the company decided it was doing something wrong. The quality of the food had slipped. Manager turnover, always high, had reached unacceptable levels. The solution, Kentucky Fried decided, was more training. The company determined that running a store required performing one hundred fifty tasks, ranging from handling customer complaints to sweeping floors. Under a new training system employees are encouraged to master all jobs. First they view filmstrips, then answer written questions. Managers grade the tests, then show the employee how to perform the task.

The material is presented in simple English. In one film Colonel Sanders gives a pep talk about the role of Kentucky Fried Chicken workers. After viewing it, employees are asked to circle the right answers: "The Colonel tells us we should: (a) Greet the customers with a smile; (b) Treat our customers as we like to be treated; (c) Serve our customers hot, tasty food; (d) All of the above." As employees progress through the film series their progress is monitored on a chart displayed in the store.

The company credits the training program with improving the cleanliness and efficiency of its stores. While the training may help workers perform their simple tasks better, more important, it gives employees a sense of their importance in the organization. The course provides some recognition, a pat on the back, an incentive in a job that otherwise offers few rewards.

During the 1982 elections the nature of franchise jobs came into some prominence. In a front-page article *The New York Times* noted that the wives of unemployed steel workers were taking jobs in McDonald's outlets, trying to make ends meet on minimum wages. Former Vice President Walter Mondale warned that Americans might be failing their children by trapping them in minimum-wage jobs. Unless basic industry is preserved, he said, the next generation might be "sweeping up around Japanese computers and spending a lifetime serving McDonald's hamburgers."

Some economists argued that the move into low-paying franchise and service jobs may have a more severe deadening effect on the overall economy than first appears. A car manufacturer supplies jobs not only for its own employees but also for many others in a variety of industries. In order to build an automobile, Detroit must make purchases of textiles, rubber, steel, glass, and other products. The fast-food restaurant or beauty parlor sends relatively fewer job-creating ripples throughout the economy. "The real danger is that the service industries don't have any regenerative power," Edmund Ayoub, chief economist of the United Steelworkers union, told *Newsweek*. "If you serve a hamburger at McDonald's you don't generate any jobs beyond that."

Jane Jacobs, in her book *The Economy of Cities*, examines this job-multiplier effect when she discusses how cities grow. In order for a city to develop new jobs it must have unique products that it exports to other cities, she argues. Money earned with exports allows the city to import. However, a city that simply exports will achieve only limited growth. A resort town whose sole industry is tourism depends on exports: selling services to outsiders. Most goods and services used in the town, such as gasoline and pillowcases, must be imported. If the town began producing pillowcases instead of importing them, money formerly spent on imports of pillowcases could buy other things. The town would be richer. A city grows most quickly through a combination of increasing exports and replacing imports with local production. This is how new jobs are created.

Franchised beauty parlors or fast-food outlets do not participate in this job creation. The franchise outlets import supplies and business ideas but do not usually provide any exports. (Parent companies do export services and expertise to cities around the country, where franchisees purchase them. Franchisees import this but do not export anything in return.) Jacobs cites Los Angeles in the late 1940s as a city that grew by replacing imports and developing exports. Thousands of new businesses were started in the postwar period in Los Angeles. One new company produced sliding glass doors for local house builders, who no longer had to import doors. Later the company grew to export its product, and it expanded, providing new jobs.

Writing in 1969, Jacobs cautioned that the U.S. economy was due for a period of stagnation and unemployment. Not enough capital was being invested in the kind of development that would produce new jobs, she argued. The country could live lavishly for a time, squandering money that should be used to nurture more employment. Eventually the bills would come due. In the early 1980s Jacobs' words came to seem hauntingly prophetic. While the overall economy suffered, as Jacobs had predicted, franchising and a few other areas prospered. There is nothing paradoxical about this. Though the causes of the economic problems were complicated, the great chains contributed their share to the slowdown. The powerful marketing programs of the franchise companies pulled money into businesses that offered low productivity and could do little to help generate the goods-exporting jobs the country needed. The more money spent on hamburgers and haircuts, the less there would be available for houses and cars. People who were increasingly poor, who were driving older cars, would buy fast food on strips that gleamed more brightly than ever.

Where the Chains Went

A trip up Stefko Boulevard in Bethlehem, Pennsylvania, begins at the Lehigh River, where the road parts from Third Street and crosses a bridge over the water. Badly in need of repairs, the bridge is closed to trucks. To make sure no one violates the warning signs, a cable is strung over the bridge, limiting clearance to six feet, barely enough room for a car. The view from the crossing is awesome. Straddling the river in both directions is the two-mile-long Bethlehem Steel plant—an endless landscape of towers, pipes, and rusting corrugated metal buildings. Some of the structures emit the low roar of steel making; many others are silent. The plant began 1982 with 11,000 workers; by the end of the year only 6500 remained on the payroll.

Stefko is a main route between the mills and the suburban homes of steel workers northeast of Bethlehem, a city of seventy thousand. A decade ago the road was a racetrack during the morning and evening rush hours. Now the press of traffic is less intense. Still, Stefko remains a good example of a prosperous strip. Every sizable city and town in the country has its strips, natural habitats for businesses that thrive on customers stopping briefly, then moving on. Strips offer prime locations for franchised businesses. Often clustering together, franchise outlets stand out from the local units that struggle to maintain positions on the roadsides. The strips began to appear in the 1930s and 1940s as traffic increased. They came into flower in the 1950s, a time when energy was wildly squandered. People drove freely along the strip, stopping when they wanted and buying a range of products. Teenagers of driving age became experts on the subtleties of the strips, knowing where the right hangouts were and when cops were most likely to patrol. Sometimes strips with special functions formed. Fast-food strips appeared near colleges or along certain thoroughfares. Motel strips emerged at key locations, such as a day's drive from Chicago along the interstate.

Bethlehem's Stefko Boulevard, unlike many of its counterparts around the country, nourishes an unusual mix of businesses. Along the two-mile stretch of road it is possible to see stark signs of what may be the nation's future. At Stefko's source in the river valley lies industrial depression. As the boulevard climbs to a ridge its roadsides brim with franchised prosperity. A driver traveling up Stefko leaves behind the steel mills and encounters Bethlehem's new municipal service center, a Chevy dealer, and Taylor Truck Rental, which features Jartran trucks parked in the lot. Then comes Suburban Realty, a carpet store, and a range of local businesses perched on the sloping hillside—Dave's Family Market, Sun Beer Distributors. About a mile from the mill the two-lane road reaches the hilltop and levels out. There, on a flat spot where it is easy for drivers to turn off, sits a Midas Muffler outlet. Next to it is a 7-Eleven. Here the serious retail action begins. For the next mile franchised businesses dominate.

Stefko widens into four lanes. On the right there is a strip shopping area called Stefko Center. The shopping center hosts Radio Shack, Elaine Powers, H & R Block, and a Carvel ice-cream outlet. Up the street there is a Dunkin' Donuts and a

Century 21 office. Across the way from Stefko Center stands a McDonald's, where a yellow banner promotes Egg McMuffins. Then in quick succession there is a Burger King, a Gino's, and a Pizza Hut. Down a few blocks Maaco repairs cars. Farther out another shopping center stands boarded up. In front of it an "AM/PM" convenience store survives. Abruptly the franchises stop, leaving the roadside to a decaying drive-in theater featuring horror movies. The road shifts from four to two lanes and becomes a country road surrounded by residential areas.

The first franchise, a McDonald's, came to Stefko in 1960. At the time the shopping center was operating but the roadside was nearly empty. There was a local operation called Mr. Burger, and farther down the hill a family-owned drive-in offered burgers that were brought out to cars by carhops. The Stefko McDonald's was one of three in that part of Pennsylvania. There were no McDonald's in New York City, 110 miles to the northeast, or in Philadelphia, 100 miles to the southwest. The Bethlehem store sputtered at first, as the franchisee, who managed a factory full-time, supervised the outlet only during his off-hours. To improve sales the local operator hired Don Mast, who had started with McDonald's in 1958, managing one of the chain's first units in the Chicago area. A dedicated company man, Mast and his children had attracted hamburger customers by dressing in clown suits and giving away gifts in the parking lots of stores. The new manager came to Bethlehem in 1962. Soon business at the Stefko unit picked up as McDonald's gained loyal customers.

Mast is a round-faced jolly man with white hair, who talked to me in his house on a quiet street a few blocks from the fast-food outlet. His conversation was interrupted by the barking of his three large dogs and by several members of his family who wandered through his living room. "At first we were out there by ourselves," Mast recalled. "The only other store on Stefko Boulevard was Mr. Burger. He was a local guy. He was selling a fifteen-cent hamburger like we were. Then as we picked up he immediately dropped his price to ten cents. He folded before too long. It was a case where he didn't have good management. He gave hamburgers a bad name. He had bought Australian beef and word was out that he was using kangaroo meat, even though Australian beef is fine. When he was gone we used to laugh if a car came down Stefko on a Sunday—they would have to pull into McDonald's. There was no other reason to be out there."

Traffic on Stefko picked up. With the mills working steadily, Bethlehem was becoming suburbanized. In the neighborhood behind McDonald's the modest houses on quiet streets were filled with prosperous working-class people. In the late 1960s Don Mast began to face other competitors. Burger King opened a block away; then Kentucky Fried Chicken appeared. By the mid-1970s, Don Mast was something of an anomaly in the McDonald's organization. As a longtime manager, he was well paid by the chain's standards—a middle-aged man in a job normally held by young people. He enjoyed more responsibility than most franchisees permitted their managers. In 1976 he was let go, as the franchisee put his son in charge of the outlet. Out of work, Mast naturally turned to the only business he knew, fast food. He decided to open his own outlet downtown.

Bethlehem's city government had decided to support construction of a mall that would revive the downtown area. For years new shopping centers and developing strips were pulling business away from downtown Bethlehem. The decisive blow to the center city came in the early 1970s, when several malls opened up. The main streets of Bethlehem now were relatively unimportant commercial locations. The dollars had moved to sites near the intersections of the highways. The main highway for the area is U.S. Route 22, which runs east and west, connecting Pennsylvania with New Jersey. At the intersections of major north-and-south roads with the highway several state-of-the-art malls sprang up, air-conditioned magical worlds that soon became prime locations for retail outlets of all kinds, including franchise chains. Though the region's economy stagnated, retail outlets thrived. During the ten years ending in 1982 the number of jobs in manufacturing of metals in the Lehigh Valley dropped 16,900 to 94,000, according to the Pennsylvania Department of Labor. The jobs in retail trade rose 7,300 to 40,600.

To compete with the powerful mall environments, city officials proposed building a huge downtown mall of three or four blocks that would involve knocking down some existing businesses. Opponents of the plan argued that building a downtown facility would not attract people away from the shopping malls, and the few small businesses remaining in the city would be pushed out. Some politicians suggested providing public support for a convention center and hotel that might bring the downtown business. While they debated the merits of the proposals, a Holiday Inn located on the outskirts of town near the main highway began expanding its banquet facilities and was soon hosting conventions. The public facility now seemed redundant. As a compromise the mall was limited to a structure covering one block in the heart of town.

Mast opened a fast-food outlet he called Big M. "I was the first place to open in the mall," Mast remembered. "I worked with my wife and my two kids. We designed the place. We laid it out. We fabricated the equipment and had it made up to our specs. We had great expectations. They had brought in consultants from Texas who looked the mall over and said they couldn't believe it. It was an absolutely fantastic idea. All we needed was some people in the mall. But a restaurant cannot operate inside an empty building. We sat there for a year waiting for customers to show up. They sold the mall in a sheriff's sale. They are supposed to open offices there and a few stores."

Mast was out of business. Five years later he had just about finished paying off the debt he had accumulated. He had set up a refrigeration business, doing work for Holiday Inns and local restaurants, repairing and maintaining walk-in coolers, refrigerators, and ice-cube makers. Nonetheless, Mast remains loyal to McDonald's. He talked with pride about the way he ran the chain outlet and eagerly told how he attended an early session of the company's university. He did not see a connection between the rise of the suburban franchise operations and his failure downtown. He insisted that independent restaurants like his Big M could still be profitable in Bethlehem. "If you have a good product and you run the place well you can still do business here," he said. Despite the recession, he said, the restaurant business was still prospering. "Once in a while they still have to take the family out, even if they're unemployed. Mom has to get out of the kitchen. How better can you do it than to take the kids out and get a hamburger?"

Throughout the country chains have selected sites similar to those chosen in Bethlehem. Early chain builders seized prime roadside locations that in the 1950s were surrounded by empty lots. Ray Kroc, McDonald's founder, sometimes took to the air to scout locations for his restaurants. Flying in a small plane, he would look for church steeples and schools, signs of the advancing middle-class families whose business the hamburger salesman sought. The first hamburger outposts would be located on large, cheap plots isolated from other businesses. By the 1960s the competition for space became more intense. The fast-food outlets lined up in pulsating rows. Alongside the restaurants were the new muffler shops and motels, and then a profusion of other franchise chains: health spas, beauty salons, dry cleaners.

As it has become increasingly difficult to find good locations, chains of all kinds have developed procedures for deciding where to build. Before accepting a site Blimpie counts the pedestrians and cars going past. While thirty thousand cars a day would be a good figure for a suburban location, subjective factors are also considered. A site with a traffic count of only twenty-four thousand might be chosen if there is a college across the street that could provide the steady lunch customers the chain seeks. For smaller chains that lack research staffs, one technique for finding a good site is to locate next to an outlet of a big company. Economy motel chains often build next to a Holiday Inn, hoping to pick up the overflow and to compete for those less interested in amenities than in price. Wherever a McDonald's or Burger King opens, outlets of lesser chains sprout, faithfully believing that the big operators must know the best sites.

McDonald's does carefully survey an area before locating a new store. In areas where there are already McDonald's units, opening a new outlet usually will take business away from other company stores. To predict the impact of adding another store, McDonald's surveys customers at existing units. If customers are driving four or five miles and going out of their normal traffic patterns to reach the store, then it is likely a new unit might prosper.

Before Minuteman Press selects a new site it sends a research team to the area to check with the Chamber of Commerce and the post office. The staff determines how many businesses are in the community and if the area is growing. The company looks for sites in center cities or locations on the main streets of suburban towns near industrial parks. In towns, Minuteman locates near a bank or post office, buildings frequented by executives and their secretaries, who are prime customers for printing work. Since the quick printer's best clients are businesses, it avoids malls, which attract concentrations of housewives and children.

Franchise companies tell prospective franchisees that site selection is a difficult art that no novice can hope to master. The chains trot out pages of computer printouts showing convincing research. Site selection is crucial for the success of retail outlets, which is why many chains are conservative and choose obvious locations clustered near competing units. There are two basic rules for site selection: (1) the best locations are near the interchanges of major highways; (2) long secondary highways connecting downtowns with interstates and neighboring towns are likely sites for franchise rows. Having mastered these difficult principles you should be able to take a map of a strange city and pick the areas where franchised outlets will be concentrated. In nearly every city of any size in the country you will be greeted by franchise strips in the places you expected to find them. The problem in most cases is not finding the site—it is raising the money and developing the political muscle to get into the good locations. Prime spots tend to go to strong local or national businesses.

For the student of franchise site selection, Louisville, Kentucky, offers fertile territory. The headquarters town of Kentucky Fried Chicken, Louisville spawned a number of other franchise chains. Its strips, like the thoroughfares of most major American cities, are lined with representatives of the major chains. Holiday Inns and Ramada, Chi Chi's and Bonanza, Radio Shack and 7-Eleven are all here. In 1960 the Louisville area had a population of one million and two franchised fast-food outlets. By the 1980s the population was still one million, but there were two hundred franchised units and new ones were constantly being added.

Until the postwar period Louisville had been run by the old plantation families who had owned the basic industries: whiskey distilleries, cigarette factories, and steel mills. In the 1950s people from the farmlands of Kentucky began pouring into the city to work in factories that were opening. General Electric moved in and hired fifteen thousand people. International Harvester hired another fifteen thousand, and Ford took on around twenty thousand. Many of the new immigrants had entrepreneurial backgrounds. They had been traders in the rural areas, buying and selling hogs and tobacco, and they mastered quickly the ways of the city. Hundreds took the plunge into franchising. Louisville entrepreneurs started chains like Convenient Food Mart and Long John Silver's. They signed up for franchises of Kentucky Fried Chicken, enabling the company to set a record in 1965 by opening one thousand units in one year.

One of the immigrants was George Clark, a farm boy who began trading cattle when he was ten and borrowed money for the first time from a bank at fifteen. In Louisville, Clark sought to purchase a franchise. In 1960 he looked at Midas and McDonald's but lacked the money to buy either outlet. Working as a civilian for the Air Force, he was thirty years old, with a wife and young children and a net worth of zero. After examining many franchises Clark and a partner settled on Burger Queen, a chain with a dozen outlets. They paid five thousand dollars and promised to give 3 percent of their gross as royalties. Borrowing money, they opened up the store on Shelbyville

Road, about ten miles outside of Louisville. Clark had made a lucky guess. In selecting the site he had correctly anticipated the advance of the suburbs. "At the time the site was really out in the weeds," he recalled. "People who were developers knew that that was going to be a real hot spot for suburbia. You could see them dividing up these big fields. It was going to come but it was still on the very fringes of happening. At the time we were actually in the town of Middletown. Now Middletown is part of Louisville. They've grown together."

From the rising subdivisions, families in station wagons headed out for hamburgers. The Burger Queen prospered, convincing Clark and his partner they had mastered the fast-food business. Their confidence growing, they opened a second store, but the new outlet floundered, encountering competition from McDonald's and other growing national chains. For three years the Burger Queen partners struggled with the two stores, making about twenty thousand a year on the first unit and losing about the same amount on the second store. Then in 1965 Clark decided to give up competing against the emerging national chains. He moved down the road twenty miles to the town of Shelbyville, where Colonel Sanders had been based. In the small community Burger Queen had the market to itself. In 1965 the Shelbyville outlet grossed five hundred thousand, a huge sum for the time. Clark was on his way. Buying out the chain from the franchisor, he began opening stores in places that looked to be too small to support fast food. Some of the towns had populations of only twenty-five hundred, but they were in counties of twenty thousand. "We would try to be as close as we could get to the courthouse and the Baptist church," Clark explained. "Those are the two best locations in every one of those little towns. We were on Main Street or the highway coming in to Main Street." Burger Queen was the first fast-food company to enter Harlan, Kentucky, the depressed coal-mining area in the eastern part of the state that has been the scene of bloody union battles since the 1930s. Clark saw that people with money from the mines or even welfare could be sold fast food. His near-monopoly lasted a decade. The national chains ignored the small towns until the mid-1970s. The large companies concentrated on the richest suburban strips, where traffic was greatest and incomes higher.

Two decades after Burger Queen started its expansion on Shelbyville Road, the strip has been heavily developed. It is now lined with shopping centers, suburban subdivisions, and dozens of franchised outlets. In my exploration of the highway I was fortunate to have the assistance of Grady Clay, former editor of *Landscape Architecture* and a lifelong student of cities. In 1982 Clay was chairman of the committee that selected the Vietnam War Memorial for Washington, D.C. A gray-haired, engaging raconteur, Clay was real-estate editor of the *Louisville Courier-Journal* in the 1950s and 1960s. He watched the development of Louisville suburbs and chronicled how some people made fortunes during the move outward, while others had their lives badly disrupted.

In the 1950s the big development started around Louisville as business people of various stripes began buying up farmland to build housing subdivisions, shopping centers, and, in some cases, franchise outlets. "There was a tremendous rise in traffic, and that was attracting all kinds of pin hookers," Clay noted. "A pin hooker is a Kentucky phrase for a speculator who buys tobacco at the markets and carries a pin hook to stick samples on. It's a derogatory term for pissant, someone who's small and perhaps untrustworthy. The pin hookers and the big operators all were out there working the strips. A lot of people saw the strips as a great place for investment. This was when a lot of small businessmen with surplus capital—the doctors, lawyers, and lots of other people—began forming companies to get into the strips."

Farmers and people who had inherited small pieces of land had little idea of the rapidly rising values of their property. Some sold out cheap. A few made enough money to retire in style and send their grandchildren to college. Much of the action focused on Shelbyville Road. As Clay explained, the road extends twenty-five miles east from Louisville, heading toward the rich farmland of the bluegrass country, and ends in

Shelbyville, the seat of the next county. The highway was once a turnpike where market gardeners traveled, bringing their produce to the city.

We began tracing the highway at its origins in Louisville, driving along Frankfort Avenue, which runs parallel to the railroad tracks. On our right there were liquor stores, locksmiths, and local businesses that did not appear particularly prosperous. In this older, less appealing part of town there were few franchise outlets. The small businesses were jammed together with older houses. There was one Kentucky Fried Chicken. In this headquarters town of the company, KFC has more outlets than any other chain. Some are located on sites like Frankfort Avenue that are not prime territory. We passed used-car lots, an appliance dealer, and a small, unpretentious shopping strip. Then Frankfort forked right and became Shelbyville Road. Signaling the shift was a Midas outlet, a big modern facility. Across the way was a Burger King. We had left the seedier city territory and moved into the financially fresher air of the suburbs. The franchises had started.

We entered St. Matthews, which, Clay explained, was a typical suburban town. A bank occupied a building that was the site of a fast-food outlet that had folded, Clay noted. For the first time on our journey the roadside was not continuously developed. There were grassy areas along the highway, and houses and a church. As we moved out of the town there were larger businesses: a big Chrysler dealer and a Baskin-Robbins. Large signs announced the stores. In one small strip center there was a Radio Shack Computer Center and a few doors down a regular Radio Shack. We passed Long John Silver's, Pizza Hut, Godfather's Pizza, and Howard Johnson's. There was a Sizzler Family Steak House right next to a Ponderosa Steakhouse. Then we moved into grassy subdivisions. These areas are higher-income suburbs, housing Louisville's professionals and businesspeople. An old community along Shelbyville Road called Anchorage has an average annual family income of $64,000. In some stretches the houses were set back, separated from the road by grass and trees. "That frontage is controlled by the planning and zoning commissions," Clay explained.

If the zoning commission had not prevented some development, I asked Clay, would the road be completely filled with businesses? "Absolutely," he replied. The commission forced the strip development to remain in certain areas and it allowed the grassy areas to go untouched. In this way development along Shelbyville Road was somewhat controlled. The strip had areas of concentrated development where the franchised outlets congregated. Some amenities were preserved for the upper-middle-class residents. Limiting development helps maintain land prices; this tends to keep out marginal businesses. Most outlets on Shelbyville Road seemed to be well-kept local operations or big shiny outlets of the national chains.

We then headed for the second leg of our trip to observe a strip that, unlike Shelbyville, has gone largely unregulated. Dixie Highway is a notorious strip in Louisville, running thirty-five miles south of the city to Fort Knox. During World War II, when one hundred thousand people were stationed at the military base, the road was called "Dixie Die Way" because there were so many accidents involving drunken soldiers. There are still twenty thousand people based at the military post, and the road generates considerable traffic and money. "In World War II, I was stationed at Fort Knox and commuted back to Louisville on weekends," Clay explained. "At the time there was practically nothing here. There were a few farms and an occasional house. We would go for miles and see nothing but farms and woods on the high ground. As the traffic to Fort Knox picked up there started to be liquor stores, filling stations, and then other business. The franchising didn't really start until the 1960s."

For the last four decades developers have built whatever they chose along the strip. Dixie Highway runs through a poorer area than Shelbyville Road. While local pressure helped Shelbyville maintain pockets of suburban amenities, Dixie Highway is a confusing jumble of all kinds of businesses and residences. "When the strip was under intense development in the 1950s, the planning commission was chaired by a wonderful old gentleman, a country hardware dealer with this lovely folk wisdom and folk blarney," Clay recalled. "He just believed that anybody was entitled to do anything they wanted to do with their property, especially if they had inherited it or lived on it a long time. He was very persuasive. Mr. George Summerfield was his name, a wonderful old man and a delightful citizen of the nineteenth century. His attitude was reinforced by a local judge, who also believed that a man was entitled to do what he wanted with his property. This combination of a nineteenth-century judge and a nineteenth-century chairman meant that Dixie Highway became a most outrageous example of strip zoning."

Dixie Highway begins as 18th Street in Louisville, heading through a poor black neighborhood of rundown houses. It passes the huge Philip Morris tobacco facility, then heads by a string of ghetto businesses: a fried-chicken joint, a package store. The first franchise outlet is a Martinizing dry cleaner's, with bars over the windows and doors. Then 18th Street becomes Dixie Highway, moving past houses with grass and trees. A McDonald's located on a strategic corner in the suburban town of Shively signals the beginning of the franchise concentration. The strip is a hodgepodge, with national chains appearing in clusters mixed with local businesses. There is a Famous Recipe Chicken chain outlet and an A & W, then the local operations of Brownie's Used Cars and Cycles Unlimited. The businesses are mixed in with houses, many of them vestiges of the time before the stores arrived. There are remnant country houses that have been converted to offices and little shops. In some of the homes people still live as they have done for the last thirty years, when their property was surrounded by farmland.

Constant traffic feeds the Dixie Highway businesses. Industrial employment in distilleries and other businesses to the west of the highway provides surges of customers. Some people suggest Dixie has a bit too much traffic for optimum sales. During peak hours it is hard to stop and pull over. At the intersection with Interstate 264, a crucial highway node, there is a Holiday Inn and nearby the formidable chain presences of Captain D's Seafood Restaurant and Pasquale's. In one section there is Bojangles, Midas, McDonald's, and Kentucky Fried Chicken, all lined up next to each other. A bit farther on is a Wendy's, and a Taco Bell performing its mission of bringing Mexican food to Louisville. All of the outlets, local and national, brandish bright signs that leap out at a passerby, assaulting the senses, demanding attention.

As we drove, Clay pointed out that different jurisdictions administer various sections of the strip. The local jurisdictions were determined to squeeze out of the strip every cent possible in sales for businesses and tax dollars. "As you pass through each jurisdiction you'll see different things happening to the road," Clay said. "You have a sidewalk for a half a mile, then it stops and there's a different kind of sidewalk or none at all. The quality of the curbing changes. If you look at these things you will see that different games are being played with the road."

In 1937 Dixie Highway was flooded. Memories of the deluge depressed land values, and the low prices attracted developers. Later a levee was built to protect the area, but the floods still contributed to the road's low-class image. Today, with few zoning restrictions along the highway, land is plentiful and prices are lower than on Shelbyville Road or in the city. Builders are not required to provide amenities such as large parking lots or grassy spaces around stores. In this relatively low-cost environment, if a business fails, the owner can quickly fold up and then start up again a mile down the road. For the franchise entrepreneur seeking to build an instant chain, such a strip is a perfect location. The risk is relatively low, and there is sufficient traffic so that success is possible. On Dixie Highway businesses start and die constantly.

Heavily developed strips have not always been welcomed. As happened on Shelbyville Road, communities have sought to limit the growth of strips. In some cases there were noisy zoning battles. The ugly and dirty strips cheapened the image of a town, citizens argued. Spurred by a new concern for the environment, upper-middle-class suburban towns began banning flashy colors and large signs. Local garden clubs insisted that fast-food outlets improve their lots before building. Prince George County, in Maryland, outlawed construction of fast-food restaurants except in shopping centers.

In Oregon the state legislature has periodically struck at fast foods by introducing bills that would outlaw throwaway containers used to serve fast foods and condiments. The bills, introduced unsuccessfully in 1979 and 1980, were developed by environmentalists who pointed out that the city dump in Portland is nearly overflowing, and that fast-food restaurants were creating garbage problems.

In communities where there had been no opposition, concern mounted as more and more gaudy outlets crowded in. "A lot of these places say, 'We'll allow fast-food operations if they take the red roof off the building and make it neutral or if they give us a lawn out front with trees,'" noted Raymond Poelvoorde, president of Lippincott & Margulies, a consulting firm that has helped design outlets for Hardee's and Kentucky Fried Chicken.

Resort towns have been particularly firm in resisting the inevitable invasion of franchised chains. Aspen, Colorado, a haven for well-off vacationers, maintains tight guidelines on signs and keeps out some businesses. The town grudgingly permitted a Holiday Inn with the stipulation that only a small sign could be displayed. After observing the motel in operation, some residents began campaigning to close the outlet, fearing it was destroying the town's scenic atmosphere. A local Kentucky Fried Chicken store was shut down after residents complained that the greasy smell tainted the fresh mountain air.

The pressure to tone down outlets did not come only from civic activists. Franchisees were less willing to buy outlets that seemed in poor taste. As the price of fast-food stores climbed to over a quarter of a million dollars, more of the operators were prosperous doctors or investors. They were hesitant to tell their friends at the country club they owned an unsightly franchise restaurant. By the mid-1970s, the companies accepted minor compromises. The eye-catching designs of earlier days were no longer as important. With the increasing use of television advertising, the names and identities of the major chains had become so well known it mattered less how big their signs were. If Kentucky Fried Chicken or Burger King opened in a warehouse, customers would still come clamoring.

The fast-food companies accommodated regulatory boards in a variety of ways. To make units less conspicuous they designed exteriors that matched surroundings. On college campuses some chains adopted stone facades similar to those of nearby buildings. Near seaports they decorated units with nautical themes. Besides appeasing zoning officials, the efforts to give outlets more of a local identity appealed to customers who had found the standardized chains sterile.

In most communities fast food was able to thrive by making limited concessions. Companies kept flashy signs but covered exteriors with subdued shingles. Just as orange and red were once popular fast-food colors, the new vogue came to be "earth tones," shades of brown and gray that gave hamburger stands a more permanent feel and offended fewer eyes. Inside, the chains embraced the ski-lodge look, with hanging plants and natural wood.

Critics of the franchise outlets may be dismissed as elitists, self-styled aesthetes who do not appreciate the wishes of most people and the needs of capitalist expansion. But it is not clear that the harshness of strips is only a little harmless capitalist frolic. Lady Bird Johnson, with her highway beautification program in the 1960s, touched on the need for a clean environment. In recent years scientists have been exploring a young discipline called environmental psychology, where they have attempted to determine, among other things, the effects of the built environment on people. Does a glaring strip take a toll on the people who travel along it every day?

The humanist psychologist Abraham Maslow of Brandeis University conducted experiments indicating that the environment can affect an individual's mood, energy level, and ability to perform tasks. To test the effects of surroundings on people, Maslow placed subjects in three rooms. One room was "beautiful," one "average," and the third "ugly." The beautiful area was spacious, with large windows and comfortable overhead lighting. The ugly room was a small janitor's storeroom with harsh lighting and a clutter of supplies. The average room was a professor's office with battleship-gray walls and metal filing cabinets. Subjects were shown pictures of people and asked to say whether the person portrayed looked weary or zestful. Many subjects in the ugly room said that the people in the portraits looked fatigued and displeased. Subjects in the average and beautiful rooms on the whole took a more optimistic view of the pictures, saying they showed well-being. The examiners administering the tests in the ugly room showed signs of boredom, fatigue, and irritability. In the beautiful room they had feelings of comfort and pleasure.

It might be argued that Maslow's research should not be used in condemnation of strips. Beauty is in the eye of the beholder, and many people might find strips beautiful or at least inoffensive. However, Robert Thayer of the University of California at Davis and Brian Atwood found in a study what some might consider obvious: More of their subjects derived pleasure from roadside scenes of nature than scenes of typical roadside structures with billboards and businesses. The idea that ugly structures can have ill effects on people will come as no surprise to architects who have long believed this. In view of the work of the environmental psychologists, citizens should have an input into how strips will be developed. Businesspeople who make their livings by positioning themselves along public highways should be required to protect the public's psychological health. While few people may be driven mad by lines of pulsating outlets, the overwhelming impact of the strips surely does not contribute to motorists' peace of mind. Determining whether or not a business is unsightly may involve a subjective judgment. But zoning boards routinely make subjective judgments. In an effort to determine what best serves a community's interests, a board might consider testimony from environmental psychologists.

The harm done by franchise strips is not limited to assaults on the senses. Franchises have destroyed the local businesses that served as informal community centers and places for people to make contact. On the strip the customer is encouraged to drop in and leave quickly. When the fast-food restaurant replaces the neighborhood diner, and the chain hair salon eliminates the local barber, there are fewer chances for people to make casual contacts. This may be a minor side effect of franchising, but it can be crucial in the life of a city.

Contact with other people is vital for everyone. This is why solitary confinement in prison is regarded as one of the most extreme forms of punishment. Some psychologists argue that the most important requirement for happiness is having three or four close friends, people the individual sees regularly and who understand the details of the person's daily life. "An individual can be healthy and happy only when his life contains three or four intimate contacts," wrote Christopher Alexander, an environmental planner. "A society can be a healthy one only if each of its individual members has three or four intimate contacts at every stage of his existence."

Most friendships start between people who are in regular contact, so that the people meet a number of times without making any special effort to do so. A number of studies found that students living in dormitories liked the people best who lived near them. The farther apart students lived, even on the same hall, the less likely they were to be friends. Robert Priest and Jack Sawyer, writing in the *American Journal of Sociology*, reported on a study of male students at the University of Chicago. "Roommates were more liked than floormates and floormates more than men in the same house," they observed. "Roommates liked roommates in 92 percent of cases, while they said they liked those eight to thirteen rooms away 47 percent of the time."

Of course, people may have repeated contact with others who share no common interests, and no friendship will develop. But if people of common interests do not meet they cannot possibly start friendships. Informal connections in casual circumstances are crucial. "If contact leads to recognition, recognition to liking, liking to friendship, and friendship to social activities, then it can be said that contact leads to happiness," wrote C. M. Deasy in *Design for Human Affairs*.

Deasy aims his work at architects and planners, who, he says, can do important work in designing bus stops, building lobbies, and apartment laundry rooms to facilitate people meeting each other. The designers of franchise facilities clearly aim to reduce contact. The franchised hair salons or dental outlets set in strips or malls are designed so that the customers feel like strangers and do not establish regular relationships with workers in the outlets. Franchised fast-food restaurants and motels have made impersonal service a trademark. Franchise companies believe an impersonal atmosphere enhances profits, and they may be correct.

This raises a peculiar question: Do customers actually prefer more impersonal outlets? In an earlier chapter we observed that consumers are drawn to chain outlets instead of independents because of advertising and marketing. An additional factor in the appeal of chains may be that they help people *avoid* human contact. Christopher Alexander writes that in America what is often considered normal behavior is strikingly like schizophrenia. The schizophrenic withdraws from people and loses sight of dependence on others. Alexander suggests that many people withdraw when confronted by stress, too much information, and the need to make complex personal decisions without the support of traditional values. People shut out other people. They do not like visitors to drop in unannounced, since they prefer to be prepared to face guests. They welcome the chance to avoid conversation with waitresses or hairdressers.

The fast-food habit may do particular damage to the socialization of families and friends. College students now dash off to fast-food restaurants instead of eating in dormitories or with friends. Family members usually eat separately. When they go on a fast-food outing there is very little time actually spent sitting and eating together. In Bethlehem, Pennsylvania, I talked to David Amidon, a professor of urban history at Lehigh University who was voted the best teacher at the school by a class of alumni that graduated ten years earlier. A large roly-poly man, he sat talking in a sleeveless T-shirt. On his desk were several empty cups from McDonald's. Hundreds of Lehigh students travel several miles every day to get fast food, Amidon said. The professor, who is married and has four kids, said he eats fast food six or eight times a week, often by himself. Half his business goes to McDonald's. Despite his reliance on fast food, he feels reservations.

"Do you like McDonald's?" I asked him. "I must," he said. "I think it's a seduction that has some very negative effects on people. Families are weakened by the fact that everybody can eat at their own pace. When I was a kid I ate meals at home with my family. That's a good tradition. It builds families. Eating fast food has some obvious advantages as far as organizing your life. But I think there's no question it's undermined the solidarity of our family. I don't eat with my family as often as I used to. If I'm working at something at dinnertime and I'd really like to keep on, I give a call home and say I'll catch something to eat later."

By the early 1970s the national chains occupied most of the best locations on the suburban strips. In order to continue growing they would have to invade center cities and small towns. Chains had long viewed the inner cities as foreign territory. Cities lacked the crowds of middle-class children fast-food outlets required. Real estate downtown seemed prohibitively expensive and parking space scarce. When Dunkin' Donuts tried to enter New York City in the 1960s it did poorly. The chain's suburban success had come from mothers in station wagons taking home donuts a dozen at a time. Faced with New Yorkers who came in for one donut and a cup of coffee, the chain outlets floundered.

Despite the obstacles, there was considerable pressure on the franchise companies to enter the cities. The chains' appetite for growth had always been voracious. The more outlets sold, the more royalties flowed to the parent's corporate headquarters. In an expanding chain there were new opportunities for existing franchisees to open more units and for their managers to be promoted. When it became clear a company was not growing, morale dipped. Franchisees looked elsewhere for investments. Store managers defected to rival companies that seemed to offer opportunities for advancement.

Incentives to expand intensified for many chains. As the companies reached substantial size, many of the founding entrepreneurs sold stock in the 1960s. In one stroke they became wealthy and gained capital to build the companies further. The price for the infusion of cash was that, as publicly owned companies, the chains faced constant pressure to increase profits. Wall Street investors have little interest in past performance or long-range potential. What matters is the current balance sheet. If this quarter's profit is lower than last quarter's, the once-hot company will be considered an also-ran, and its stock price might fall. Of course, most American companies are expected to grow. But for the chains the pressure is particularly severe, since franchising's main appeal is that it promises rapid growth. And because the companies have attained such spectacular results, investors expect the show to continue. If profits climbed 50 percent last year and only 30 percent this year, the company's management must be slipping, the experts will say.

For chains the easiest way to increase profits is to sell more franchises. With growth possibilities slowing in the fertile suburbs, the chains found themselves focusing increasingly on areas that had once seemed inhospitable. The franchise companies did indeed face formidable problems in their march to conquer urban areas.

The squeaky-clean image the fast-food companies pursued became badly tarnished in the cities. While suburban stores sought to serve middle-class families in a spotless environment, the city units soon found that most of their customers were the poor and minorities. The new stores were dirtier and noisier than the original outlets. Restaurants designed to discourage loitering nevertheless became lounges for drug dealers and petty criminals. In New York and Chicago stores hired guards, and franchisees kept guns behind counters.

Unions, seeing the chains as exploiters of low-wage labor, picketed fast-food restaurants. Community groups, concerned that the charm of their neighborhoods would be destroyed by franchised eyesores, fought construction permits in zoning boards. New Orleans refused to lease or sell city-owned land to Burger King when it wanted to enter the French Quarter. When Gino's tried to replace a café in Washington's Dupont Circle, residents formed the "Ad Hoc Committee to Prevent Ginocide." The biggest target for the opposition came to be McDonald's. Around the country horrified community groups protested the arrival of the hamburger giant. McDonald's was singled out partly because it was the biggest of the fast-food chains. In addition, the company's powerful promotional campaigns, featuring All-American bands and cheery-faced young people, had proved effective. At a time when patriotism was at a low point in the closing days of the Vietnam war, for many people McDonald's came to symbolize all that was wrong with the country. Blacks saw it as a white company coming to exploit ghetto neighborhoods. In middle-class areas residents viewed the chain as a crass corporation willing to earn profits at any cost. Small businessmen complained that McDonald's drove up real-estate prices and pushed them out of neighborhoods. In Cambridge, Massachusetts, community groups howled when McDonald's tore down one of the city's two pre–Civil War Greek Revival landmark buildings. More than twenty other fast-food outlets opened within a four-block radius of the new store, transforming the section from a prosperous shopping area with a wide variety of shops to a fast-food haven.

In 1974 New Yorkers delivered a petition with ten thousand signatures to their mayor. The protesters argued that the fast-food outlets would encourage drug addicts to loiter on street corners and that hordes of hamburger eaters would scatter paper wrappings around the neighborhoods. The corner of 66th Street and Lexington Avenue was the site of what came to be a particularly fierce dispute, which reporters named "the Battle of Lexington." McDonald's tore down a funeral parlor and began working on the site. As had happened in other areas, the community greeted the construction with a protest. But this was no ordinary neighborhood. The 66th Street area is home for some of the richest, most powerful people in the country, including bankers such as David Rockefeller, network television executives, and Wall Street lawyers. Such luminaries were not about to tolerate a hamburger intrusion. Theodore White, author of *The Making of the President* series and a resident of the neighborhood, argued that the coming of fast food would ruin the area. He warned Ray Kroc in a letter that "the enmity of this community is not a matter to be taken lightly."

McDonald's abandoned the project in what was a rare defeat for the company. Elsewhere in New York and cities around the country, wherever McDonald's sought to build, communities could not prevent it. Relying on batteries of high-paid lawyers, McDonald's fought whatever legal obstacles communities imposed. The company would keep construction secret, often building behind bare walls. Workmen were not permitted to tell passersby what was under construction. By the time communities figured out the ploy and mounted resistance, the restaurants were in operation. For McDonald's, the costly move into the cities proved worthwhile. The stand built across from New York's Madison Square Garden set a company record soon after it was built, selling $190,000 in one month. By the fall of 1974 there were twenty-two McDonald's outlets operating in New York City. The hamburger giant was soon joined by an increasing number of chains, such as Kentucky Fried Chicken, Arby's, Burger King, and Dunkin' Donuts.

The chains, quickly exhausting the most obvious sites, began putting stores in locations previously unheard of. Fast-food outlets appeared in zoos, office buildings, and hospitals. In 1976 McDonald's opened an outlet in Chicago's plush Water Tower Place, site of the Ritz-Carlton Hotel, a Halston boutique, and other expensive stores and condominiums. It soon became clear that many of the customers in the swank seventy-five-story complex had never visited a fast-food outlet. "More than once," *Business Week* reported, "fur-coated dowagers sat waiting to be served, only to be told they had to step up to the counter like everyone else.''

Discovering it could be very successful in surprising places, McDonald's changed its criteria for locating stores. In the late 1960s new store sites had to contain fifty thousand residents within a three-mile radius. By the early 1970s the company had abandoned this rule. Since most customers stopped at the store in connection with some other activity, the chain began locating stores according to traffic patterns. Now it is common to see two McDonald's outlets within a few blocks of each other. In Milwaukee the company has one store in a mall and another across the street.

Announcing that there was no foreseeable limit to the number of outlets it could build, McDonald's aimed at smaller and smaller population areas. The company now enters towns of ten to fifteen thousand people, places that in the past had been thought too small to support outlets of the leading fast-food chain. There are more than ten thousand such towns in the United States, and most don't yet have a McDonald's.

Other chains have been designing special outlets for small markets. Burger King developed modified store models that franchisees can use to handle the lower volumes of smaller towns. Playboy, trying to develop franchised clubs in smaller markets, commissioned a design firm to draw plans for clubs that could be economical in towns such as Greensboro, North Carolina, and St. Petersburg, Florida. Half the size of the package offered in large cities, the newer design does not include a large showroom but offers more seating in relation to the total space of the club.

Everywhere outlets have become more concentrated. Over the last decade, Washington, D.C., has become crowded with fried-chicken chains. In 1981 *The Washington Post* reported a "fried-chicken war." The competition was particularly heavy in black areas of the city, where "it is almost impossible to make it down a mile or so of any major commercial street without encountering some kind of chicken outlet." In one stretch of Benning Road the paper counted a dozen stores. The leaders included Chicken George—a chain named after a character in Alex Haley's *Roots*—Church's Fried Chicken, Popeye's, Bojangles, and Kentucky Fried.

For many chains shopping malls offer ideal locations. By 1980 there were eighteen thousand malls in the country. The climate-controlled worlds of these enclosed shopping areas are populated by a wide array of franchise outlets, ranging from Athlete's Foot to Elaine Powers. Competition for places in prosperous malls is fierce, since strong sites guarantee store owners a healthy traffic flow and reduce the need to advertise. In the struggle to lease the best sites, franchised outlets have a decided advantage over independent operators. Mall developers, seeking proven businesses, favor the brand-name drawing power and financial resources of the chains. "Without a financial statement showing $250,000 to $500,000 in net worth, you can't get a lease in any major shopping center," Harry Nedell, chairman of Meineke Discount Muffler Shops, told the *Houston Business Journal*. "It's impossible. They don't even look at you. And they always want a concept they can count on."

Great Expectations, a CutCo Industries subsidiary, locates its unisex hair salons only in malls, since they attract the young, casual customers the chain seeks. "In a good mall our store is likely to do well," says Norman Bander, the company's franchise director.

The problem for Bander is to find the right mall. "If the mall is the first mall in a population area of seventy thousand or more, there is a good chance it will be a good site," Bander observes. "I cannot always be sure it will be successful, but it normally would."

New malls become focal points for their communities, drawing people into a fantasy world of waterfalls and brightly colored signs. Strollers buy ice cream cones and engage in shopping as a form of entertainment. By the 1980s most sizable towns had at least three malls, and the process of selecting the best sites began to be more difficult. In an existing mall Bander checks the sales records of stores and the rent. Most malls today have track records of several years. Few new shopping malls have been built in the last five years because of high interest rates, and Great Expectations has been finding its new sites as malls raise rents, forcing out former tenants. A Great Expectations needs around nine hundred square feet, a space that may cost about eighteen thousand dollars a year in a good mall. For the franchisee to do well, the store must gross about two hundred thousand a year.

Within the malls, companies search for the best locations. Most businesses prefer the main corridors. Failing to obtain the most visible spots, they will accept sites on arteries off the main corridors but near entrances. Fast-food companies often cannot win the prime sites. "Mall developers want food operators off main corridors, since they feel that food is secondary," explains Patrick A. Terhune of Philly Mignon, a sandwich chain.

One increasingly common solution for fast food's location problem is the food court, where a group of restaurants in a mall cluster around a common seating area. Facing companies such as Charlie Chan, Orange Julius, and a variety of pizza chains, Philly Mignon has been successful in the courts, which offer the food outlets greater visibility. The company leases court sites in cities such as Boca Raton, Florida, Pittsburgh, and Plano, Texas. For Philly Mignon, a small chain trying to expand into new cities, malls are the key to the company's efforts to make its name and steak sandwich well known. The first unit in a new city is usually located at a leading mall. "The basic strategy is to go into a mall to build awareness," Terhune notes. "Then we move to freestanding units or strip centers and downtown locations."

At the same time that the chains moved into malls and small towns, they also headed overseas. American highways might be clogged with outlets, but the booming markets of Europe and Japan were untouched by franchising's modern representatives. In 1968 Holiday Inns opened a unit in Holland, its first

European motel. The company invaded Japan in 1973, and the following year reached into South America. By 1981 the chain had 212 motels overseas in 58 countries.

Other chains hurried to join the rush overseas. In 1971, 156 U.S. franchise companies had more than 3300 outlets abroad, according to the Department of Commerce. By 1980 the figure had climbed to 279 firms with more than 20,000 outlets. There were more than 3400 outlets in Japan, 2000 in Great Britain, 450 in Africa, and 900 in Mexico. In 1980 the Department of Commerce sponsored a trade mission to Kuwait and other Persian Gulf states so that companies could locate franchisees. The chains making the trip included Kwik Kopy, Midas, and Wee Donuts.

Most American companies rely on native franchisees who know local laws and business conditions. Hertz sold franchise rights to Australia and New Zealand. The chain licenses Thailand to one of the country's wealthiest families. Malaysia went to a local auto company. The franchisees are subject to the same standards and must use the same signs as Hertz dealers in the United States. The companies have found many foreign investors eager to adopt the franchise way. CutCo Industries had no plans to enter Japan, since it knew nothing about the country's business or hairstyles. But when a Japanese entrepreneur showed up wishing to buy a license, the company gladly sold him the rights to open five units. The Japanese franchisee is required to use the same procedures as American CutCo units, though he will use local Japanese products.

Fast-food companies joined the charge abroad in full force. Giant outfits were determined to enjoy the same growth in Europe they had seen at home. Entrants in the overseas derby included Wendy's, Kentucky Fried Chicken, A & W, Shakey's, Pizza Hut, Dunkin' Donuts, McDonald's, and Burger King. While most American industries have failed to penetrate Japanese markets, fast food has established a solid Asian outpost. Young Japanese have embraced Western eating habits. In Tokyo more than one thousand stands sell hamburgers, pizza, donuts, and other American staples.

Kentucky Fried Chicken led the efforts to win over a nation raised on fish and rice. In 1970 the first fried-chicken outlet came to Tokyo, and by 1981 there were 324 stores accounting for $200 million in sales. The company recruited ninety franchisees, who now must spend around four hundred thousand dollars to open a new store. The chicken that has captured a Japanese following is identical to the American product, and the company's marketing program is similar to the U.S. effort. Kentucky Fried Chicken blitzes the country with about five million dollars a year of television ads. With American music playing in the background, the commercials convey the idea that this chicken was developed in the heart of Kentucky. In front of each store stands a life-sized model of Colonel Sanders, who is portrayed as a master chef. To be sure, the company has made concessions to the Japanese culture. Stores serve smoked chicken and yogurt as well as the Colonel's standard fare. When the Japanese balked at pasty potatoes and gravy, the chain switched to french fries.

Though McDonald's once trailed its chicken rival in the move overseas, the hamburger giant today presides over the largest foreign franchise empire. The chain's 1185 stores abroad brought in $1.3 billion in revenues in 1981, or 19 percent of McDonald's total. There were 155 outlets in Germany, 18 in Hong Kong, and 123 in Australia.

To expand overseas, McDonald's has had to educate foreigners about its system. Before the arrival of the fast-food companies, hamburgers in Europe had been aimed mainly at the cosmopolitan few who appreciated American culture. Although Europeans at first found the thin hamburgers strange, they were swayed by American advertising know-how. Thanks to its huge flow of profits at home, McDonald's could invest heavily in wooing the Europeans. However, a group of Swedish leftists proved difficult customers. In 1975 they greeted the opening of McDonald's in Stockholm by setting off bombs in two stands, as a protest against American imperialism.

When it arrived on the Continent, McDonald's had to train European suppliers in the mysteries of patty production on a large scale. Wary producers could not believe that any company would possibly require the quantities the strange hamburger chain said it wanted. Potential franchisees were also skeptical. While in America investors tripped over each other trying to win a coveted franchise, in Europe the company faced a difficult sales job. In capital-scarce England, few entrepreneurs were willing to part with a quarter-million dollars to sell what was considered an exotic dish. The idea of franchising itself was unfamiliar.

McDonald's persevered, however. At first, in order to meet company specifications, it brought in french fries from Canada and pies from Tulsa. Franchisees were trained in the company's standard production and marketing techniques. Managers from around the world were sent to Hamburger University, where they were indoctrinated in Ray Kroc's philosophy. To handle the students the training center was outfitted with translation facilities.

Wherever it went, the company brought Ronald McDonald to entrance children. The clown now speaks ten languages. In Japan he is called Donald McDonald, a name local customers can pronounce. But not all the familiar McDonald's trademarks translated well. Big Mac rendered into French became *Gros Mec*. Someone told the company too late that the name was a slang expression for "big pimp."

Holiday Inns also faced a bumpy journey when it traveled abroad. Ensconced in suites at their Memphis headquarters, company executives envisioned their great green and orange signs attracting hordes of travelers in exotic places around the globe. The world was coming more and more to resemble the United States. The formula that proved wildly successful in Pittsburgh would surely win followers in Paris. Holiday Inns began building precise replicas of its American units in the Common Market countries. Motel coffee shops served hamburgers. Ice machines were conveniently stationed. As it had done in Tennessee, the company selected roadside sites on the outskirts of cities.

But Europeans failed to appreciate the flower of American

franchising. From 1971 to 1975 the fifty-one European Holiday Inns lost $28 million. "There is no way a chap in Memphis can run a hotel in Europe," explained David Lewis, a Holiday Inns franchisee from South Africa, sent to Europe to straighten out the mess.

The motel chain faced formidable problems in adapting to a new environment. The first units were built in poor locations. European cities had not become dispersed like their American counterparts. Business travelers and middle-class families, prime motel customers, had little use for the suburban Holiday Inns. David Lewis, arriving to head the chain's European effort, was perplexed to find one unit situated at "the crossing of two roads that don't go anywhere." The motels themselves proved unappealing. Accustomed to uniformed bellhops bringing room service, Europeans were confused by ice machines, a bit of American technology that was not popular on the Continent. The standard American brick facades seemed drab to French and Belgian customers used to variety and regional nuances. For Holiday Inns labor costs in Europe seemed astronomical. The American company that relied on low-paid maids confronted strong European unions, who demanded higher wages and made it very difficult to lay off employees. The chain did make concessions to local demands, and by the 1980s it was operating profitably abroad.

Franchising has spawned a trade press in Europe. *World Franchising*, a British publication, carries success stories and news of chains that may remind an American of home. In the January 1983 issue, Prontaprint announced it was starting a £500,000 national TV campaign featuring a comedian named Dick Emery. It was the first instant-print company advertising on British TV. Emery was scheduled to play different print customers, such as a businessman who comes in looking for letterheads and a punk rocker who wants to get posters for a concert. Another *World Franchising* article told of a successful franchise entrepreneur tackling a new challenge. Ray Allen, who founded Kentucky Fried Chicken in Britain, had developed a concept for an orange-juice kiosk. "The kiosk is a giant seven foot diameter fiberglass orange, which opens like a clam," the magazine reported. "Sitting on its counter is an Orangematic 36 machine, which takes in up to thirty-six whole oranges per minute, and, in view of customers, automatically 'squeezes' out the juice. At the end of the day the clamlike kiosk can be snapped shut and locked."

The article noted that the first franchisee, an ex–sales manager in the textile industry, had opened in Blackpool, where he had taken in £927 his first week, selling standard cups at 65 pence and jumbo cups at 95 pence. The franchise costs twelve thousand pounds. Allen, who is fifty-four, met Colonel Sanders in 1963 and won the master license for Kentucky Fried Chicken for Britain, Europe, and Australia. By 1973 he had an interest in more than fifty company-owned stores and oversaw one hundred fifty franchise units. He sold out to Heublein and became a tax exile, moving to Jersey in the Channel Islands. He now drives around Jersey in a white Rolls-Royce bearing the license plate KFC 1.

In other news of note, *Franchising World* reported that a conference for prospective franchisees attracted one hundred companies to London, including Alfa Joule (an energy-saving system), Mr. Slade dry cleaning, and Oliver's hot bread and coffee shop. The French Franchise Federation held a four-day exhibit in Paris, where one hundred fifty companies exhibited, including La Boutique de marie claire and Midas.

As the American chains moved abroad and into cities, they began altering their buildings. Designed to serve the middle-class suburban families of the 1950s, the franchise outlets were changed inside and out.

Responding to customer complaints, Holiday Inns began redecorating roadside motel rooms. In an era when many people sought to express their individuality, travelers had tired of the standardized motel room and began to find the Holiday Inn room predictably sterile. Even franchisees—most of them millionaires—rebelled against producing uniform products. They wanted to invest in motels that were truly their own. "When I'm in San Francisco I want a hotel that reminds me of San Francisco," said Carman Robinson, a Holiday Inns executive, explaining the new attitude of customers.

Some franchisees added more tasteful furnishings. A few questioned the value of the Great Sign, symbol of the chain. Increasingly, Holiday Inns executives came to see that the orange-and-green marquee detracted from the chain's image. It might have turned away customers who associated the sign with matchbox rooms and soggy food, one executive speculated. Holiday Inns staff members joked that the garish sign was so out of date, it might qualify as a fashionable object of 1950s art. In response to these concerns, the company has begun replacing its famous signs with modern, energy-efficient models.

Fast-food chains altered their architecture only gradually. For the last three decades McDonald's did much to shape industry standards. The early McDonald's store captured the spirit of the cars whizzing by, streamlined fantasies of glass and metal. Made of glistening tile in red-and-white strips, the hamburger outlets were surrounded by wide asphalt parking lots. The golden arches jutted through the roofs before connecting to the ground. In the 1950s the sign in the parking lot proclaimed "McDonald's" in small letters, while the word "hamburgers" appeared in big type. Americans had not yet been taught to crave what would soon become their favorite food. And in the days before television advertising, the name of the company was still less well known than the product it sold.

In an age when cars were objects of beauty and excitement, customers were content to pick up hamburgers at the store windows and bring them back to their spacious vehicles, where the wide seats served as dining rooms. In winter, sales dropped as customers scurried up to the drive-ins and employees inside shivered as they handed out hamburgers.

In the first decades of the fast-food expansion, the chains paid little attention to the design of their drive-ins. Many companies were content to copy competitors' stores. Hardee's instructed its architect to create a red-and-white-tile building with big windows and a sloping roof—a duplicate of the prosperous McDonald's layout. As the fast-food industry became more crowded, chains began using the architecture of their stores to establish distinct identities. Companies chose bright colors or odd-shaped roofs in an effort to stand out in the roadside lines of competitors, each trying to win the attention of passing motorists. Pizza Hut relied on its bright red roof shaped like a Caribbean hut, while Burger King showed a picture of a jolly monarch. Such designs proved successful in the suburban franchise rows.

But by the mid-1960s the traditional fast-food building seemed inadequate. McDonald's and the other chains were now well-established businesses in the suburbs of large and medium-sized cities. No longer content to be seen as drive-ins, the franchise companies began altering their architecture, hoping to persuade customers that the fast-food outlets had become "restaurants."

In 1966 McDonald's opened a unit with inside seating in Huntsville, Alabama. The experimental operation featured a narrow counter with stools and a few tables. By 1968 the company had altered the pilot unit to create what would become the standard fast-food store for a generation. Borrowing elements from the drive-in and from the traditional small restaurant, the new McDonald's resembled the decade-old suburban houses that sheltered fast-food customers when they were not eating hamburgers. The exterior was solid brick with expanses of glass allowing approaching customers to observe the action inside. The enormous arches that once towered above the stores were shrunken and placed on the signs, vestiges of the drive-in era. The sloping mansard roof, a traditional French design, added a touch of dignity. Inside, the one hundred twenty seats offered patrons something of a sit-down restaurant experience.

Parents, tired of frisky children spilling food on car backseats, welcomed the renovated fast-food stores. Though the company at first did not mandate the new design, it displayed the sit-down store in television advertising. Franchisees who adopted the new image saw their sales dramatically rise. Still, some operators remained skeptical. Having grown accustomed to the regular profits old-style units produced, they clung to the original design, only gradually making modifications, such as adding brick facades or partly removing the arches.

The chains invested heavily in decorating a few important sites. On a corner in Providence, Rhode Island, Burger King renovated a men's clothing store built in 1876. Since the unit faces three banks, the company decorated the fast-food restaurant to resemble a bank during the 1890s. Instead of plastic booths, there are imported Italian chairs with velvet seats. Walls are covered with mahogany woodwork. The more comfortable seating has created problems. Customers linger longer than normal, causing management to request that patrons sit for only twenty minutes during lunch hours. A McDonald's franchisee spent a million dollars building a model nineteenth-century riverboat moored on the Mississippi River in St. Louis. Complete with smokestacks and sidewheels, it is located, appropriately enough, near the Gateway Arch, a site that attracts three million tourists a year. Opponents tried to block the store, arguing it would interfere with tasteful development of the riverfront area. The company proceeded at full speed.

Small chains, seeking to remain competitive with the major operators, followed the design trends. In the late 1970s Blimpie, the submarine chain, became concerned that its outlets did not look "professional" compared to the national companies. The Blimpie stores had been decorated in orange, brown, and yellow, striking colors that had begun to seem harsh and perhaps outdated. In addition, the Blimpie logo, which was designed to resemble a blimp airship, confused many people, who thought it looked like a fish and associated the stores with fish. To solve the problems the chain hired a design firm to create a modern look that would project an image compatible with wholesome sandwiches. Blimpie adopted a simple oblong logo, and the stores were redecorated with natural woods, hanging plants, and color schemes of dark green, yellow, and red.

For all the changes, few outlets would win architectural prizes. Like fast food itself, most franchise structures are designed by parent companies to be cheaply produced and easily standardized. Chains develop basic plans that can be used to develop hundreds of sites around the country. The end result of such mass architecture is usually at best a harsh, undistinguished box. The interiors of most restaurants are still dominated by gaudy menu boards and various promotional signs that give the impression of being in a magical fantasyland.

As the pace of expansion increased, chains developed ways to build units faster and cheaper. With construction costs climbing, companies became reluctant to build expensive outlets from scratch. Now they often renovate existing stores. When a pizza outlet fails it may be transformed into a fried-chicken store. Every town has a site that constantly changes hands, as one optimistic franchisee after another takes a chance. Relying on renovations it is possible to develop a substantial chain without actually building any new structures. Blimpie, whose sales are much lower than national chains', never builds new units. The chain tries to hold renovation costs to around fifty thousand dollars. The low price tag means Blimpie can attract franchisees who could not afford the quarter of a million dollars needed to build a major hamburger outlet. An increasingly popular approach for chains is to convert abandoned gas stations whose locations on busy intersections and wide parking lots make natural franchise sites. The fifty thousand service stations that have been closed in the last decade have become cheap alternatives for restaurants, muffler shops, and other outlets.

Some of the chains that do continue to build use prefabricated units. Besides cutting costs, this permits outlets to be built with dizzying speed. In 1980 G.W. Jr.'s, a chain serving hamburgers and hot dogs, set an official franchise record when it built an outlet in Austin, Texas, in six days. The company achieved this speed as a result of a special effort designed to beat the previous mark set by Hardee's, which had put up a unit in Atlanta in nine days. Materials were carefully organized in advance, and construction crews worked around the clock. Building faster and faster throughout the 1970s, the chains expanded their empires. They were becoming more dominant in their markets—and bringing new wealth to their shareholders.

Growing Pains

10

In the late 1960s, a wave of optimism swept Wall Street. Businesses roared ahead on what seemed an endless ride upward. The economists, it was believed, had finally discovered how to break the cycles of boom and recession that had long plagued the economy. Around the country many confident Americans observed that the drive to reach the moon and the campaign in Vietnam were both proceeding toward their goals.

Viewing the heady prospects, large and small investors began pouring money into stocks in the kind of buying binge the country had not seen since the 1920s. Prices for "growth" stocks skyrocketed to fantastic levels. Investment counselors bragged of doubling their clients' money in a single year. Sophisticated operators and small-time entrepreneurs compiled paper fortunes in a game where it seemed no one could lose. In this wild atmosphere Wall Street became infatuated with franchising, which was seen as a bright new industry. Prices of restaurant stocks doubled and tripled in 1968. Howard Johnson's and Holiday Inns were viewed with intense interest. The excitement over franchising did have some foundation: Sales and earnings of many chains were climbing at incredible rates. The only limits to growth seemed to be a shortage of low-wage labor.

But the joyride could not continue indefinitely. Franchise investors experienced the same mood changes that infected the nation's ghettos, college campuses, and military. They began the decade full of hope and ended the period disillusioned. By 1970 franchising's image was severely tarnished. On Wall Street millions of dollars slipped through investors' fingers, while around the country tens of thousands of would-be franchisees watched helplessly as their life savings vanished.

The optimism had started to rise sharply in the middle 1960s, when franchising had begun to make its presence felt around the country. Excitement about the industry was mounting. In 1969 a group of Harvard Business School students reported that forty thousand people a year were purchasing franchises, and 90 percent of the new operators were surviving. The figures were alluring indeed. Increasingly, the public was coming to see franchising as a pleasant path to a secure future.

New companies constantly opened, moving into every service business imaginable. There were franchises for tuxedo rentals, burglar alarms, and undertakers. An entire franchise economy was developing. *Business Week* reported that scores of companies were opening up to *service* franchise companies. Dean Roach, a Philadelphia businessman, quit running two franchise operations, Open Pantry and Mr. Grocer, to set up a company called Second Philadelphia Corporation, a name chosen for its respectable ring. The business located and developed sites for outlets and then helped with marketing. Other firms specialized in finding land, putting up buildings, or financing outlets. There were lawyers and insurance dealers who claimed expertise in franchising. Industry officials predicted the formation of giant franchise conglomerates, consisting of a range of food, lodging, and service chains—all franchised. The skills involved in running a franchise chain were the same whether a company sold fast food or leased equipment, the experts argued.

Compelling chain ideas, such as employment agencies and convenience stores, attracted investors, who rushed to plunk down their cash. In a few months a chain could be started, open a few outlets, and then begin selling stock. Wall Street investors, mesmerized by the promise of franchising, raced to grab the new issues.

In April 1965 McDonald's stock went on sale at 22½. The first day of selling the price rose to thirty dollars, and by the end of the month it had reached fifty dollars. McDonald's mustered its already considerable public relations forces to tell the story of the chain's financial success. Company officials spoke around the country, emphasizing that earnings were climbing at the rate of 40 percent a year. Staggered by the figures, investors made McDonald's one of the hottest stocks of the decade. Wall Street experts suddenly considered the hamburger company as solid an investment as IBM or General Motors. In 1968 McDonald's stock climbed to sixty dollars, an unheard-of price for a twelve-year-old company with only $50 million in sales.

In 1966 Kentucky Fried Chicken stock sold at fifteen dollars. Two years later, with 1500 takeouts operating, the stock had climbed to ninety dollars. Holiday Inns and dozens of other chains soon emerged as premier companies. Pension funds and insurance companies, the major repositories of the nation's wealth, began pouring funds into franchise stocks. At the same time heavy industry, the keystone of American prosperity, was attracting less attention. It would be more profitable, Wall Street was saying, to invest in hamburgers and motels than steel and airplanes. By betting on franchising the financial community accelerated a shift that would become painfully obvious several years later, when an increasing number of once-gleaming mills and factories began shutting down.

One way to attract investors, franchise salesmen discovered, was to name chains after celebrities. Franchising reduced the time needed to build a national chain, and using a celebrity speeded the process of developing a brand name. While most national companies had to spend millions for years to make their names household words, a chain named for a celebrity could win instant recognition. Companies rushed to sign on entertainment and sports stars. The list of celebrity operations included Tony Bennett Spaghetti restaurants, Fats Domino's New Orleans Style Chicken, and Mantle Men and Namath Girls. Though the stars lent their credibility, they generally understood little about the projects. In the euphoria of the time they had little or no conception of the problems their enterprises might encounter. Lured by familiar names, hundreds of small investors risked life savings on the new chains, many of them poorly conceived and underfinanced.

The South and Midwest became the spawning ground of many of the new companies. By 1969 there were thirty-four franchise operations based in Nashville alone. Perhaps the most ambitious of these efforts was initiated by John J. Hooker, a former candidate for governor of Tennessee, who was inspired by Colonel Sanders to develop a fried-chicken franchise. A high-powered promoter with a down-home manner, Hooker chose as his representative Minnie Pearl, the folksy star of the Grand Ole Opry, who was tired of her show-business career and enthralled by the franchising idea. Hooker persuaded Minnie she could promote the best chicken in the country and become better known for fast food than for comedy. "I had gotten to the point where most people get to after a while in show business," she later told a Senate hearing. "They are tired of the one-nighters, and they are tired of the continual pressure of making planes and making all the efforts that you make."

Providing Hooker with instant credibility, Minnie met every new franchisee personally and presented an autographed picture that said "I care." The rights to a Minnie Pearl outlet cost ten thousand dollars. By the end of 1968 Hooker had sold licenses for 405 stores. Within three years the total climbed to 1840 units. There seemed to be no limit to what the ambitious chicken salesman could accomplish. In a frenzy of activity he set out to build a franchise empire.

Hooker latched onto Mahalia Jackson to represent a roast

beef franchise that would aim at black customers. He planned a transmission-repair franchise and began a chain of day-care centers. In May 1968 Minnie Pearl stock went on sale; excited investors snatched up the new issue. Minnie Pearl was said to have a special method of preparing chicken that was certain to sweep the country. Although only a dozen stores were actually in operation, Hooker announced plans to open another thousand units. The stock began selling at twenty dollars a share and by the end of the day it was priced at forty. Eventually it would peak at sixty-eight dollars. The annual report for 1968 showed the company with revenues of $13 million and healthy profits of $3.5 million. But the good picture was achieved by some accounting that treated the money coming in from sales of franchises as current income—income that of course could not be realized in future years.

By the end of 1969, 263 stands were operating and only a few showed profits. To the amazement of hundreds of trusting investors, Hooker's company announced losses for 1969 of $30.8 million. In 1970 Hooker resigned to run for governor again. His Republican opponent argued with some persuasiveness that the chicken salesman had not demonstrated his reliability as a businessman.

Quickly the Minnie Pearl empire collapsed. The accounting practices Hooker employed—and other shady chains also adopted—came to be called "Minnie Pearling it," a phrase that *The Wall Street Journal* said may be the company's most lasting contribution to fast food. By 1970 Hooker's stock was priced at fifty cents, cheaper than his chicken, which was selling for ninety-nine cents a meal. In retrospect Hooker's dream of using chicken to further his political career may look preposterous. However, a few years after the Minnie Pearl chain failed, John Y. Brown rode to the governorship of Kentucky on the strength of his fortune and reputation derived from success at Kentucky Fried Chicken.

Not all the celebrity franchises vanished. Roy Rogers' Roast Beef and Edie Adams' Cut & Curl proved good investments for some. Still, in the late 1960s tens of thousands of operators

were wiped out in what was a major bloodletting in all kinds of
franchises. Companies that had rushed into businesses with
poorly conceived ideas disappeared. In 1970 alone, more than
one hundred franchise companies folded. After paying handsome fees for fast-food stands, franchisees discovered the parent company that was supposed to provide supplies no longer
existed. Some solid companies that later prospered overex-
panded in the feverish atmosphere, saturating market areas
with more outlets than could be supported. Lum's swamped St.
Louis with restaurants. Dunkin' Donuts sold units in Indiana
that quickly folded. Unlucky franchisees went under. The recession of 1970 made matters worse, drying up sales throughout
the economy.

Besides the more or less legitimate operators, thieves of all
stripes joined the rush to capitalize on the glamour of franchising. Many of the scams demonstrated impressive creativity. In
one ploy reported by *Dun's Review*, a phony company ran ads in
newspapers promising big profits for those who purchased a
license. Respondents were invited to bring their spouses to a
motel, where they met salesmen. The company representative
would inform an eager couple that the last license had just been
sold. In any case, he would say, the husband lacked business
experience, and quite frankly did not appear to have the management ability and intelligence needed to run a franchise.
Leaping to her husband's defense, the wife would protest. The
salesman would confess to having second thoughts, saying he
hadn't appreciated the couple's determination. Because of their
sincerity he would gladly accept a cashier's check. The investors would turn over the check to the salesman, who promptly
vanished.

Some of the largest scams were the pyramid schemes that
became something of a fad in the late 1960s and early 1970s. In
1972 *Business Week* estimated there were one hundred twenty-
five pyramids operating around the country. In these schemes
the parent company would sell distributorships to franchisees
who purchased the right to sell the dealerships to other sub-
franchisees. Like a chain letter, each new distributorship paid a

fee that was divided between the parent company at the top and the franchisee who made the sale. Eventually the pyramids collapsed when it was discovered that the companies sold few—if any—actual products. The heads of the company would be rich while franchisees at the bottom would have lost their savings.

In 1964 William Penn Patrick, a thirty-three-year-old former door-to-door utensil salesman, began Holiday Magic Inc., one of the pioneering pyramid ventures. Patrick claimed to have been passing by a garage in San Rafael, California, when he smelled an intriguing scent. In the garage he found boxes and boxes of fruit-scented cosmetics, which he promptly purchased. Instead of selling the perfume, Patrick chose to sell perfume distributorships, and he became a multimillionaire by building a web of franchises. Federal authorities who later investigated the pyramid empire were astonished by the complex maze of four hundred subsidiaries. Patrick's companies included Leadership Dynamics Institute, which offered a motivational training program for franchisees. Most of the subsidiaries consisted of a desk and a secretary.

A right-wing ideologue, Patrick spent half a million dollars running for governor of California against Ronald Reagan in 1966. He managed to poll 3 percent of the vote. In the course of his political career Patrick called for the hanging of Supreme Court Justice Earl Warren. Patrick was killed in 1973 while flying a World War II fighter plane.

Glenn Turner, one of Patrick's students, learned the business so well he went on to found what became the biggest pyramid of all. At his peak in the early 1970s, Turner traveled by private plane, surrounded by an entourage of forty regional vice presidents, area distributors, and hangers-on, who idolized him with religious fervor. The followers claimed the franchise operator had led them on the path to wealth. Like Turner, they flaunted their new prosperity. Flashing hundred-dollar bills, they drove late-model Cadillacs and wore white half boots, mink cufflinks, and loud suits of kelly green and deep violet. An eighth-grade dropout with a harelip, Turner started with a five-thousand-dollar loan from an uncle and built up an empire he claimed was worth two hundred million dollars five years later in 1972. At the time thirty-three state attorney generals were accusing him of fraud and thousands of franchisees said they had lost money in Turner's schemes. Faced with so many bitter enemies, Turner maintained a thirty-two-man security force and was constantly accompanied by burly bodyguards. This did little to discourage the legions of devotees.

Turner was a populist somewhat in the mold of George Wallace, though unlike the Alabama governor, the entrepreneur appealed to blacks as well as whites. The franchise operator had polished his approach while selling sewing machines among the poor blacks and whites of the rural South. He employed humility and self-deprecating humor to disarm customers. In 1967 Turner set up his base of operations in Orlando, Florida, near the future site of Walt Disney World, a likely spot for a business peddling dreams.

He began selling distributorships for five thousand dollars to franchisees, who would then sell subdistributorships to others for two thousand dollars. Turner sold hundreds of licenses before he settled on what product the company would handle. After reading that mink oil is the closest thing to human skin oil, he found a mink supplier and launched his Koscot brand of cosmetics. The distributor handled one hundred thirty mink oil products, such as Kleansing Kream and Nail Kote, which were sold door-to-door by "beauty advisers" who reported to the franchisees. One major problem was recruiting the sales staff. Since thirty thousand distributorships had been sold, the country was saturated. Thousands of franchisees went bankrupt, unable to recruit salespeople. Some state attorney generals accused Turner of fraud. With so many distributorships, the states argued, Turner had to realize his franchisees stood no chance of earning their money back. Turner promised distributors they would make one hundred thousand dollars a year, a feat the New York Attorney General later calculated would require franchisees in the state to sell fifty million distributorships in two years. New York won a consent decree forcing Koscot to repay 1604 investors. Other states carried out similar actions.

Turner won followers by speaking to groups in school auditoriums around the country. He traveled at a frantic pace, sometimes working in four cities a day, seven days a week. The "GO" (Golden Opportunity) meetings began with some of Turner's followers warming up the audience, explaining how the great man had changed their lives, leading them from financial insecurity to wealth. Then Turner would make his entrance, dashing down the aisle and leaping onto the stage as his supporters yelled "Go, go, go" and stomped. "I want to make everyone a millionaire," Turner would shout. "That's how much love is in my heart for people."

Speaking to his blue-collar audiences he would attack college graduates, saying that despite their educations many were not making much money because their heads were full but their hearts were empty. "The only reason you aren't great is because someone told you you can't be great," he would preach.

The frauds like Turner and the business failures of the early 1970s put a cloud over franchising. Potential franchisees and bankers began to grow leery of investing in the chains. The stocks of most of the sixty public fast-food companies began to decline. A dozen state and federal investigations began searching for remedies. A Senate subcommittee chaired by Senator Harrison Williams held hearings in 1970, calling a parade of famous people who had lent their names to franchises, such as Johnny Carson and Jackie Robinson. The senators also listened to experts and small investors who told tales of shady deals and questionable procedures.

John Y. Brown, head of Kentucky Fried Chicken, testified that people buying franchises were among the most gullible investors. Brown, who had probably sold more franchises than anyone else, noted that many franchisees had little business experience and sought outlets after hearing rags-to-riches success stories. "These small businessmen very often scrape up every dime they can borrow, beg, or steal," Brown said, "and put it all on one dream and hope of a franchise concept that very likely could have been misleading and misrepresentative and fraudulent."

Thomas H. Murphy, publisher of *Continental Franchise Review*, explained to the senators that many parent companies had been unprepared to handle the operations they built. He told the story of Dutch Inns of America, a motel company that sold seventy licenses in 1968 priced at twelve thousand dollars each. In return for the fee the parent promised to furnish the motel, staff the unit, and provide initial operating capital. The company incurred liabilities for furniture and supplies of about fourteen million dollars. Its financial statement showed assets of a quarter of a million dollars. For some of the unfortunate franchisees, this was their second loss at the hands of a questionable motel chain. The novice investors had recently purchased franchises from Congress Inns for twelve thousand dollars. Since Congress never managed to open, most of the franchisees lost their money and were left sitting with vacant lots. Dutch Inns salesmen, aware of the would-be operators' predicament, offered to help salvage the franchisees' initial investments.

Armed with evidence from various investigations, the Federal Trade Commission began seeking a way to clean up the industry. In 1979, after seven years of work and delay, the FTC finally issued regulations mandating that franchise companies disclose key information. At least ten days before a contract is signed, franchisees must be presented with a document that describes the business experience of the chain's officers, lawsuits against the company, and any previous bankruptcies. The company must explain all franchise fees and continuing payments an investor is required to make. It must reveal the number of franchises already sold and the number that have been terminated. If a chain wants to provide information on franchisees' profits, it must back up the figures with data.

It is not clear how effective the regulations have been. The FTC, which has a small enforcement staff, can prosecute a company only for failing to make a disclosure or for providing false information. By the end of 1981 the FTC had brought only three cases against companies and had four more prepared to go forward. Since disclosure documents do not have to be registered with the government, the FTC must receive a franchisee complaint before it can take action. But by the time an operator recognizes a fraud he will have already lost money and may stand little chance of getting it back. In addition, there is no law against franchisors' demanding outrageous conditions, such as high fees. If the franchisee does not understand the terms but everything is spelled out, the document is binding. A company wishing to sell stock at ten dollars a share must comply with rigid disclosure regulations tightly enforced by the Securities Exchange Commission. If the same company wants to sell franchises for fifty thousand dollars, its activities will not necessarily be scrutinized by any government body. Enforcement of franchise regulations appears to be on a hit-and-miss basis.

Although the FTC has no way of knowing how many companies are actually using franchise disclosure documents, the commission believes the regulations have been effective. In the first half of 1979 the FTC received an average of twenty-seven complaints a month about illegal franchising operations. By the first half of 1981 the figure had dropped to three a month. Asked if the rule has discouraged criminals, John Tifford, the FTC lawyer in charge of franchising, said that the same thieves are probably around but they may have moved on to new areas, such as land swindles. Tifford said it could be that the regulations have made his job easier but created problems for FTC officials in other areas.

One concrete result of the move toward regulation is that newspapers have come under pressure to screen franchise advertisements. In the 1960s, respected publications such as *The Wall Street Journal* regularly carried notices of companies promising annual incomes of fifty thousand dollars in return for an investment of ten thousand. Now the advertising managers of most major newspapers require some evidence backing franchise claims. Consequently, the ads have offered more modest rewards.

While the disclosure documents may have frightened off

some fly-by-night operations, they have also made it more difficult for the small company starting out to challenge the increasing clout of the established chains. If Colonel Sanders
were starting out today he would be forced to spend up to ten
thousand dollars on legal expenses and filing costs in order to
produce disclosure documents. This alone would probably be
enough to prevent him from attempting to sell franchises. If the
would-be chain builder did manage to scrape up the money, he
would then face the problem of explaining his complicated past
and shaky present. An honest man, the Colonel would have to
confess in writing that, yes, he had been involved in a business
failure or two in his time. And, well, he hadn't sold too many
franchises yet and didn't have much income. Meanwhile, the
established chain faces no such disclosure burdens. If the company's officers have a history of corruption and the operation is
about to go bankrupt, the chain has little obligation to provide
this information to prospective franchisees.

Unsatisfied with the federal rules, fifteen states have passed
disclosure requirements and enforcement powers for regulators. New York has enacted one of the toughest laws, though
companies with fifty million dollars in assets are exempt. Under the state's rules the signer of a franchise disclosure statement is criminally liable for any errors in the document. The
filing must be approved by the state attorney general before
any licenses can be sold in New York. By the end of 1981 the
attorney general's office had received three hundred disclosure
documents and had approved only about one hundred. Some
were sent back because they were unclear or lacked information, while one application was rejected because a company officer had a felony record.

The tougher New York law was prompted by the continuing
spate of franchise ripoffs. From 1972 to 1980, fourteen thousand
would-be operators in the state lost a total of forty million dollars to franchise companies. The largest of the schemes was Futuristic Inc., which the attorney general's office put out of
business in 1979, when it won a court order forcing the company to pay three million dollars to franchisees. Altogether

New Yorkers invested twelve and a half million dollars in the phony grocery company. Founded in 1973, Futuristic claimed to be a franchise business that would enable customers to order groceries over the phone. According to its promotions, the bogus company would open twenty-five warehouses around the state and run massive television campaigns advertising lower prices than those offered in supermarkets. After paying fees of a thousand to fifteen thousand dollars, franchisees would sign up customers on the plan who could phone in orders. The franchisees would receive commissions for all food purchased.

Futuristic salesmen recruited franchisees by stopping people on the streets in poor neighborhoods and asking if they wanted to earn fifty thousand dollars a year. Thousands said yes. They were told to come to "interviews," which turned out to be mass hard-sell meetings. Groups of fifty to four hundred people who attended the meetings were mesmerized by speeches touting the company. Over four thousand people paid Futuristic for the chance to represent the company. Most of the franchisees lived in the same neighborhoods. They found themselves tripping over each other trying to sell groceries that never existed.

The frauds and economic problems of the 1970s that bankrupted hundreds of investors may have provided franchising bad publicity, but for the strong companies the huge shakeout was a blessing. With much of the competition gone, the surviving chains could become more powerful than ever. Seeing hundreds of outlets fold, industry observers confidently announced the fast-food expansion had ended. Through it all, however, McDonald's continued to prosper, increasing its earnings by 30 percent or more year after year. Other rich chains showed similar progress. By the 1980s the strong companies had come to dominate their markets more tightly than ever. More and more the independents were falling by the wayside.

The trend toward concentration of wealth was hardly limited to franchising. In nearly every industry fewer and fewer businesses were taking larger shares of the markets. By 1965 the nation had 412,000 businesses. The twenty largest manufacturing corporations held 25 percent of all corporate assets and 32 percent of profits after taxes. In packaged consumer goods fewer large companies offered breakfast cereals, coffee, paper products, toothpaste, and shampoo. Much of this concentration could be attributed to national television advertising. Regional beers collapsed before the onslaught of the national companies. Budweiser and Miller did not necessarily offer better beer, but they did clearly mount powerful network advertising campaigns. Only a limited number of brands can be advertised on TV because the amount of airtime is finite—by 1974 one hundred companies accounted for 76 percent of network television ads.

To join the ranks of the elite one hundred, franchise companies must compete with the painkillers and cosmetics for increasingly expensive airtime. At most, two or three franchise companies in each field will be able to use network TV and gain the decided advantage it offers. The winners of the race to television become dominant. With three hamburger chains now using national television and each year gaining greater market shares, it is unlikely that a fourth chain will ever gain access to national TV unless one of the leaders stumbles and falls out of the TV ranks. Besides enjoying access to TV, large companies hold other crucial advantages. They can pay for the best sites. They can survive downturns in the economy, absorbing losses for a period that would kill off smaller companies. Large companies obtain loans more easily to finance expansion. All this helps to explain why the big grow bigger.

In franchising the growth was not limited to parent companies. A few franchisees were beginning to reach large proportions themselves. The early franchise salesmen appealed only to small investors seeking one restaurant or one muffler shop. Wealthy individuals had little interest in franchising; they had better places to put their money. As the chains prospered, doctors and real-estate operators began to express interest in what seemed to be a gold mine. People who had made fortunes in one franchised chain wanted to invest in new companies. To accommodate the wealthier breed of franchisee, the companies began selling packages of more than one outlet. An investor could buy rights to put up a certain number of restaurants in a particular city, state, or region. This big-money approach allowed chains to grow faster than ever.

When David Thomas began expanding Wendy's nationally he relied on area developers. Thomas was not interested in the small entrepreneur who dreamed of opening one stand in Brooklyn. The company wanted the substantial investor who could build one hundred fifty units covering the New York metropolitan area. Wendy's franchisees included Jack Massey, the former chairman of Kentucky Fried Chicken, and James Patterson, founder of Long John Silver's seafood chain. These experienced developers understood fast food. They helped Wendy's set records for growth.

The chain did not need to sell thousands of individual units in order to build a national system. By negotiating a few dozen contracts with developers, Wendy's blanketed the country in several years.

From its beginning in 1972, Century 21 hoped to go national quickly. Starting from a base in Orange County, California, the company sold area franchises for the San Fernando Valley, San Diego, and then five regions in Southern California. The license for San Diego originally cost only five hundred dollars, but soon the price shot up. The company's founders realized that the first regions were not large enough to permit truly explosive growth. So they packaged all of Northern California as one region. In its second year Century 21 sold an Arizona region, then Virginia, Florida, and Texas, hopping around the country trying for national coverage that would permit economical use of television advertising.

The holders of the regional franchises had purchased the right to develop their territories. But instead of building hundreds of new brokerages, they opened the regions by selling licenses to individual local operators. The company now has thirty-three regions. Local operators pay 6 percent of their gross to the regional franchisees. Then the regional offices send

15 percent of their take to national headquarters. By 1980 Michael Shinn, a local Century 21 operator in Denver, had expanded to run eleven offices with three hundred fifty full-time agents and an office staff of fifty. In 1979 he paid four hundred thousand dollars in franchise royalties.

From its headquarters in Roanoke, Virginia, American Motor Inns oversees an empire of fifty Holiday Inns located from Maine to Florida and in the U.S. Virgin Islands. With sales of $161 million in 1982, the franchisee is a substantial company whose shares are traded on the American Stock Exchange. American Motor Inns has a full-blown modern corporate hierarchy that features sixteen vice presidents, a training program, and an internal inspection operation. Corporate headquarters has a staff of eighty, including six computer programmers and operators. In 1980 the company spent ten million dollars on room furnishings, buying two thousand mattresses. In recent years, venturing away from its basic Holiday Inns operation, the franchisee built a Sheraton Inn and developed a growing business telephone division.

Like all franchisees, American Motor Inns must pass Holiday Inns inspections and constantly refurbish its units. A vice president who acts as liaison with the parent company is on the phone almost every day talking to Holiday Inns officials. He constantly asks questions about new regulations or seeks help with problems. Relations between the chain and franchisee are carefully structured, with particular executives overseeing certain areas such as real estate or reservations. But when American Motor Inns started, the communication channels were hardly formalized.

In the early 1950s Adolph and Joel Krisch, struggling to turn profits from a pawnshop in Roanoke, Virginia, decided they needed to start a more promising business. At the time the interstate highway system was being built, and the brothers resolved to tie their future to the spreading ribbons of concrete. The Krisches discussed business possibilities such as selling concrete or producing industrial road equipment. But with no manufacturing experience and little cash, they settled on building a motel. "When we decided to go into the hotel business, I took a twenty-five-hundred-mile drive to towns comparable to Roanoke," Adolph recalls. "We took pictures of hotels. We measured rooms and so forth. Coming through Bessemer, Alabama, I saw this Holiday Inn and I was very impressed with it."

With seventy-five rooms, the Alabama hotel was bigger than anything Adolph had seen. Inquiring about the owners, he contacted Holiday Inns' Memphis headquarters. In 1956 the company's franchise system was not yet organized, and Adolph had trouble persuading a Holiday Inns representative to come to Roanoke, which was farther north than the company had gone. The would-be franchisee convinced the company to sell him a license for the seventeenth Holiday Inn in exchange for a three-thousand-dollar note. The struggling young chain accepted the IOU, then forgot about it. Three years later Adolph reminded the parent and paid off the debt.

Krisch is not proud of his first motel. "It looked like shit," he explains.

The small brick unit Adolph and Joel built could never meet the standards the company later imposed. Since the motel had no restaurant, Adolph would visit the grocery store every morning to buy donuts, coffee, and orange juice, which he gave free to guests. Faced with little competition, the unit immediately thrived. "Everything in this world is luck and timing," Adolph sermonizes. "We happened to be very lucky. We got into this at exactly the right time."

In 1960 the Krisch family opened a second motel in Roanoke, downtown near the civic center. From 1962 to 1967 the brothers built motels one after another. The family won the exclusive rights to develop Holiday Inns in Baltimore, where the company eventually built eleven units. In one thirty-six-month period they developed fifteen units. "Don't ask me how I did it; I was younger then," Adolph observes. "In the beginning my brother and I did everything. We were the personnel department, the buyers, and site selectors. We did all the financing. When we needed help we hired people."

The brothers scouted out sites and bought lots only when

both agreed enthusiastically. If one partner had mixed feelings they passed up the property. In this way if a motel failed both would share the blame. Since the Krisch brothers' Holiday Inns were located so that they were clearly visible to drivers on the increasingly crowded highways, most sites produced handsome profits.

During the years when the Krisch family expanded out from its Virginia base, other Holiday Inn owners were also building empires. In 1981 the chain listed twenty-four large franchisees that together owned 354 motels. Among the biggest were Brock Hotel Corporation, with fifty units, and United Inns, which owned thirty-seven.

For the ambitious franchisee, ownership of a chain can be a way to move into a bigger league. The operator can use the profits pouring in from secure franchised units to build a new business. Collins Foods, a company little known outside the restaurant industry, is one of the largest franchisee companies, with $265 million in sales in 1981. It is the biggest Kentucky Fried Chicken franchisee, with 231 outlets, and it also owns Sizzler Family Steak Houses, a chain of 137 company-owned outlets and 341 franchised units. The Kentucky Fried Chicken outlets are concentrated in California, Florida, Illinois, and Australia. Revenues from the chicken stores helped build the steak operation. Jim Collins, chairman and founder of the company, has been a fast-food pioneer, developing ideas for inspections and manager incentive programs that have been adopted throughout the industry.

Collins opened the Hamburger Handout self-service drive-in in 1952 in Culver City, California. In 1960, he obtained a franchise from Colonel Sanders with the idea of selling take-home chicken along with the hamburgers. When it became clear the two products did not mix, Collins focused exclusively on chicken. In 1962 Collins became the Colonel's franchise agent in Southern California, selling licenses to investors and developing some outlets himself. Altogether the former hamburger merchant helped build more than two hundred forty chicken units on the West Coast.

In the shifting world of the chains, it is not uncommon for a company like Collins Foods to wear more than one franchise hat. Shoney's, one of the richest fast-food operations in the country, has at various times been a franchisee, a subfranchisee, and a parent of a chain. With sales of $383 million in 1983, the company is one of the most profitable restaurant operations, highly regarded by Wall Street analysts for its solid record of steady expansion through periods of poor economy and rising hamburger prices. In 1984 Shoney's owned or franchised 1084 restaurants in states stretching from Pennsylvania to Florida and west to New Mexico.

For two decades the mainstay of Shoney's was Big Boy, the hamburger operation now owned by Marriott. Big Boy was founded as a loose-knit franchise chain, where operators were required only to use quality products and serve the double-decker Big Boy hamburgers. Along with the words "Big Boy," franchisees could display their own names on store signs. In 1953 Alex Schoenbaum founded Shoney's Big Boy, a franchisee with rights for ten states, centered in West Virginia. Ray Danner, a drive-in movie theater owner whose business was killed by TV, became intrigued with the curb service Big Boy offered. In 1959 Danner bought from Schoenbaum the right to open several Shoney's Big Boys in Nashville. An aggressive entrepreneur, Danner was not bound by tight regulations that would stifle later franchisees. He soon outstripped the company that had sold him the license. For Danner's first Big Boy he bought a slightly used restaurant with 175 seats, located in front of a shopping center. He added a drive-in area, making the outlet an unusually large Big Boy. To fill the place he started luncheon specials featuring two choices of meat and six vegetables. Adding steak and baked potatoes, he opened more units and fully developed his territory in middle Tennessee. In 1966, unable to acquire more Shoney's territory, Danner bought the rights to franchise Kentucky Fried Chicken in Louisville. Seeking to grow faster, Danner sold stock in his company in 1969, and the same year he started a chain of his own, called Mr. D's.

While Danner pushed ahead, the original Shoney's company

stagnated. By 1971 it became clear that Alex Schoenbaum was in trouble. To save the struggling operation, he merged with Danner Foods. Having taken control of Shoney's ten-state Big Boy territory, Ray Danner began adding more outlets. In 1975 Mr. D's was changed to Captain D's, with an emphasis on seafood. The new chain grew rapidly, and by 1980 it boasted more than 330 outlets, compared to 320 for Shoney's.

By the early 1980s Danner began to feel limited by his franchise territory. Opening coffee shops called Shoney's that did not bear the Big Boy name, he moved into areas licensed to other Big Boy operators. After a Big Boy franchisee sued to stop the expansion, Shoney's relinquished its Big Boy franchise. The Shoney's name had become more valuable than Big Boy's, Danner believed. "No one says they're going to Shoney's Big Boy Restaurant; they say they're going to Shoney's," Danner told *The New York Times.*

Large companies, always on the alert for takeover targets, began eyeing chain operations in the late 1960s, when franchising was a darling of Wall Street. Buying an established fast-food or auto-service chain offered easy entry to rapidly growing markets. By selling out, franchise chain owners reaped instant, enormous fortunes. For the owner who came from a poor background and had started his business on a shoestring, selling to a corporation was a fantasy come true. After pocketing the cash, a few of the entrepreneurs stayed on to manage the companies for the new corporate owners. Some became disillusioned as they saw their creations become sterile copies of the original businesses.

Kentucky Fried Chicken was one of the first major franchise operations acquired by a corporate buyer. In 1971 Heublein purchased the fried-chicken chain for $280 million worth of stock. The largest share of the money went to John Brown and Jack Massey, who bought the company from Colonel Sanders in 1964 for two million dollars plus stock. The Colonel, who no longer owned any stock in the company, grumbled that he had been shut out of the richest gravy. Heublein seemed likely to help the chain expand faster than ever. The corporation had proved itself a powerful marketer, running strong campaigns that had helped make its Smirnoff vodka and A-1 Steak Sauce leading brands.

Delighted with the sale, Brown remained with the chain. Soon he resigned, though, as he became disillusioned with the company. An entrepreneur, Brown had prided himself on providing incentives to company employees, allowing them to participate in the excitement of building up the chain. The new corporate owner installed a regimented operation, ending the system of bonuses that had allowed area managers to make as much as ninety thousand a year. "Heublein turned it into a cold, insensitive business," Brown complained to *Forbes*. "I found professional management people very distasteful—they were always having meetings and never deciding anything."

One after another, fast-food chains were acquired. Since the giant corporations had no interest in swallowing small businesses, they made bids only for mature chains that had already eliminated much of their competition. The hamburger and chicken companies were the first to reach tantalizing size and be snapped up. Then pizza and Mexican chains, later generations of franchise companies, grew and were purchased. Food-processing giants particularly sought to enter fast food. Giant companies who already exercised enormous control over food supplies gained even more power. Sales of products such as bread and breakfast cereals were no longer growing rapidly. In fact, grocery stores were losing sales to fast-food chains. Rather than fighting the expanding restaurant companies, the food processors elected to take them over. Pillsbury bought Burger King, while General Foods acquired Burger Chef and United Brands purchased A & W. Pepsico bought both Pizza Hut and Taco Bell. Royal Crown swallowed Arby's.

The corporate acquisitions were not limited to fast food. IC Industries purchased Midas, and Imperial Group Limited of Britain bought Howard Johnson's. TWA purchased Century 21 and Dunhill Personnel System. For good measure the airline spent eighty million dollars to buy Spartan Foods, Hardee's largest franchisee, which operates two hundred forty outlets.

With these acquisitions TWA hoped to enter stable consumer businesses that would provide earnings growth during periods when the airline business sagged. Franchise chains that remained independent went on buying binges themselves. Holiday Inns acquired Perkins 'Cake & Steak, a franchise chain with three hundred seventy-five outlets in thirty states. In a move that was controversial within the company, the motel chain invested three hundred million dollars in purchasing Harrah's, the only casino company with a stake in all four U.S. gambling centers: Las Vegas, Reno, Lake Tahoe, and Atlantic City. Kampgrounds of America bought Sir Speedy, a printing company. H & R Block, having already saturated the country with tax offices, bought Personnel Pool of America, an employment agency supplying temporary nurses.

Chains that are already strong as independents become more powerful after they are acquired by conglomerates. By joining a giant corporation the franchise company can obtain access to larger supplies of cash. It will have a clear advantage battling against independent chains. The new corporate owner may decide to spend heavily on television advertising or promotions. This puts pressure on the franchise founder who resists selling out. As more franchise companies have become parts of conglomerates, life has become more difficult for small chains. Entrepreneurs must face competitors that are divisions of giant multinationals. Just as the independent motel has been forced to affiliate with a chain, the independent chain is being pushed to join a larger entity. The recessions of the 1980s may have accelerated the trend of mergers. Large companies are better able to survive periods of sluggish economy and high interest rates. For the troubled small competitor, merger is an attractive route to financial health.

In a market dominated by giants it becomes more difficult to begin new franchise ventures. Bankers are reluctant to finance someone embarking on a campaign against billion-dollar companies. The survival rate of such new projects is tiny. The large corporations themselves rarely attempt new franchise chains— they leave this work to restless entrepreneurs who are willing to take huge risks. The corporations seek to acquire a proven product rather than gambling on an uncertain commodity. In markets such as motels and restaurants, fewer and fewer new entrants survive.

Large companies do face risks in acquiring franchise chains. The rapid growth a young operation achieves may not continue indefinitely. As a chain covers the entire country, it becomes progressively more difficult to expand at a high rate. While it may be possible for a chain with thirty units to grow 30 percent a year, it is difficult for a chain with three thousand units to expand 30 percent annually. After acquiring Pizza Hut, Pepsico struggled to maintain the chain's incredible growth record. Some large companies were ill-equipped to manage a fast-food chain. General Foods found itself sailing in unfamiliar waters as its Burger Chef company stagnated. To its shareholders' dismay, Heublein discovered that selling chicken was a very different business from promoting vodka. Under the wealthy corporation's rigid guidance, Kentucky Fried Chicken outlets deteriorated. Morale of managers declined. Earnings of the once highly profitable company slipped. After receiving drubbings in the marketplace for several years, Heublein sharpened its operation and watched the company again achieve fat earnings. In 1982 Heublein was itself acquired by a larger company, R. J. Reynolds.

The rise of national businesses has sharply altered the economies of small towns, draining their investment capital. With the increase in automobiles in the 1950s and 1960s, many small-town businesses faced competition from operations outside their local areas. People might travel thirty miles to deposit money in larger banks. The advance of K mart, Kentucky Fried Chicken, and regional banking meant that small businesses could not count on local support. "The small towns were transformed into vassals of the larger cities," said Grady Clay, the former editor of *Landscape Architecture*. "The first casualty in this process is a lessening of local venture capital. The surplus that might have gone into local businesses gets pulled off into distant owners. A sizable portion of the profits that would go to locally owned business now go to outsiders," observed Clay, who has watched many local business people go bankrupt over the years as outside businesses take their places.

Just as franchise companies take profits out of communities, sending the money to shareholders and central management, the chains also take away political power. In an era when money buys votes, those who control corporations influence politicians. The chains have grown increasingly skilled in manipulating the levers of political power. That franchising has managed to avoid strict federal regulation after years of scandal and losses by investors is a tribute to the tough lobbying powers of the International Franchise Association. A cousin of the National Rifle Association and other Washington lobbying groups, the IFA in its own limited area is an unchallenged force. With a budget of one and a half million dollars and a staff of twenty, the association protects the interests of three hundred eighty-two of the largest franchise companies. By all accounts it loses few political battles.

William Cherkasky, the executive vice president who directs the IFA, is a savvy Washington veteran, having spent fourteen years on Capitol Hill, first as administrative assistant for former Senator Gaylord Nelson, Democrat of Wisconsin, and then as executive director of the U.S. Senate Select Committee on Small Business, which reviewed franchise regulations. Although he worked for a liberal Democrat, Cherkasky impressed the franchise organization with his aggressiveness and was hired in 1981. Cherkasky, who ran his own business in Wisconsin before coming to Washington, said he supports franchising because it enables small-business people to survive. "The tragedy of small business is that eight times out of ten any small business started today will be out of business in five years," he noted. "The competition is fierce for small businesses. They are shilly-shallied around by the government. They don't have economic buying power. They don't have national advertising. They don't have anything."

Franchising is an alternative, he said, although he did not pause to consider that the growth of chains may be a reason why life is so difficult for the small-business person. Few Washington lobbyists are as sanguine as Cherkasky about their areas of concern. Asked if there was any pending legislation troubling his organization, Cherkasky said no. "We really don't have any major concerns," he said. "The FTC has been very helpful to us. They are favorably disposed to our way of doing business."

The IFA's staff includes lawyers and lobbyists who monitor legislation and quickly react to the first sign of a bill affecting franchising. They testify at hearings, talk to regulators, and raise money for election campaigns. In 1978 Representative Abner Mikva, a Democrat of Illinois, introduced legislation that would limit the power of franchisors by forcing them to show cause before terminating licenses to franchisees. Under many franchise contracts the company can throw out a franchisee who has built up the business. Then the company is free to take over a lucrative outlet. Mikva and his cosponsors faced heavy lobbying pressure. In 1979 Mikva told PBS that the franchise companies had been spending a "barrelful of money in election campaigns" to defeat the legislation. "Last time they were very heavily in my district as they were in many others of my cosponsors," he said. Mikva retired from the House to the security of a federal judgeship, and the push for legislation was abandoned.

Franchising Political Action Committee, the IFA's fundraising organ, is careful to reward its friends. In 1980 Representative James Scheuer of New York was the PAC's largest recipient, with a donation of sixteen hundred dollars. In 1982 he was given a thousand dollars. As chairman of the House Subcommittee on Consumer Protection and Finance, Scheuer was responsible for franchise legislation. Speaking at the IFA's annual convention in 1980, the Congressman said the FTC regulations need not be tougher and denounced the Mikva bill. The existing franchise rules are "entirely consistent with a careful, limited view of regulation," he told the group. Scheuer has proved an outspoken ally, introducing legislation for International Franchise Day. "Franchising's contribution has been one of consistent quality and service offered by individuals strong enough to work and free enough to dream," he noted in his resolution.

The IFA PAC distributed only $14,050 for the 1982 elections, but the association's power was magnified, since individual franchise companies make donations. The Holiday Inns corporation gave $24,950. Holiday Inns franchisees donated $67,000. The franchisees' largest contribution went to Orrin G. Hatch, the conservative Republican Senator from Utah who received four thousand dollars and is perhaps franchising's favorite legislator. McDonald's contributed $125,385. Hatch again was the most loved recipient, with five thousand dollars. Hardee's contributed $9,525 to the democratic process. Jerrico, the parent of Long John Silver's, offered $28,250, including a high contribution of two thousand dollars to the Hatch reelection effort. Southland, parent of 7-Eleven, gave $24,058. Days Inns of America Civic Responsibility Group donated sixteen hundred dollars to several representatives of the chain's home state of Georgia.

Having silenced opponents in Washington, the IFA has done most of its lobbying lately in states where a series of bills has been introduced to protect franchisees and limit the power of franchisors. When a troublesome bill appears, the IFA begins its lobbying by sending a letter to the chairman of the committee considering the bill or the state attorney general. In some cases legislators agree to withdraw the bill or make an amendment. If the recalcitrant legislators persist, the IFA calls up member companies in the state and prevails on them to testify or reason privately with the politicians. "Say the bill is in Texas," Cherkasky explained. "If we can't reach an informal agreement, then we go to our members like Radio Shack and 7-Eleven and tell them we need them to call the chairman and the members of the committee. If they do that and we still don't get any action we hire a lobbyist who knows his way around the legislature. In most cases a simple phone call or a visit by our staff to two or three people in the state capital is enough to make sure no damage is done."

Cherkasky then ticked off the states where he recently set

aside attempts at franchise regulation bills. "Texas we just finished. Connecticut we just finished. Massachusetts we're done with. California we're almost finished. We found compromises or we got the bills withdrawn or killed. We didn't lose any."

Part of the reason for the success of the IFA lobbying effort is that in many cases the people seeking franchise regulation are largely unorganized. Prospective franchise buyers and consumers do not have tightly structured, well-financed lobbying groups. While IFA representatives make appointments with state officials, the interests of the other side may go unrepresented. If small-business people get pushed around by government, as Cherkasky observes, it is partly because large corporations want it that way.

The IFA confines its lobbying activities to legislation that is specifically related to franchising. The organization leaves lobbying on matters that affect its members, such as the minimum wage, to other groups, such as the National Restaurant Association, which disbursed $109,250 in 1982. In 1978 the National Restaurant Association received some political fund-raising assistance from Colonel Sanders, an entrepreneur who fumed at government interference. Under the Colonel's name the NRA sent a letter saying, "What you need—what all of us in the food-service industry need—is a whole new batch of Congressmen! Legislators who understand the problems of businessmen today . . . Elected officials who believe, as you do, in the American system of free enterprise."

The minimum-wage lobby came close to achieving a major goal in May 1972, when the House of Representatives passed what some called the "McDonald's bill," which instituted a subminimum wage. Under the legislation employers could hire sixteen- and seventeen-year-olds as well as full-time students for 80 percent of the minimum wage. Fast-food chains lobbied hard for a measure that would be a major windfall for employers of teenagers. President Nixon backed the bill, calling it anti-inflationary. The AFL-CIO replied convincingly that minimum wages were hardly the cause of inflation. The Senate rejected the measure and it never passed. Franchising's most famous political involvement came in 1972, when Ray Kroc of McDonald's gave the Committee to Re-elect the President a sum that Jack Anderson reported to be $255,000. The donation made Kroc one of Nixon's biggest contributors and won the hamburger magnate an invitation to a White House dinner, where guests included such important business executives as Henry Ford.

In the Senate Watergate hearings, Maurice Stans, of the Committee to Re-elect the President fame, testified that he had visited Kroc in Chicago for about forty-five minutes. He suggested that McDonald's chairman make the donation. After the contribution became known, critics charged that McDonald's had received other favors besides a free White House dinner. In 1971 McDonald's raised the price of the Quarter-Pounder from fifty-three to fifty-five cents, and the Quarter-Pounder with cheese from fifty-nine to sixty-five cents. The company did this at a time when the Nixon administration had adopted price controls. Shortly after the hamburger chain's move, the Price Commission of the Cost of Living Council ordered the increases rolled back. McDonald's fought the order. In September 1972 the Price Commission reversed itself, permitting the increase. For the company this represented a victory that could bring millions in added profits.

Congressman Benjamin Rosenthal of New York charged that the Price Commission had favored the hamburger company because of the political donation. Rosenthal said that the hamburger deal, like the IT&T scandal, was an instance in which the Nixon administration gave special treatment to a corporate contributor. In March 1974, special Watergate prosecutor Leon Jaworski included Kroc's gift in his investigation of illegal political activities. The House Judiciary Committee decided to drop the question from the impeachment hearings. The incident did make clear that the franchise company had taken its place among the ranks of the nation's most influential companies.

Kroc denied any wrongdoing. In his autobiography, *Grinding It Out*, he expressed regrets about the donation. "There's one other mistake I made that I mention only because so many jack-asses have brayed about it. That was my $250,000 donation to President Nixon's campaign in 1972. I let myself be talked into that by Nixon's fund raiser, Maurice Stans, and it wasn't until later that I realized I had made the contribution for the wrong reason. My motive was not so much pro-Nixon as it was anti–George McGovern. I should have known at the time that this went against my rule of not trying to make a positive out of a negative action. The worst thing about the donation was the subsequent implication by some sons of bitches that I made it in order to get favorable treatment from the federal price commission in regard to the price of our Quarter-Pounder. As my friend and lawyer, Fred Lane, says, 'This has been thoroughly investigated by the Watergate Select Committee, the Government Accounting Office, the Department of Justice, and the House Committee on Impeachment, and none found any hint of impropriety.' I use this language because my own is un-printable."

If the controversy raised questions about the hamburger company's integrity, investors gave no indication of losing faith in the chain's earnings power. Throughout the 1970s, while the financial markets suffered a series of setbacks, stocks of McDonald's and leading franchise companies remained in favor much of the time. Money that could have gone into local businesses and heavy industries poured into the construction of franchise chains and helped them to offer more minimum-wage jobs. In 1974 Senator Lloyd Bentsen of Texas scolded financial institutions for causing havoc in the economy by wildly bidding up the prices of certain glamorous stocks while ignoring fundamental industries. Bentsen noted that the physical assets of U.S. Steel were vastly greater than those of McDonald's, yet the total value of the hamburger chain's stock was about the same as the steel giant's. By the end of 1978, observed securities analyst Robert Emerson of Fred Alger & Company, the market value of McDonald's stock was greater than the total figure for American Airlines, United Airlines, Eastern Airlines, Pan American, and TWA. In the *Forbes* listing of leading companies for

1982, McDonald's ranked 244th in sales but in the market value of its stock it rated 58th. The chain was ahead of companies such as Xerox and Pepsi-Cola, whose sales and assets were vastly larger. Holiday Inns ranked a respectable 207th, putting it higher than larger companies. Franchising had not lost its magic.

Some observers argued that the hottest growth chains of the 1980s would be in financial services and health, rather than traditional areas of food and lodging. In 1983 *Forbes* added William Willard, head of Computerland, to its list of the four hundred richest Americans, all worth over a hundred and twenty-five million. Computerland is the largest computer retailer, with three hundred stores that registered sales of about four hundred million dollars in 1982. The franchise chain is one of two exclusive dealers of the IBM Personal Computer. The company has been able to take a large lead over independent computer stores, thanks to aggressive marketing and contracts it signed with large suppliers.

Another new franchised field is banking. In 1982 First Interstate Bancorporation began franchising its name, attempting to build a national system that would advertise on television and offer customers a network of services. First Interstate, which is based in Los Angeles and has thirty-nine billion dollars in assets, sold two licenses. First National Bank of Golden, Colorado, with one hundred twenty million in assets, purchased an exclusive license for its community. American Security Bank in Honolulu, with seventeen branches and four hundred forty million in assets, acquired franchise rights for Hawaii. Banks joining the chain change their names to First Interstate Bank of their home city or state.

Customers can use automatic teller machines at any unit to get cash and make deposits. By joining the chain, franchisee banks have access to large computer facilities and expensive equipment. Banks might affiliate as an alternative to being completely swallowed in mergers. The parent company receives fees and hopes to gain eventually the clout of national television advertising. This brand-name identification is becoming crucial for banks. With deregulation, financial services companies such as Prudential and American Express—whose names have long been familiar to television viewers—are beginning to compete against the banks. The day may come when a few major institutions and chains dominate banking services. A franchised bank could reach into cities and towns around the country, where it would be a major force in local economies. If banks consolidate into a few big chains that dominate finance the way McDonald's and Burger King control hamburgers, consumers seeking attractive lending rates would have a limited selection of sources.

The same kind of conglomeration could happen in medicine. In a chain, doctors might be forced into employee status, with less freedom to make decisions on patient care. Humana, a Louisville hospital company with one billion dollars in annual sales, started MedFirst, a chain of health centers that are basically franchising for doctors. The company provides a well-stocked building with examining rooms and X-ray units. A doctor runs the facility, paying the company 51.5 percent of professional fees and 30 percent of hospital fees. The office is open from eight a.m. to eight p.m., seven days a week.

Around the country there are six hundred fifty profit-making emergency centers that offer potential for building chains. Dr. E. R. Dunsford of Jacksonville, Florida, told *The New Physician* magazine that his operation is a "convenience place." It is "like going to a 7-Eleven for a loaf of bread instead of to a Safeway," he said.

Noting that many kinds of medical practices are being attempted, the magazine said some new health chains are emphasizing fast-food-style marketing. "If the terminology begins to sound like that in a fast-food kitchen—terms like 'McMedicine' or 'Doc in a box' or 'Kentucky Fried medicine' are being tossed around—there's good reason. Ready or not, medicine has entered the marketing era, in which the fine line between a product, like a Big Mac, and the traditional health service blurs."

People are being conditioned by fast food to want fast medicine. Dr. Enzo DiGiamcomo, vice president of medical affairs at Mercy Hospital in Springfield, Massachusetts, told the magazine that consumers today are asking: "What can medicine do to do things quickly? People want to get in and out of surgery and other care just like people want to go to McDonald's for a quick bite."

11

The Franchisees Rebel

In the late 1970s the Carvel ice cream chain announced a new marketing program that seemed certain to attract crowds. On selected days customers who bought a sundae would receive a second one free. Such television promotions had proved effective in the past and helped the chain grow to seven hundred fifty outlets. Tom Carvel, the chain's gravel-voiced founder who narrated its commercials, had become a minor celebrity in some Northeast television markets where the spots ran. The unpolished advertisements often featured stumbling testimonials by children and other amateur merchandisers.

But the New York State Attorney General's office was not amused by the advertising campaign. In a complaint filed in 1979, Assistant Attorney General John Desiderio argued that Carvel was acting in restraint of trade by coercing franchisees into participating in the memorable advertising program.

The problem, the attorney general argued, was that under the chain's contract, franchisees were required to buy all their supplies and equipment from the company or from sources approved by Carvel. However, the attorney general alleged, there were no approved sources where franchisees could buy directly. Carvel franchisees were actually required to purchase all their supplies "from Carvel at Carvel's high prices." Dealers were charged royalties on the ice-cream mix purchased from the company. New franchisees paid fees based on a minimum of ten thousand gallons, whether or not they actually used the full amount.

The attorney general alleged that franchisees were compelled to participate in the "Buy one, get one free" campaign. When the television campaign began, ice-cream lovers appeared at the stores expecting free sundaes. Franchisees who refused to honor the televised commitment risked facing crowds of justifiably angry customers.

Carvel told *The Wall Street Journal* that it denied the charges and said that its methods of franchising already had been thoroughly tested before the Federal Trade Commission and the courts and were found to be proper. A Carvel spokeswoman said that seventy franchisees decried the civil suit and said that they stood to be damaged by the adverse publicity. "They're little people and they have a lot to lose," she told the newspaper.

But according to the newspaper, the attorney general's office said that some franchisees had complained to the state's anti-monopolies unit, which had conducted an eighteen-month investigation of Carvel. To keep franchisees in line, the attorney general charged, the company used a variety of rough tactics, harassing store owners.

In December 1985 the case ended with a settlement. The attorney general dropped the lawsuit. Carvel admitted no wrongdoing and said it would allow franchisees to make some purchases from other suppliers. The attorney general's office said that the antitrust problem had been cleared up. The company said the withdrawal of the case was a victory. "There was no finding of any wrongdoing, just total vindication," Eric B. Kaviar, an attorney for Carvel, told *The New York Times*.

The Carvel case was hardly the first sign of franchisees' discontent. Over the last decade operators have come increasingly to question some of the promises made by franchise salesmen. What attracts so many investors to franchises like Carvel is the security chains claim to offer. Among franchising's boosters, it is an accepted truism that the operator affiliated with a chain has a better chance of success than the independent. In its 1983 membership directory, the International Franchise Association, the leading trade group, notes that "the success rate of businesses owned by franchisees is significantly better than the rate for other independent-owned small businesses." In 1980, the IFA reported, .7 percent of its members' franchisees closed because of business failures and another 1.1 percent closed for other reasons. The Department of Commerce claims that in the decade ending in 1981 less than 5 percent of all franchisee-owned outlets failed each year. In contrast, most independent businesses last less than three years. To many would-be franchisees the statistics might sound reliable. After all, a Holiday Inn or a McDonald's is more likely to prosper than a Joe's Motel or a Bob's Burgers. Hundreds of thousands of small investors flock to buy chain outlets because they believe they are purchasing security. However, there is considerable reason to question the government statistics on overall franchise failure rates.

To begin with, if you believe the Commerce Department's 5 percent figure, conduct a simple experiment. Select twenty franchised outlets near your home. A year later check to see if nineteen are still standing. Anyone who regularly drives along a highway strip will notice that the signs enticing motorists constantly change.

Determining the exact turnover rate is difficult. David Gladstone, executive vice president of Allied Lending Corporation, argues that the failure figures are surely higher than the Department of Commerce suggests. Gladstone is unusually qualified to assess chain survival rates, since his investment company, among other activities, specializes in loans to franchisees. A participant in the Small Business Administration franchise program, Allied is, in effect, a small bank making loans to entrepreneurs who have been turned down by conventional institutions such as banks. Since Allied can not accept savings deposits, it pays a high price for its money and charges more for loans than banks do.

In 1983 the company was making about seven or eight loans a month for a total of about one and a half million dollars. Gladstone has loaned money to franchisees of forty-five different chains, including Wendy's, McDonald's, Dunkin' Donuts, and Ben Franklin. He usually finances outlets of established chains with more than two hundred units. Before lending any money Allied thoroughly investigates the chain and its industry. The company maintains extensive files detailing, for example, how many donut shops have failed and what profits a store of a particular size should produce. The research involves phoning franchisees. "If the chain has a hundred franchisees, we'll call fifty or seventy," Gladstone says. "We ask, 'Do you know anybody that failed?' The franchisees know each other and how the chain is doing."

Sometimes franchisors mislead lenders about the success of franchises, Gladstone observes. Despite his research and caution, Gladstone says that 3 percent of his investments fail. He believes the Department of Commerce figures are based on incomplete data. "They probably don't follow chains that open one year and close the next," he says. "They also must not count cases where the franchisee shuts down and the franchisor takes over the outlet or sells it to someone else. The bank may lose money and the franchisee may go broke, but the unit won't be listed as closed."

Bankruptcies commonly occur in cases where the franchisor collects a franchise fee from the investor, but the unit is never opened because the company folds or the investor runs out of money. "There are two kinds of companies," Gladstone cautions. "There is a group that is in the business of selling franchises. They just want to collect a quick fifteen-thousand-dollar fee. That is the type to avoid. Another group is in the business of collecting royalties. They want the franchisees to last over the long term."

In the latter category of reputable chains there are solid com-

panies that offer franchisees about a 90 percent chance of surviving, Gladstone says, though he hesitates to name them. He
points out that of the eighteen hundred chains there is a group
of a half dozen premier companies—including Midas and
McDonald's—where the annual failure rate is less than 1 percent. At the moment some of the computer store chains have
been enjoying 1 percent rates. This may change as the number
of computer outlets increases and good sites are occupied.

At this point, if you know anything about business and long
to make a fortune, you may be panting wildly with excitement.
Finally it is here, the goose that lays the golden egg, then stands
up and hands it to you. The elite franchises offer investments
where you are almost—though not quite—guaranteed success.
An annual failure rate of less than 1 percent is truly phenomenal. And you may conclude that your time could more profitably be spent running a Midas Muffler shop rather than reading
the rest of this book. You are probably, of course, correct. However, be advised that thousands of other people are similarly
enamored of the muffler and hamburger businesses and are at
this very moment waiting to get a franchise. In addition, as was
clear in the chapter on franchisees, being associated with a
large, successful company is not necessarily an existence that
will fulfill many people's dreams.

Franchisees who are not associated with the very top chains
face considerable uncertainties. Old chains collapse, new ones
are started. The *Franchise Opportunities Handbook*, published
annually by the Department of Commerce, is the most complete listing of franchise companies. Each year the government
distributes about thirty thousand copies of the book, which
serves as a standard reference for prospective franchisees and
people in the industry. Most companies selling outlets are
listed. To obtain a rough idea of the turnover of chains, compare the 1980 volume with the 1982 edition. In 1980 there were
897 chains listed, while the figure climbed to 1023 in 1982. Of
the companies included in 1980, 243, or 27 percent, were no
longer listed in 1982. The 1982 book contained 362 companies,
or 35 percent, that had not appeared in 1980. Companies that

are no longer listed have not necessarily folded. A few may have temporarily stopped selling franchises.

Several years ago Congress became curious about franchise closings. In May 1981 the House Subcommittee on Commerce, Consumer, and Monetary Affairs, chaired by Representative Benjamin Rosenthal of New York, held hearings on the high failure rates of loans to franchises made with Small Business Administration guarantees. Under the SBA program the government provides loan guarantees for small-business people who cannot obtain financing any other way. In an economy dominated by giant corporations the little guy needs a hand, the theory goes. But as so often happens, government benefits were finding their way into the coffers of the richest companies. From 1967 to 1979 the SBA guaranteed eighteen thousand franchise loans totaling $1.3 billion, with money going to outlets of such small businesses as McDonald's, Burger King, and Western Auto. Many of the franchisees had been turned down for loans by banks who considered the deals risky. Undeterred, franchise salesmen turned to Uncle Sam, who made it possible for thousands of outlets to open. Having secured the SBA loans, the new dealers paid royalties and fees to parent companies. Then in many cases the franchisees went bankrupt. The franchisor companies suffered limited direct losses and seemed to have little incentive to reduce default rates. In testimony before Rosenthal's committee, Henry Eschwege, director of Community and Economic Development of the General Accounting Office, used strong language condemning some big companies. "They are in effect running a scam on a lot of well-intentioned small businessmen," he said.

At the request of the subcommittee, the General Accounting Office determined that in the SBA program 10 percent of franchises defaulted, while only 4 percent of the independent businesses receiving similar assistance were failing. And some franchises were defaulting at rates considerably higher than average. In a group of thirty large franchise companies GAO found default rates ranging from 11.6 to 33.3 percent. At Tastee Freez ten out of seventy loans defaulted, while five of thirty-one loans to Ramada Inns defaulted and six of forty-one loans to Bresler's 33 Flavors failed. Among small companies, Turf Tenders defaulted on five out of five loans, Mister Softee failed on four out of six loans, while Duraclean International defaulted on thirteen out of twenty-six.

The congressmen were curious why chains were suffering such problems. It seemed particularly strange that the SBA was experiencing failure rates no private bank could long tolerate. In the hearings Representative Rosenthal pointed out that the defaults might drop if the parent companies were forced to be more cautious in selling outlets. "If these loans are risk-free to the franchisor and if franchise fees and operating equipment costs are paid to the franchisor 'up front,' then some franchisors may be more interested in selling franchises than in selling ice cream, hamburgers, or other franchise products," Rosenthal said.

In making loan decisions, the SBA had no files on the track records of franchisors. Some companies' outlets were defaulting all around the country, while the SBA continued assisting franchisees entering the highly risky ventures. SBA loan officers were required to issue a certain number of loans but were not held responsible for defaults. A former SBA loan officer explained that he requested a promotion in 1977 and was told he would have to approve ten loans a month instead of his current average of eight. Since his wife was pregnant he increased his total and was promoted in 1978. Later in 1978 he again asked for a promotion and was told he would have to raise his quota to twelve. He achieved thirteen and was promoted in May 1979.

One of the more conspicuous failure rates was achieved by the New York City SBA district office, which approved thirteen loans to Burger King outlets between September 1973 and November 1976. By 1981 eleven of the franchises had defaulted and the government had lost two and a half million dollars. The House committee's staff prepared a memo noting that the franchises failed because of poor locations chosen by Burger King, which was "experimenting." Confident of the national chain's expertise, the SBA had not bothered to check the potential of the new sites. The congressional staff noted that Burger King "made no attempt to save these businesses or help them once it was realized that there was a problem. Instead, the company tried to 'shop in the bargain basement' for the used equipment once the franchises failed."

The report went on to question the value of the government subsidy program. "Burger King is owned by Pillsbury. In 1974–76, when these loans were made, Pillsbury's profits were rising from $28 million to $41 million. Pillsbury was expected to show $103 million profits in 1980. As of May 1981 the SBA has made a total of $24 million of loans and guarantees to Burger King franchisees. The SBA is supposed to be a lender of last resort but due to its rules and regs on franchising, neither Pillsbury nor Burger King were asked to bear the risk involved in making these loans and guarantees—despite the fact that both were obviously in a position to do so.

"An SBA printout received by us indicates that even after these defaults the SBA guaranteed one hundred loans to Burger Kings, mostly elsewhere but also in New York City. The Miami SBA district office guaranteed fifteen loans. They advised us they were unaware of the New York City situation."

Despite the high default rates it is not fair to suggest that franchise companies are completely indifferent to the fate of franchisees. Companies indeed prefer franchisees to succeed and send royalties to the home office. But for many chain builders franchisees serve as cannon fodder, foot soldiers to be expended in battle. If the company thinks there might be a market for a product in a certain area it can find operators who will invade the community. If the experiment fails and the franchisees go bankrupt, well, that's too bad—in business there are always risks. In this way tens of thousands of individuals have lost their investments. As long as some outlets survive, the chain can continue trying new areas. It is out of the trial and error financed by many franchisees that a few successful chains and franchisees emerge.

While failures may do little damage to parent companies they can ruin the lives of franchisees. This was amply demonstrated by testimony of several franchisees to the House sub-committee investigating franchise loans. The dealers had invested in Zip'z, an ice-cream company that obtained forty-eight loan guarantees through the SBA. By 1981 twenty-six had defaulted. Barbara Boghetich told Representative John Conyers of Michigan, a committee member, about the nightmare she endured when she entered the world of franchising.

"We had a big dream although we had limited resources. We had no experience in running a business, and so we decided to buy a franchise because that would give us the benefit of somebody who had business experience. We ordered a booklet from the government which lists all your different franchises and what they do and where to write for information. We wrote for many of them and it took us about three months to decide on Zip'z. Zip'z was not in that booklet but it had advertised in *The Wall Street Journal.*"

John Conyers: "What made them so interesting?"

Boghetich: "One was the fact with an ice-cream franchise, it was something many people liked. Baskin-Robbins had no real competition that we could see around the country on a national basis. You had several hamburger franchises that were successful. You had several chicken franchises that were known nationally, and yet ice cream is enjoyed by people of all ages. We thought the idea that Zip'z had of making your own sundae was a novel one, and we were led in by a beautiful sales pitch."

Mrs. Boghetich and her husband raised twenty thousand dollars by emptying their savings account and borrowing money from their mothers. An SBA loan supplied another fifty thousand. In 1978 Mrs. Boghetich began searching for a location, driving around Chicago for several months, looking at possible sites. She found one, but the company rejected it. Finally she received approval for a site in a new shopping center. The store opened in June 1978. The couple soon discovered that the company had already offered the site to a franchisee who refused it because he believed the surrounding communities could not grow.

From the beginning the project floundered. Remodeling the

store cost five thousand dollars more than expected. Traffic at the shopping center proved disappointing. An apartment complex scheduled to be built near the shopping center was canceled when the county turned the area into a flood plain and park. Students from nearby high schools rarely patronized the store because traffic patterns made it difficult for them to visit the shopping center. In winter, sales vanished. Then Mrs. Boghetich's husband died in January 1979.

Zip'z predicted the store would do $120,000 a year in sales, but it never climbed past $47,000. By late 1979 it had become clear the loan could not be paid off. When Mrs. Boghetich first talked to SBA about obtaining the loan, the agency said the couple would have to take a second mortgage on their house. Officials assured her that even if the business failed the government would never seize someone's home and would probably settle for five cents on the dollar. In September 1980 Mrs. Boghetich closed the business. The SBA liquidated the store, selling forty thousand dollars' worth of equipment for thirteen thousand. The government also sold the woman's house. "I will never be able to buy a house again," she told the committee. "My life is finished. I lost my husband. I was going bad in business. I had to work sixteen hours a day, seven days a week. And I did not know whether I was coming or going and nobody else cared. And I still have nightmares at night."

In October 1982 the House subcommittee issued a report recommending that the SBA take steps to minimize franchisee failures. The committee suggested the agency monitor failure rates and require franchising companies to share the risks in guaranteeing loans. In January 1983 the SBA wrote to Congressman Rosenthal, saying, in effect, that it would not change its basic policies. To the committee's recommendation that franchisors participate in loans and loan guarantees, the SBA said that franchisors should not be required to act as lenders, though this might be done in some cases. SBA said it did not have the resources to develop a body of information on franchises, as the committee suggested. The SBA did say it had dropped its system requiring officers to meet quotas for numbers of loans issued. Soon after the communication Rosenthal died. The matter of the franchise loans was allowed to drop. The hearings seemed to produce no substantial results.

Periodically Congress rediscovers the issue of franchisee failures. Previous investigations, which were discussed in earlier chapters, focused on fly-by-night operations and con artists. But Rosenthal's hearings concentrated on legal businesses— substantial ongoing companies that year in and year out induce thousands of people to part with their savings. For all the congressional warnings and occasional scandal story in the press, the stream of potential franchisees eager to invest never seems to slow.

In recent years experienced franchisees have become more assertive in their disputes with parent companies. Through the 1960s, most franchisees were novice investors, willing to follow the dictates of the parent companies. Uncertain how to operate a business, many new dealers faithfully followed their corporate leaders over financial cliffs and into bankruptcy. As franchisees of established companies prospered, they became less dependent on the parent company. Having mastered the mysteries of operating a muffler shop, franchisees were no longer awed by the chains' expertise. They resented new regulations emanating from corporate headquarters and began to feel exploited. The parent companies were expanding thanks to money the franchisees were risking. After saving for years, investors purchasing franchises held high expectations, anticipating fulfilling lives as independent businessmen. They quickly grew disillusioned, often finding themselves mere employees of severe bosses. As chains grew larger and more bureaucratized, the parents came to be more rigid in dealings with franchisees. They were less willing to bend rules and sometimes balked at providing services they had promised.

The operators' anger was fueled by the imbalance that exists in any franchise chain. Parent companies almost always hold more power than franchisees. Richer and more sophisticated than the operators, parents decide how the chain's profits will be divided. Since the franchise contract is usually drawn up by the parent, the terms are usually one-sided. However, in the 1970s franchisees began to discover that they could exercise some clout. Increasingly they turned to the courts for assistance. The number of franchise lawsuits climbed quickly. A new body of law developed, and lawyers appeared who specialized in franchising.

In 1977 Arlene Anthony did battle with McDonald's. One of the few women to own an outlet in her own name, she had purchased the fast-food store before her marriage. When her husband, Don Anthony, opened up a delicatessen sixty-five miles away from the hamburger outlet, the company objected, claiming there was a conflict between the two businesses. While franchisees in earlier years meekly followed corporate dictates, Mrs. Anthony hired a lawyer. "I was threatened that if I did not force my husband to sell his interest, which I could not do, that they would litigate beyond our capacity to pay," she told PBS. Mrs. Anthony also claimed that the company said that if she did win, McDonald's would build other restaurants near hers so that the Anthony outlet's business would decline. Before the case went to trial a settlement was reached. While both sides refused to discuss the settlement, Anthony kept her unit and she and her husband got a second one. The deli was closed.

Disputes often develop because franchisees and parents have different sources of profits. The parent, which collects royalties based on total sales, seeks to maximize sales. The franchisee is interested only in his profits. This becomes a source of conflict when chains select sites for new outlets. Franchise companies may seek to open more units in an already profitable area. If one franchisee is achieving, for example, one million dollars in sales in a town, the company may want to put a second store in the area. With two units operating, total sales in the town for the chain might reach one and a half million. But faced with competition from its own company, the first store may see its sales drop to seven hundred fifty thousand. The company would increase its royalty income, but the first franchisee would experience a decline in profits. McDonald's, Dunkin' Donuts, and other companies have been accused of this practice. Franchisees are usually powerless to prevent such incursions.

In instances where parents were milking excess profits from chains, franchisees formed associations to protect their businesses. Occasionally the skirmishes escalated into full-scale civil wars that nearly toppled chains. In 1982 Arthur Treacher's, the fish chain, came close to bankruptcy as angry franchisees withheld royalties. The chain, which at one time boasted seven hundred units, had slipped to four hundred, with two hundred seventy of them franchised. In December 1981 Arthur Treacher's reported that 90 percent of its franchisees were refusing to pay about fourteen million dollars in royalties. Some outlets had taken down their signs. Agostine Malerba, a franchisee who owned seven outlets, told *The Wall Street Journal* that he had covered his signs with black tarpaulin and banished the name from menus and paper cups. "These days the name Arthur Treacher's doesn't mean much," he said. Other franchisees had gone so far as to add unapproved items to their menus, such as Alaskan crab legs, spaghetti, and tacos. In April 1982, Mrs. Paul's, owner of Arthur Treacher's, was forced to sell the chain, which had become nearly insolvent.

The franchisees had been locked in disputes with the parent company even before Mrs. Paul's acquired the chain in 1979. Arthur Treacher's was founded by Orange-co. Inc., a maker of juice concentrate based in Florida. Under Orange-co., Arthur Treacher's traveled an uncertain course, switching advertising agencies and managements repeatedly. Franchisees paid five thousand dollars for outlets or a hundred thousand for the rights to a city. At first the company provided adequate training and assistance, the franchisees say. But the franchisees charged in court that the support diminished because of the parent's "incompetence, mismanagement, corruption and self-dealing." Arthur Treacher's closed regional offices and fired many of the experienced employees who had assisted the franchisees in the field. The franchisees also charged that the company "improperly diverted assets and wasted funds provided by the franchisees, and desperately needed in the system, on numerous ill-conceived and untested projects." After several experiments failed, the company decided to convert the traditional fish and chips outlets to "family-style seafood restaurants." This effort further enraged franchisees, who said they were not given adequate supervision to make alterations and that the costs of conversion were underestimated. The chain was short of cash and Orange-co. was in no position to provide funds, since it had lost eleven million dollars trading orange juice futures in 1977.

Franchisees cheered when Mrs. Paul's purchased the troubled company for five million dollars. But the good feelings quickly vanished after the new owner cut off the chain's suppliers of Icelandic cod, the high-quality fish that had been Arthur Treacher's primary product. The parent claimed the suppliers were including inferior fish parts, such as belly flaps, in the fishcakes. The franchisees, questioning this explanation, said Mrs. Paul's hoped to use the fast-food chain as a market for its precooked fish at a time of stagnant supermarket demand. But the franchisees did not want to serve the precooked Mrs. Paul's fishcakes.

A month after the purchase by Mrs. Paul's, franchisees met with Edward J. Piszek, chairman of the company. The meeting ended with both sides fuming, telling several different versions of what transpired. Franchisees say the chairman had presented a table spread with Mrs. Paul's reheatable products, including fishcake sandwiches and flounder. From now on, the chain would be selling these products, he is reported to have said. The franchisees, however, found the food inedible. The company says it never intended to *force* the franchisees to sell the products. The chairman merely *suggested* that the operators might want to add new items to the menu. Mrs. Paul's claims the franchisees had been hostile and closed-minded before the meeting started. "From the beginning they wanted a guarantee of profitability," Richard Baker, Arthur Treacher's president under Mrs. Paul's, told *The Wall Street Journal.* "I think they figured with Mrs. Paul's their wildest dreams would be realized."

The chain deteriorated rapidly. Most of the franchisees refused to use Mrs. Paul's fish and withheld royalty payments. Many sold their businesses or closed after going bankrupt. Arthur Treacher's will go nowhere, franchisees said, unless a corporate parent invests in catchy advertising and new product ideas. Finally Lumara Foods bought the chain from Mrs. Paul's, promising to ease relations with franchisees.

As disputes in chains grew more bitter, franchisees began to form associations that could do battle with powerful parent companies. In 1970 there were only a handful of associations. By the end of the decade the total had climbed to more than forty. Many formed in response to severe abuses by chain parents. Harold Brown, a Boston attorney and champion of franchisee associations, claimed that many parent companies were earning unfair profits selling supplies to their operators. Brown told a Senate hearing that Howard Johnson's imposed huge markups on products it forced operators to purchase. The company bought gallon containers of maraschino cherries priced at $1.50, changed the label, and resold them to franchisees for $4.50.

The franchisee associations sometimes spouted rhetoric reminiscent of the labor movement. Fast-food operators talked of protecting their rights against the all-powerful companies. In fact, many of the franchisees were dedicated capitalists with strong anti-union sentiments. Most were small operators simply trying to protect their limited profits. A few had become wealthy and wanted to preserve their assets.

Harold Forkas, a Midas Muffler dealer, was already a millionaire when he began to believe the chain needed an association. Midas had been good to Forkas, he conceded, but he began to grow frightened by developments in the company. Midas had been founded in 1956 by Nate Sherman and his son Gordon. Pipe manufacturers who recognized the muffler business as a growing market for their product, the Shermans set up a system of distributors. Like most early franchise operations, Midas offered its dealers only a loosely drawn contract. Franchisees who sold the gold Midas mufflers paid no royalties. Either party could cancel the agreement on thirty days' notice with no cause. The system worked because the fiery elder Sherman was basically fair to his dealers. Even when he wasn't, the operators usually made money. Once Sherman forced his dealers to sell tires, an effort that failed miserably. Still, the operators considered Sherman a benevolent dictator whose powerful advertising campaigns helped the entire chain grow as explosively as the suburbs where it was based.

After growing up poor, Forkas worked for Coca-Cola for seventeen years, quitting in 1957 to join the new muffler chain in Suffolk County, New York. By 1970 he owned seven Midas shops. Though pleased with his new prosperity, Forkas worried about the chain's future. The younger Sherman had tired of working under the control of his now elderly father, and he sought to seize the company. When Nate Sherman refused, father and son waged a proxy fight for the ownership of Midas. Watching on the sidelines, Forkas rooted for the younger man. The franchisee feared that if the father won, he would retire and sell out to a conglomerate as so many other family-controlled companies had done. Forkas had seen another auto service franchise languish and collapse after it was absorbed by a giant company. The Midas dealer was not prepared to let his recently acquired fortune vanish. He decided to organize franchisees into an association that would protect their investments.

At his own expense, Forkas set out traveling around the country, recruiting operators. Some dealers reacted hostilely when they heard about a proposed organization that sounded suspiciously like a union. Forkas himself inspired wariness. A fast-talking salesman and aggressive New Yorker, he was asking franchisees to take a risk that could endanger their businesses. Forkas argued his case fiercely. He had no intention of forming a union, the Midas dealer told fellow franchisees. In fact, Forkas had become interested in the association idea when he and other dealers in the New York area had formed a regional operators group to fight a union-organizing campaign. "I was not out to hurt Midas," he said, a decade later. "I was out to work with Midas, but we would protect our own interests."

Soon Forkas won over dozens of dealers. Learning about the

growing movement, Nate Sherman was furious. The elderly chief executive viewed the dealers as his children, and he was deeply offended that they would question his authority. Though Sherman fumed about the association, he did not directly threaten the organizers. The Midas chief needed Forkas and the other dealers as much as they relied on him.

Sherman had decided to tighten the franchise contract. He sought to install a modern franchise agreement that would require dealers to pay a licensing fee and royalties. To ensure cooperation he announced the formation of a dealer advisory board that franchisees would elect. The board would help win franchisees over to the new contract. It would also counter the growing association, serving as a sort of company union. When the ballots were counted, all the new representatives were members of the association. Sherman, who still refused to accept the association, agreed to talk to the advisory board. The new contract that emerged called for an initial franchise fee of ten thousand dollars. Royalties would be 10 percent, with half that going for national advertising. In return for these concessions, Sherman offered the dealers twenty-year contracts that could only be terminated for cause.

Gradually Midas ended its stance of refusing to meet with the association. The company recognized that the association could become a tool for running the chain and maintaining control over the dealers. As long as the operators were permitted to make money they would support the chain's policy. When Canadian manufacturers began selling pipes and other parts at lower prices than Midas, the chain's dealers turned to the foreign suppliers. The company, its profits dropping sharply, appealed to the dealers association, which pointed out the price problem. Midas reduced its prices and the association urged its members to buy from the parent, even though some Canadian companies offered better deals. When the parent company is strong, the association argued, the entire chain benefits from more advertising, training programs, and product development. Franchisees shifted their purchasing to Midas.

Like the Midas dealers group, the International Association

of Holiday Inns has no legal veto over its company's policy and it cannot strike. However, the parent company has learned that regulations are easier to enforce if the operators support them. Holiday Inns constantly engages in a tug-of-war with the franchisees. The parent urges the operators to spend more on their units and for corporate activities such as advertising. The franchisees, meanwhile, seek to reduce their expenses and enhance their own profits. The Holiday Inns association has a strong organization, with fourteen committees and a paid staff. It is funded by dues paid by franchisees of two hundred fifty dollars a year for each hotel unit.

The parent recently proposed that all motels install pulsating showerheads, a step that would have upgraded motels but cost franchisees money. Learning about the policy change, the association committee on standards howled its opposition. After considerable arguing back and forth, the franchisees compromised, agreeing to install pulsating showerheads in all new units as they are built. In another controversial regulation, Holiday Inns proposed standardizing all food in motel restaurants, including the size of fruit. The franchisees objected to the extra work and expense the project would involve. The parent modified the standards. In 1978 Holiday Inns issued a new franchise contract that would have tightened the company's control over the chain and taken power away from franchisees. Outraged franchisees refused to sign. One particularly irksome regulation said that if a franchisee died the license would revert to the company in six months. The company backed down, allowing the franchisee's estate to continue to own the license.

The Holiday Inns and Midas operators associations are unusual organizations in the franchise world. There are only about half a dozen chains in which independent franchisee associations negotiate with parents as equal partners. In other companies operators have little recourse. If the parent imposes an odious regulation the operators can protest but normally the parent will win the round. The company can use its inspectors and lawyers to pressure operators to obey. Parent operations have often used their powers to discourage the development of independent franchisee associations. Operator-activists have been harassed, and in a few cases forced out of business. Reacting to the heavy-handed tactics, California passed legislation protecting the right of franchisees to join trade groups.

According to Timothy Fine, an attorney who represents franchisee associations, in 1980 Taco Bell moved to oppose an association franchisees were forming. He claimed that company executives told operators that the association would not be healthy for the chain, and that Taco Bell has exerted subtle pressures against the organizers. While the chain is not about to endanger the source of its profits by closing outlets, he alleged that it has dropped hints to franchisees that troublemakers may not be permitted to open additional units, and franchisees who refuse to support the association are rewarded for their good behavior with licenses for more outlets. Fine conceded it is necessary for parent companies to maintain standards, but he argued there are two ways to accomplish this. "You can achieve product control by reasoning with franchisees," he says, "or you can snap a bullwhip."

It is a fact that the company refused to negotiate with the franchisee association. However, Rodney Hatler, a Taco Bell vice president, said that the chain did not attempt to discourage franchisees from joining the association. He said that the association has had little impact on the company and that Taco Bell has formed an advisory council where franchisees can present their views on company policy.

In recent years a major concern of franchisee associations has been the question of renewal or termination of licenses. Under most early contracts companies could take away licenses on short notice. Franchisees such as the Midas operators lived in constant fear of losing their livelihoods. Their concern was justified. In 1971 Ralston-Purina decided franchising was not profitable for its Jack-in-the-Box chain. The huge food processor gave thirty days' notice to the owners of six hundred forty-two franchises that their licenses had been terminated. They were forced out of business.

In the late 1970s some franchisees accused McDonald's of harassing them, by trying to take over units that were operating in profitable areas. In 1979 McDonald's terminated Dennis Walker, who ran three successful units in Kansas City, a growing hamburger market. For Walker, obtaining his first unit in 1971 was a dream come true. In a six-year period he achieved sales of six million dollars, but he failed to report $38,000 to the company. Of this sum, McDonald's would have received $2,581 as royalties. Walter claimed he wasn't trying to defraud the chain; he simply made a mistake. The company told *The Wall Street Journal* it had lost confidence in the franchisee when the audit revealed his inaccuracy.

Under most current franchise agreements the companies can terminate contracts only when the franchisee fails to meet requirements such as maintaining sanitary standards and paying royalties. However, at the end of the contract term companies can refuse to renew at their whim. If a store is profitable because the franchisee has worked hard for twenty years, the company can simply take it over. Parent operations can use the threat of nonrenewal to force franchisees to toe the line.

Advertising is another area that has troubled franchisee groups. Dealers, paying heavily into national advertising funds, become angry when they feel the campaigns are not effective. In most companies there is little they can do to change a campaign. They may suggest firing the advertising agency or changing television ads. But the power to control advertising normally belongs to the parent. Disputes over advertising expenses nearly destroyed A & W in the 1970s. As the struggle sapped the chain of energy, the number of A & W units dropped from 2608 in 1969 to 1437 in 1979. The legal battle started in the mid-1970s when the company accused the franchisee association of misusing advertising money. The association countered by saying the company was not supporting advertising as it had contracted. For two years the parties battled in court to determine how advertising money would be controlled. Franchisees exhausted themselves attending depositions. Company executives, occupied with legal matters, allowed the chain to slip behind competitors. Finally in 1978 the two sides agreed to establish a committee consisting of three franchisees, three representatives of the company, and an advertising professional from outside who would arbitrate disputes. Any advertising must be approved by the committee.

Franchisees have looked to antitrust laws for some protection against companies forcing purchases of overpriced products. As the courts have ruled, operators may be required to buy from parents only if the product is truly specialized. Parents cannot dictate where franchisees buy generic products, such as napkins, which can be produced by anyone. In a settlement with Howard Johnson's, the Federal Trade Commission ruled the company could require franchisees to purchase the chain's ice cream. Customers come to outlets expecting genuine Howard Johnson's ice cream, the commission reasoned. Other food items that are not trademarked may be purchased from the cheapest supplier.

In the battles with parent companies few franchisees have been able to win more than limited concessions. The greatest threats to the chain's power have come from franchisees who are sizable corporations themselves. Throughout the 1970s Burger King feuded with its largest franchisee, Chart House, a company whose revenues rose from $47 million in 1971 to $313 million in 1980. The franchisee was headed by Bill and Jimmy Trotter, sons of a wealthy Louisiana rice broker, who bought a Burger King outlet in 1963, a time when the company exercised little control over its franchisees. Recognizing the money-making potential of fast food, the brothers built more and more outlets. By 1971 they operated one hundred Burger Kings, bringing in sales of thirty-two million dollars. In 1967, while the Trotters expanded, the founders of Burger King sold their chain to Pillsbury for eighteen million. The new corporate owner, seeking to bring direction to a chain that had been growing haphazardly, found itself on a collision course with the Trotters. The brothers had set their eyes on sixteen outlets operating in Chicago. Five franchisees who controlled the territory wanted to sell.

For the brothers, moving into the northern city represented a chance to expand into a rich, undeveloped territory. But Pillsbury also coveted the area and wanted to purchase back the franchise rights. One night during a snowstorm Bill Trotter flew to Chicago and bought out the five franchisees for eight million dollars. The next day a Pillsbury executive arrived to find he had been beaten.

The Trotters, who named their company Chart House after a steak chain they developed, were not content to remain a franchisee. In 1972 they offered to buy the Burger King chain from Pillsbury for one hundred million dollars. The company refused. Meanwhile, Burger King floundered, operating at low profit levels, while McDonald's continued its rapid climb. Chart House, which enjoyed wider profit margins than its parent, bought nine Burger King outlets in Boston from franchisees and thirteen in Houston. Burger King sued, arguing it had not been granted its right of first refusal in buying outlets from franchisees. The parties compromised, with Chart House keeping the Houston unit and releasing the Boston operation. But the difficulties did not end. In 1974, attempting to improve efficiency, Burger King told franchisees to install the "hospitality system," the approach used by McDonald's where each store uses more than one cash register. At the time Burger King customers had to wait in line at one register.

While the new system would be expensive for the franchisee, the parent argued it would create more sales. Chart House was not persuaded. In the franchisee's view, the additional cash registers and clerks would increase sales but not profits. Since the parent company received a percentage of sales, it was not concerned with the franchisee's costs or profits. Chart House relented only gradually, adding additional registers as sales increases seemed to make the extra equipment economical.

While Burger King jousted with Chart House in the mid-1970s, the chain began to face another upstart operator, Horn & Hardart, a venerable New York restaurant company that bought franchise rights in Manhattan. In the 1930s Horn & Hardart became known for its Automats, the gleaming Art Deco cafeterias that many believed were the wave of the mechanized future. Customers viewed food displayed behind windows, then shoved the appropriate number of nickels through slots and pulled out their selections. By the early 1970s enthusiasm for Automats had declined, as customers abandoned cafeterias for trendier restaurants and fast food.

To salvage the struggling company, Horn & Hardart struck a deal with Burger King, converting their Automats to fast-food outlets. For Burger King, Horn & Hardart offered an attractive vehicle for breaking into New York. The Manhattan-based company already owned real estate in prime locations. More important, it had experience in the trickiest restaurant market in the country. While the Burger King executives in Miami knew little about the Big Apple, the local franchisee was expert at the mysteries of operating in the city. The hamburger chain was well aware that many fast-food companies had failed in New York, not having known where lunch crowds congregate or how to deal with local workers and zoning officials.

Observing the Manhattan expansion, Barry Florescue, a Burger King franchisee, became intrigued with Horn & Hardart's potential. A heavy-set accountant who talks in a low voice, Florescue had bought his first hamburger license several years earlier. The young entrepreneur had been involved in a Florida real-estate project when he heard about two Burger Kings that were losing money. To the accountant the struggling outlets represented an opportunity to earn quick profits. He bought the restaurants and soon became infatuated with fast food. Working eighteen-hour days, he pushed the businesses into the black, remodeling antiquated facilities and promoting products by giving away prizes. Then he acquired three more units in Suffolk County, a suburb of New York City.

Examining the Manhattan franchisee, Florescue concluded Horn & Hardart would not be able to exploit its Burger King license. The cafeteria company had almost run out of money. With its capital drained from years of weak revenues, Horn & Hardart was handicapped in its effort to enter the fast-food arena. Florescue approached the company and offered to invest. The management refused. In 1977 Florescue waged a bitter proxy fight and took control of the company. After installing himself as chairman of Horn & Hardart, Florescue began to move, pumping money into the company. With creditors at the door, he won a two-year loan from Burger King and began pouring money into fast-food restaurants. In 1978 he built three Burger Kings and began planning others. By the end of the year Horn & Hardart was operating profitably.

In 1977, as Florescue eyed more fast-food sites, Burger King appointed a new president, Donald Smith. The chief executive had been recruited from McDonald's, where he had been senior vice president and a likely candidate to head the chain eventually. Hiring Smith was a coup for Burger King. He had gained a reputation for being perhaps the best store operator in the fast-food business, always able to make an outlet more profitable. Burger King was dropping further behind McDonald's and losing sales among young adults to Wendy's. The new president seemed the ideal cure for the chain's disease.

At thirty-six, Smith was a supremely confident executive. He had enjoyed a meteoric climb to the top ranks of the hamburger business, having started at the bottom and excelled at every job he held. While in school he worked at A & W, barbecue outfits, and chicken restaurants. In 1966 Smith was running a small hamburger chain in Minnesota when he was spotted by a McDonald's executive, who hired him to be assistant manager of a store. Working long hours, lavishing attention on details, Smith moved swiftly up the McDonald's organization. He headed West Coast operations, then supervised an eight-state area centered in Washington, D.C. After lifting the region from the worst to best performer in the chain, he was brought to corporate headquarters in 1973.

Smith set about rebuilding Burger King in the McDonald's mold. Replacing eight top executives with McDonald's veterans, he centralized corporate control and began aiming products at children. The parent company, Smith believed, must dictate how things would be done. If each franchisee freelanced, setting its own standards, the power of the chain to control its product and maximize its earnings would be weakened.

When the new president arrived Burger King had a small field staff that exercised loose control over franchisees, a system that resulted in erratic standards throughout the chain. Methodically Smith set about establishing the consistency needed to overtake the number-one chain. He reached out to franchisees, personally visiting stores and encouraging operators to remodel their outlets. Most of these efforts were welcomed by franchisees, who recognized the need to revive the floundering chain. But when Smith began imposing limitations he clashed with the increasingly powerful large franchisees. In one controversial decree the president announced that all operators must live within one hour's drive of their units. This was done ostensibly to eliminate absentee owners and ensure that franchisees play an intensive role in managing the stores. However, Chart House and other franchisees had long proven capable of overseeing far-flung outlets. The real aim of Smith's policy was to eliminate empire building. In the future no franchisee could own more than a dozen outlets and amass power that could threaten the company. Chart House, angered by Smith's edict, soon compromised. It was allowed to continue building as many units as it wanted in the Illinois territory, but the franchisee could not expand anywhere else without the parent's permission.

For Horn & Hardart the new regulations were particularly distasteful. A bitter confrontation ensued between Smith and Horn & Hardart's Barry Florescue, ambitious men in their mid-thirties whose goals conflicted. "Barry doesn't really accept the idea of partnership," Smith told *Fortune*. "I'm not sure he really has the personality of a franchisee."

"He believes that the franchisee is not a first-class citizen," Florescue said about Smith, "and that the franchisor has the right, power, and position to do whatever he damn well pleases to run roughshod over the franchisee."

The dispute began after Smith blocked a move by Horn & Hardart to expand. Under the franchise agreement Florescue could open only three New York units a year. Unsatisfied with this level of growth, Horn & Hardart turned to Philadelphia, where it decided to purchase some units. A vice president of Burger King approved the franchisee's move. The expansion into the unfamiliar city was necessary, Florescue believed. As a publicly owned company, Horn & Hardart had to show growing profits in order to satisfy its stockholders. In addition, the company, which was short of cash, did not want to concentrate all its investments in New York. As Florescue saw it, one snowstorm or power failure shutting down the city would severely damage the company, perhaps push it into bankruptcy.

When Smith vetoed the Philadelphia project, Florescue was especially incensed, since he believed the parent had already approved the expansion. With its growth limited in the East, Horn & Hardart looked to Orange County, California, a rich territory that had few Burger Kings and seemed ripe for development. A franchisee owned the development rights for the area but had been slow in opening units. Horn & Hardart sought to buy out the license. During the same period Florescue approached Arby's, seeking a franchise for New York and rights to develop units in Florida. Arby's, delighted to sign on the veteran New York company, granted Horn & Hardart considerable freedom to open units in Manhattan.

Smith, appalled by the franchisee's aggressive activities, sued to stop Horn & Hardart's move into Orange County and to prevent the Arby's deal. Horn & Hardart countersued on antitrust grounds. For Smith it was clear that the parent company must maintain control of the acquisition of franchises. The parent should not find itself in bidding wars for sites with its own operators. In addition, a franchisee with complete access to a company's methods and training procedures should not have a license and interest in another directly competing company. This was the McDonald's policy and it served to keep a tight rein on operators. Florescue pointed out most franchise companies do permit operators to hold licenses in other chains. In fact, there were longtime Burger King franchisees who owned outlets in competing chains. But Smith was determined to tighten regulations.

A federal judge ruled in favor of Burger King on the Orange

County issue, and the two parties settled other questions. Horn & Hardart gave up its designs on Orange County but began to open Arby's units. The franchisee agreed not to develop any more Burger Kings without consent from the chain. For Smith this represented a victory. Limited to fourteen Burger King outlets, the wayward franchisee would never be an independent force determining its own growth. Having turned Burger King into a profitable company with tight control over its franchisees, Smith left in 1980 to become head of Pizza Hut, a company with sales problems and large franchisees seeking independence. In 1983 Smith received a significant compliment: Chart House, the troublesome Burger King franchisee, hired him as its chief executive.

Though Horn & Hardart's Florescue was angered by the outcome of his struggle with Burger King, he conceded Smith had acted in the interest of the parent company. "Whether the decisions he made were right or not for the franchisees, they were right for Don Smith and moved Burger King," he said.

Frustrated in his efforts to open Burger Kings, Florescue quickly began building Arby's units. He also sought to acquire a chain outright. For Florescue it was clear that to build Horn & Hardart into a large company whose stock would attract attention on Wall Street, it was not enough to remain a franchisee. Although the franchised outlets brought in steady, secure profits, Wall Street investors are not enamored of companies dependent on outside masters.

12

The Cost of Franchising

On many occasions in the 1970s Colonel Sanders made no bones about what he thought of the product Kentucky Fried Chicken was producing. The once magnificent gravy had been watered down to "slop," he said frequently, sometimes within earshot of reporters. Sanders appreciated the value of a dollar and was a skilled public relations man, but he could not tolerate what he considered mediocre cooking. The salesmen who bought the chain from Sanders had set out to build the business as fast as possible. Signing up hundreds of franchisees, they moved around the country and publicized the chain on television. Quality began to take a backseat to marketing efforts. All this did not sit well with the Colonel, who had personally inspected franchisees' kitchens to make certain the chicken was cooked properly.

Kentucky Fried Chicken, like the other giant franchise chains, had become an impersonal force more concerned with profit than the welfare of its franchisees or the thickness of its gravy. In their drives to build national companies, franchise entrepreneurs chose their strategies from a range of possibilities. As we have seen, the chains elected to emphasize marketing rather than developing innovative ideas. They chose a strategy of low wages and low productivity rather than achieving more efficiency through a stable workforce. All phases of the chain business focused on making the product seem special. The gleaming outlets with the bright signs suggested that the product must have a unique identity. This message was pounded home again and again on television.

In recent years companies have placed even more reliance on advertising. As John Kenneth Galbraith noted, advertising becomes particularly important when corporations strive to create markets for products that are not needed by consumers. "Outlays for the manufacturing of a product are not more important in the strategy of modern business enterprise than outlays for the manufacturing of demand for the product," he wrote in *The Affluent Society*.

Over the years, as companies sought to distinguish themselves from similar competitors, there has been an escalation in the franchise advertising warfare. Chains spend heavily on advertising, forcing their rivals to spend even more heavily. With more advertising in all media, the effect of each ad has been lessened so corporations must spend even more to achieve the same impact. This strategy may prove ill-conceived. As the car companies discovered, there may be a limit to how long consumers will believe the images created by ads. Eventually customers may begin to demand real value. In 1983 McDonald's, perhaps worried about the "quality issue," briefly featured the actor John Houseman in a television spot claiming that the hamburger chain's food is of the highest order.

Defenders of advertising sometimes insist that commercials serve the public by promoting greater sales of products, which allows companies to become larger and more efficient. Prices to consumers are lowered. However, as we noted, for many of the franchised chains, increased sales have not brought productivity growth. The prices of advertised products are often higher than prices for goods not supported by television promotions.

The only real end served by franchise advertising is a greater concentration of economic power in the chains.

Because television time is limited, only a few companies in each category can make the jump to the airwaves. Those who succeed in the race enjoy an enormous advantage. The local restaurant and the independent motel are destroyed by a barrage of electronic marketing. The products that do win the advertising sweepstakes closely resemble each other. The consumer, denied a variety of choices, must decide between Ford and Chevy, or Burger King and McDonald's. Those who control the growing chains become richer, while others fall behind.

As companies of all kinds have grown more powerful the general drift toward greater economic inequality has progressed. More and more the United States is coming to resemble a Third World country, where a small group of the wealthy reigns, served by the majority of the people who live in poverty. Throughout the service industries there is a growing disparity in incomes between well-paid managers and low-income workers. As the U.S. moves toward a dichotomized workforce, it may lose the upward mobility essential in a democratic society.

Franchise chains, more than most companies, have played a role in increasing the gap between rich and poor. The expansion of unions into areas such as fast food, motels, and beauty salons could improve the position of workers. While unions have hardly proved a cure-all for economic problems they do serve to distribute income more widely. Auto workers receive six times as much hourly compensation as people working in fast-food outlets or motels. While workers in heavy industry may be somewhat more skilled, franchise employees seem significantly underpaid. The difference in pay scales can be attributed to unions.

In manufacturing, many forward-looking companies have accepted their responsibility to provide decent wages and some security to workers. Chains have attempted to get by offering workers minimal compensation. In a publicity brochure McDonald's boasts that it "is known worldwide for the excellent training it provides franchisees, managers, and crewpeople." In fact, most employees of the hamburger giant and other fast-food chains receive little training, few pay increases, and no benefits. They stay an average of three months on the job, then quit in disgust. Organizing franchise workers is a difficult task that the unions have largely abandoned. The chains have been able to block efforts at signing up part-time and low-wage workers. Organized labor, seeking new members to fill its declining ranks, should reexamine the possibility of recruiting franchise workers.

One immediate step unions could take is to begin a publicity campaign to taint the good-guy image chains have promoted on TV. During one episode of the steamy CBS serial *Falcon Crest*, a hamburger commercial disrupted the action to inform viewers they were "Wendy's kind of people." Meanwhile, back at the show two characters debated the morality of paying California agriculture workers the minimum wage. "Angela, these people deserve equal pay for equal work," a sincere man named Chase told the head of a grape-growing empire.

"Labor is a commodity and we pay as low a price as we can," Angela retorted.

Later in the show Angela lectured the stubborn Chase about the realities of the business: "Falcon Crest is a business, Chase, not a charity."

"You don't seem to understand it isn't a charity to pay for what you get," Chase pointed out.

While the plight of farm workers has been publicized, most people are not aware that fast-food employees are paid less than many migrants laboring in the California fields. Union campaigns highlighted the problems of agricultural workers. The same kind of organizing could win more income for franchise workers.

Franchise companies, not content with paying the minimum wage, have sought legislation that would introduce a subminimum wage for young people. Lower wages would help solve the problem of youth unemployment, the argument runs. With lower costs, companies could afford to hire more young people. But the minimum wage is now at a historic low, standing at 39 percent of the average wage. Once the minimum was more than half of the average. It does not seem fair to push it lower. A lower wage would encourage companies to operate more inefficiently than they do already. There would be less incentive to train and promote workers. The youth wage would decrease jobs for the growing number of older franchise employees who work in high-unemployment areas such as Detroit. The day shifts of fast-food restaurants include many middle-aged women trying to make a living for their families.

The best solution for the employment problems of young people is to find jobs for their parents. When his parents are working at decent-paying jobs the eighteen-year-old is more likely to remain in school. If unemployed he is more likely to be viewed as a nuisance, hanging around his mother's house eating her cooking, rather than as part of a crisis. The eighteen-year-old whose parents are unemployed faces a more severe problem. The country would be stronger if more parents were working steadily earning eight dollars an hour, even if that displaced younger workers making three-fifty. The companies would protest that they could not possibly raise wages without raising prices, a move that would drive consumers back to their own kitchens and out of the motels, beauty salons, and tax offices. However, it is clearly possible for companies to operate profitably by paying higher wages. In recent years chains in most areas of franchising have achieved adequate profits. Unlike heavy industry, which has suffered huge losses, companies such as Holiday Inns and Burger King could afford to raise pay.

When Kentucky Fried Chicken moved to Japan it was forced to change its wage policies. The Japanese, accustomed to lifetime employment, would not tolerate the part-time jobs, low wages, and harsh conditions of American fast-food outlets. Kentucky Fried Chicken was forced to pay higher salaries and offer more training to employees, who are seen as valuable members of a paternalistic company. Under this system the workers can be paid more because they are more productive. Higher salaries force a company to lower turnover and take other steps to ensure each worker produces more. Production breakthroughs must be speeded up to cut costs. If a motel has a plentiful supply of low-wage maids it is under no pressure to develop systems that would improve efficiency. Part of the reason that union businesses tend to be more automated and productive is that they must pay higher wages. If pay is high, expenditures on labor-saving devices become economical. Productivity rises. Living standards improve. Profits may be *higher* for the company that pays higher wages.

Low-wage jobs may temporarily boost the profits of individual companies, but they do little to strengthen the country's overall prosperity. When Henry Ford opened his car plants he began paying wages substantially higher than other industries offered. Part of the reason for the auto magnate's generosity was that he hoped Ford workers themselves would buy cars. If franchise companies paid higher wages they might stimulate the overall economy, including their own businesses.

Franchisees often complain that, like employees, they do not receive their fair share of profits. In the franchise systems the parent companies usually maintain the upper hand. This imbalance of power intrigued a white South African lumber firm, which saw franchising as a way to profit from blacks opening stores in their homelands. The parent company developed a do-it-yourself furniture concession that sells customers kits they construct at home. The South Africans believed franchising would enable blacks to share in capitalism without taking initiatives or competing directly against white companies.

The South Africans correctly perceived the nature of franchising. Optimistic new franchisees do not always understand that they are expected to be subservient to the parent company. Boosters of the chains sometimes praise franchisees as the last of the rugged entrepreneurs. The chain system allows the individual operator to thrive, it is argued. "Franchising is the most perfect form of business I know of," James Schorr, president of Holiday Inns, told *Franchising Today*, a trade magazine. "It gives franchisees access to power; they get all the good, but they aren't handicapped by the bad."

Many disgruntled franchisees would take issue with the motel executive. Except in a few cases where franchisees have amassed empires in their own right, the local operators are forced to follow the dictates of the franchisors. Franchisees function as managers, though they share in the profits of their companies and stand to go bankrupt if their businesses fail. From the beginning of their relations with the parent companies, the franchisees are in a weak position. The potential investor approaching a franchise company often suffers from a lack of information. In some states where franchise registration is mandatory, buyers have a chance to learn whether the chain is about to go broke and if other franchisees have been hoodwinked by the company. But in many states this does not exist or large companies are spared enforced disclosure. Because franchise companies operate in many different states there should be one uniform national code administered by the FTC. Franchise chains should be required to file their disclosure statements with the FTC in much the same way that companies selling stock must pass muster before the Securities and Exchange Commission. Too many thousands of franchisees have lost their life savings. The lesson of their suffering should be learned.

Instead of working to prevent the fleecing of franchisees the government has on many occasions assisted the process. Federal agencies such as the SBA have helped the chains sell outlets. The need for this practice is questionable. In recent years there has been considerable discussion about whether the country should aid businesses or adopt an industrial policy dictating how the nation's wealth should be invested. Advocates of industrial policies suggest reviving the Reconstruction Finance Corporation, the Depression-era government operation that helped pump government money into declining industries. Some argue the funds should help failing businesses like steel, while others contend the money should be channeled to "sunrise" industries, such as high technology. The Japanese, we are reminded, have relied on an aggressive industrial policy that has encouraged the growth of their high-technology businesses.

Of course, the United States already does have an industrial policy, consisting of piecemeal programs administered by a variety of government agencies.

Through the Small Business Administration government money is funneled to giant franchise companies such as Ramada and Burger King. In this program the SBA guarantees loans to franchisees that banks refuse to take because they are considered too risky. The franchise chains, knowing the degree of risk, refuse to back loans. The parent corporations pocket the franchise fees, then in many cases watch as the franchisees go bankrupt.

The bankruptcies of thousands of franchisees represent a significant loss to the overall economy. Money is lost that could have been used to build job-generating businesses. Franchisees who invested months or years of their lives in the unsuccessful projects emerge from the experience devastated. Instead of chasing franchise dreams, many investors would be well advised to sink their savings into safer assets or independent businesses. The independent business is certainly risky, but at least the self-employed entrepreneur is not burdened by franchise fees and the need to meet bureaucratic company regulations. Too often the franchisee is saddled with the least attractive site operated by the chain. The parent company, viewing the franchisee as a novice who can be exploited, sells the operator supplies at high prices.

The SBA became involved in franchise financing only recently. Until 1969 the SBA—which is supposed to promote small businesses—did not make loans to franchisees who were considered to be affiliated with large corporations. The agency, reversing this policy at a time when the chains were exercising more political clout, created a pilot program to encourage minority franchisees. The pilot project reviewed the operations of the franchisors and determined their success records. It required the parent companies to provide specific assistance to franchisees. The agency suggested changes in the franchise contract to improve the local operators' profits and reduce the government risk. The SBA discontinued this program but continued the franchise loans. If the agency insists on continuing its industrial policy of promoting chain growth it should at least take steps to protect franchisees. The operators taking loans should be advised of failure rates. The chains that benefit from sales of outlets should be forced to assume part of the risk of the loans. This would discourage franchisors from selling outlets where the chance of success is minimal.

The General Accounting Office in its report to Congress on the SBA franchise program argued that the chains were not protecting franchisees from failure. The SBA was allowing chains to profit without taking any risk. "Other than the borrower, the franchisor benefits most from the success of the franchisee," the GAO noted. "Franchisors would have more incentive to ensure the financial success of SBA borrowers if they were required to share the burden of loss with SBA."

As it is currently structured the SBA franchise program serves little purpose except enriching a few corporations. The franchise chains are perfectly capable of flourishing without assistance and they do not face the subsidized foreign competition confronted by auto and steel companies. Government aid might be more useful to chains and other service industries in the area of research and development. The United States has a long tradition of government-sponsored research and development, dating back to the nineteenth century, when land-grant colleges began to do the work that would make American agriculture so productive. Much of today's defense and aerospace research is funded directly by the government or indirectly through government contracts. Research that widely benefits society may be too expensive for individual companies. The productivity rates of the service industries should be a matter of national concern. Many more people work in motels, restaurants, and muffler shops than on farms. Service companies have been unable or unwilling to fund the research that might increase productivity. Research grants could be channeled through existing university programs. Academic scholars now spend millions in government and foundation money examining subjects such as the behavior of mice and the psychology of the stock market. Some of these resources might profitably be directed to studying retailing systems patronized by millions of people.

The most effective source of research funding could be the companies themselves. Unconcerned about achieving product breakthroughs, the chains have largely avoided investing in research. Such expenditures need hardly be done for altruistic motives. The ultimate end of corporate research programs would be increased profits. Companies that achieve higher productivity through automation often do not pass on proportionate shares of increased profits to workers. Franchise chains that used effective research to establish systems of high productivity and higher wages might record increased profits.

Opposed to low-wage jobs and appalled at the unsightly chain outlets, communities have attempted to ban franchised units. Virtually all these efforts have failed. A few well-off communities and resort areas have managed to force the companies to tone down their signs or stay in certain parts of town. Franchise companies do not simply detract from scenic beauty. They can do considerable damage to the economy and social fabric of a community. Chains drive out the small businesses that provide jobs for local people. Independent businesses reinvest profits at home. Local operations help give communities their identities. They provide informal meeting places. Though local businesses have an obvious stake in stopping the chains, they have been reluctant to fight in courts or take actions that would impede franchising. The businesspeople have perhaps been afraid to hamper the operation of the free market. But in a system where large companies hold all the cards, where television advertising can be used to drive out superior local businesses, small operations are justified in taking stronger measures to fight for survival.

In some cases municipal governments have used zoning regulations to limit chain businesses. Communities that oppose franchise growth have the tools to stop it. Coalitions of unions who opposed the rise of minimum-wage businesses and community groups fearing destruction of neighborhoods have delayed the chain expansion. Local groups may consider the battle lost. Nearly every city is heavily populated with franchises. But the chain expansion has not stopped. For fifteen years business experts have talked about the saturation of key franchise markets. There is *no* more room for barbershops, motels, and restaurants, they have argued. The experts are, of course, correct. The country has more than an adequate supply of those businesses. Even so, the experts are confounded almost every year. Wendy's proved a giant success in the 1970s. New chains are starting all the time. Much of the chain growth comes by taking business away from the independents. For the foreseeable future the expansion should continue. Even after three decades of chain growth there are still many independents left.

Communities faced with the prospects of ever more franchised outlets should address the fundamental question of what kind of contribution the chains make. Do they improve the communities where they operate? Do they enhance overall happiness? Economic activity should provide an environment where people have good houses, schools, and transportation, where there are opportunities for culture and recreation, where people can feel a sense of community. It is difficult to see how franchise companies contribute to these goals. In recent years environmentalists and business executives have debated the value of economic expansion. The factory that offers jobs creates more pollution, the environmentalists have pointed out. There is a tradeoff between economic development and protection of the environment. With franchising the terms of the tradeoff are murky. It is not clear whether chains offer new jobs or simply replace existing local businesses and provide products people don't really need.

Xenophon Zolotas, a governor of the Bank of Greece, has written one of the more interesting books on the value of growth, called *Economic Growth and Declining Social Welfare*. Zolotas argues that in a developing country economic growth may promote happiness and social welfare. As a nation grows richer, people live longer, eat better, and are more physically secure. At a certain point, as a country becomes developed, the benefits of further economic growth diminish. In the early stages of development the introduction of a few automobiles offers faster transportation and a relief from the sanitation problems caused by horses. As the number of cars increases, traffic jams begin and pollution becomes an irritation. If more cars are added, transportation will be even slower and pollution could become a hazard. Increasing the number of automobiles no longer enhances the social welfare of the country. The costs of accidents, health problems, and slow transportation reduce the standard of living. The society would be better off with fewer cars.

Zolotas attempts to support his argument using data on measurable social indicators such as crime, health care, and divorce. Although the United States spent more of its disposable income on health over the last several years, he notes, the figures on problems such as heart disease did not improve. The increased expenditures on health may have been canceled out by greater stress and unhealthy eating habits. As the country becomes more developed it does not become healthier. The author cites studies done by the Institute for Survey Research at the University of Michigan, where people over decades were asked simply if they were happy. In 1978 fewer Americans claimed to be happy than in 1957, although the standard of living had risen over the two decades. Zolotas argues that "increases in material production merely raise the social costs of production, while keeping the level of social welfare unchanged or even lowering it."

There may have been a time when the introduction of franchised units somehow added to increased social welfare. But that time is long past. Having mobilized the forces of modern advertising and financing, the franchise chains have grown wildly around the country, going out of control like dandelions sprouting on a lawn. Like weeds, the franchised units may choke out other desirable growth. Individual franchise chains prosper. In the end, the nation as a whole may be poorer.

Notes on Sources

CHAPTER 1. CHAINS AND MORE CHAINS
Page 1. Thomas discusses his original concept in Robert L. Emerson, *Fast Food: The Endless Shakeout* (New York: Lebhar-Friedman Books, 1979).
Page 2. The quote from Thomas and material on his early years appear in D. Daryl Wykoff and William L. Berry, "Wendy's Old-Fashioned Hamburgers," Harvard Business School case study, February 1977.
Page 6. Franchise sales figures appear in *Franchising in the Economy 1981–1983*, U.S. Department of Commerce, January 1983.
Page 6. The Newspaper Advertising Bureau study is "Eat and Run: A National Survey of Fast Food Chain Patronage," July 1978.
Page 9. The number of jobs is from *Franchising in the Economy*.

CHAPTER 2. THE FRANCHISE FORMULA
Page 13. Singer's franchise experiment is described in Ruth Brandon, *A Capitalist Romance* (Philadelphia: J. B. Lippincott, 1977).

Page 14. The early growth of franchising is discussed in Charles L. Vaughn, *Franchising* (Lexington, Mass.: Lexington Books, 1979).

Page 15. The Coca-Cola story is told in Franklin M. Garrett, "Coca-Cola in Bottles," *The Coca-Cola Bottler*, April 1959.

Page 18. William Rosenberg's story is told in Robert Rosenberg, *Profits from Franchising* (New York: McGraw-Hill, 1969).

Page 21. The Block material is from an interview of Henry Bloch by the author.

Page 26. The Stanley quotes are from an interview with the author.

CHAPTER 3. IDEAS FOR SALE

Page 31. The story of Thomas meeting Sanders is in Emerson, *Fast Food*.

Page 31. A good account of the Colonel's life is William Whitworth, "Profiles," *The New Yorker*, February 14, 1970.

Page 34. The story about Ted Cullin is from Elinor Brecher, "He Was an American Original," *Louisville Courier-Journal*, December 16, 1980. The Colonel's efforts to build his chain are described in Max Boas and Steve Chain, *Big Mac* (New York: New American Library, 1977).

Page 37. Reports on Chicken Delight appear in *The Wall Street Journal*, February 29, 1972, and April 26, 1972.

Page 38. The Vittoria quote is from an interview with the author.

Page 46. The Mason quote is from *The New York Times*, May 26, 1981.

CHAPTER 4. THE IDEAL OPERATOR

Page 51. The profile of Harold Fulmer is from interviews with the author.

Page 55. Sales figures on the company and franchised units are from *Franchising in the Economy*.

Page 59. The Fulmer quote appears in the *Allentown Evening Chronicle*, December 9, 1977. A profile of Fulmer is in the *Sunday Call-Chronicle*, July 20, 1980.

Page 61. Material on Kinmoth is from an interview with the author.

Page 64. Material on Gaderick is from an interview with the author.

CHAPTER 5. THE FRANCHISE FACTORY

Page 69. The story of the founding of McDonald's is told in Ray Kroc, *Grinding It Out* (New York: Berkley Medallion Books, 1977). A good source on McDonald's is Max Boas and Steve Chain, *Big Mac*.

Page 76. A solid discussion of the service economy is in Daniel Bell, *The Coming Post-Industrial Society* (New York: Basic Books, 1973).

Page 76. Quotes from Clark are from an interview with the author.

Page 81. Charlie Chan's is discussed in *Fast Service*, May 1980. There is a discussion of frozen food in Jim Quinn, *But Never Eat Out on a Saturday Night* (Garden City, N.Y.: Dolphin Books, 1983).

Page 92. The quote is from Erich Fromm, *Marx's Concept of Man* (New York: Frederick Ungar, 1966).

Page 92. The Dubos material is in René Dubos, *So Human an Animal* (New York: Charles Scribner's Sons, 1968).

Page 93. Burger King's system is praised in *Fortune*, March 10, 1980.

Page 95. Thurow's article is "The Productivity Problem," *Technology Review*, November 1980.

Page 96. The Viegle quote is from an interview with the author.

Page 98. The Carnes quote is from an interview with the author.

Page 99. The material on Moore is in "The Millionaire Meatman," *Dun's Review*, July 1975.

Page 101. A portrait of Keystone is in "How Keystone's Handshake Turned Golden," *Fortune*, March 13, 1978.

CHAPTER 6. BATTLING BRAND X

Page 104. The account of the rise of H & R Block is from the author's interview of Henry Bloch.

Page 107. Merriman's quote is from an interview with the author.

Page 108. A good account of the early days of advertising is in Daniel Pope, *The Making of Modern Advertising* (New York: Basic Books, 1983).

Page 112. The data on hotels and motels are in Robert Moore Fisher and Royal Shipp, *The Postwar Boom in Hotels and Motels*, Board of Governors of the Federal Reserve System, March 1966.

Page 113. The Levitt quote is in Theodore Levitt, "Production Line Approach to Service," *Harvard Business Review*, September 1972.

Page 116. The Emerson quote is from *Fast Food*.

Page 116. Pizza Time Theatre's problems are described in "The Pitfalls in Mixing Pizza and Video Games," *Business Week*, March 12, 1984.

Page 120. The quote from Connor is from an interview with the author.

Page 121. Rich is described in "Bojangles Campaign by Rich," *The New York Times*, April 15, 1983.

Page 123. The Vadehra quote is in "Making a Lasting Impression," *Advertising Age*, April 25, 1983.

Page 124. General works on advertising that are useful include Wilson Bryan Key, *Subliminal Seduction* (New York: New American Library, 1981); Jerry Mander, *Four Arguments for the Elimination of Television* (New York: Morrow Quill Paperbacks, 1978); Jonathan Price, *The Best Things on TV* (New York: Viking, 1978); Vance Packard, *The Hidden Persuaders* (New York: David McKay, 1957).

Page 127. The New Jersey broker is quoted in "Franchises Slip as Brokers Find Fees Burdensome," *The New York Times*, December 27, 1981.

Page 128. Material on Playboy is in "Playboy's Catering Prowess," *Restaurants and Institutions*, April 1, 1981.

Page 133. A description of McDonald's franchise system is in *Big Mac.*

Page 136. Kroc describes his early public relations efforts in *Grinding It Out.*

Page 137. The trademark protection efforts are described in *Big Mac.*

Page 138. The Wells article is cited by Robert Choate in testimony at the House hearings.

Page 140. The summary of TV spots is in *Advertising Age*, January 3, 1983.

Page 141. McDonald's suit is reported in *Advertising Age*, September 27, 1982. Wendy's suit is reported in *Advertising Age*, October 4, 1982.

Page 141. Manning's quote appears in "The Battle of Hamburger Hill," *Madison Avenue*, January 1983.

Page 144. The Schmitt quote is in *Restaurants and Institutions*, June 1, 1983.

CHAPTER 7. NEW AND IMPROVED: FRANCHISED RESEARCH AND DEVELOPMENT

Page 145. The story of Filet-O-Fish is told in *Grinding It Out.*

Page 148. The story of chicken-pricing strategy is in "The Spectacular KFC Turnaround," *Restaurants and Institutions*, December 1, 1980.

Page 149. Louis Martino's efforts are described in *Grinding It Out.*

Page 151. Quotes on breakfasts are from *Restaurant Business*, May 1, 1981; *Fast Service*, March 1981; *Restaurants and Institutions*, October 1, 1980.

Page 153. The Hughes quote is in *Restaurants and Institutions*, June 15, 1980.

Page 156. Swart's quote is from an interview with the author.

Page 158. A discussion of drive-through windows is in *Fast Service*, September 1981.

Page 160. John Kenneth Galbraith discusses R&D in *The Affluent Society* (3rd rev. ed. Boston: Houghton Mifflin, 1976).

Page 160. The importance of small businesses is discussed in Jane Jacobs, *The Economy of Cities* (New York: Vintage Books, 1970).

CHAPTER 8. HELP WANTED

Page 162. The story of the Burger King pickets appears in *United Labor News*, June 1981.

Page 163. Earl Campbell's role is described in "Grid Star Campbell Stirs Union Debate," *Detroit News*, May 2, 1980.

Page 164. A good description of the rise of the service economy is in

Emma Rothschild, "Reagan and the Real America," *New York Review of Books*, February 5, 1981.

Page 167. A discussion of income distribution is in Institute for Labor Education and Research, *What's Wrong with the U.S. Economy* (Boston: South End Press, 1982).

Page 169. An account of fast-food jobs is in *The Wall Street Journal*, March 15, 1979.

Page 172. Emerson's ideas appear in *Restaurant Business*, May 1, 1981.

Page 175. Newman's quote is from an interview with the author.

Page 181. The article on working wives appeared in *The New York Times*, May 31, 1982.

CHAPTER 9. WHERE THE CHAINS WENT

Page 187. Professor David Amidon, in an interview with the author, provided background on Bethlehem's mall and the city's development.

Page 192. The Clark quotes are from an interview with the author.

Page 198. A discussion of the Oregon debate appears in "Oregon Update," *Fast Service*, March 1980.

Page 198. The Poelvoorde quote is from an interview with the author.

Page 205. There is a description of the battle to stop McDonald's in *Big Mac*.

Page 206. The plush McDonald's is described in "The Fast-Food Stars," *Business Week*, July 11, 1977.

Page 212. The tale of *Gros Mec* is in *Restaurants and Institutions*, October 15, 1977.

Page 213. The Lewis quote and the story of Holiday Inns' invasion of Europe appears in *Forbes*, February 15, 1976.

Page 215. The Robinson quote is from an interview with the author.

Page 215. McDonald's architecture is discussed in "They Did It All for You," *Progressive Architecture*, June 1978. Another good discussion of architecture is a master's thesis at Miami University of Ohio: James Michael Abbott and John K. Grosvenor, "Corporate Architecture and Design Theory: A Case Study of McDonald's."

Page 218. A description of G.W. Jr.'s appears in *Fast Service*, December 1980.

CHAPTER 10. GROWING PAINS

Page 221. Accounts of the boom in franchising appear in *Dun's Review*, January 1969; *Fortune*, March 1970; *Business Week*, February 21, 1970; *The Wall Street Journal*, November 1, 1970.

Page 223. Minnie Pearl's statement came during hearings of the Senate Select Committee on Small Business, January 20, 1970. At the hearings Hooker described his operation.

Page 226. Turner's story is recounted in *Sales Management*, May 15, 1972.

Page 231. A discussion of the franchise regulations is in "How the FTC Fails to Regulate," *Venture*, February 1980.

Page 231. The Futuristic case is described in *Barrons*, April 30, 1979.

Page 235. Material on Adolph Krisch is from an interview with the author.

Page 237. A discussion of Collins appears in *Restaurant Business*, June 1, 1979.

Page 238. Shoney's is described in *The New York Times*, June 2, 1984.

Page 240. Brown's quote appears in *Forbes*, August 6, 1979.

Page 243. The Cherkasky quote is from an interview with the author.

Page 244. Mikva's quote was in *The MacNeil/Lehrer Report*, June 7, 1979.

Page 248. Emerson's estimate is in *Fast Food*.

CHAPTER 11. THE FRANCHISEES REBEL

Page 255. The Gladstone quotes are from an interview with the author.

Page 264. A discussion of franchisee problems appears in *The Wall Street Journal*, January 2, 1979.

Page 265. The Mrs. Paul's takeover is described in *The Wall Street Journal*, December 23, 1981.

Page 266. The material on Forkas is from an interview with the author.

Page 271. A description of the A & W battle is in "New Concept Propels A & W Growth," *Restaurants and Institutions*, April 1980.

Page 272. A discussion of the Trotters and Horn & Hardart is in *Fortune*, June 16, 1980.

Page 276. The Florescue quote is from an interview with the author.

CHAPTER 12. THE COST OF FRANCHISING

Page 284. The Schorr quote is in *Franchising Today*, February 1981.

Index